DANCING FOR DIAGHILEV

THE LIVELY ARTS SERIES
FROM MERCURY HOUSE

LILLIAN GISH   *The Movies, Mr. Griffith, and Me*

JEAN RENOIR   *Renoir, My Father*

JOSEF VON STERNBERG   *Fun in a Chinese Laundry*

GENE FOWLER   *Good Night, Sweet Prince: The Life and Times of John Barrymore*

JOHN GIELGUD   *Early Stages*

LYDIA SOKOLOVA   *Dancing for Diaghilev*

ALSO EDITED BY RICHARD BUCKLE

The Prettiest Girl in England

The Lively Arts

General Editors: Robert Ottaway and Gill Gibbins

Dancing for Diaghilev

The Memoirs of
LYDIA SOKOLOVA
edited by
RICHARD BUCKLE

Mercury House, Incorporated
San Francisco

This trade paperback edition published in 1989 by arrangement with Columbus Books Limited, London. First published in 1960 by John Murray, London.

Copyright © 1960 by Richard Buckle

Published in the United States by
Mercury House
San Francisco, California

Distributed to the trade by
Consortium Book Sales & Distribution, Inc.
St. Paul, Minnesota

Mercury House and colophon are registered trademarks of
Mercury House, Incorporated

Manufactured in the United States of America

Library of Congress Cataloging-in-Publication Data

Sokolova, Lydia, 1896–1974.
  Dancing for Diaghilev.

  (The Lively arts)
  Includes index.
  1. Sokolova, Lydia, 1896–1974. 2. Ballet dancers — Great Britain — Biography. 3. Diaghilev, Serge, 1872–1929. I. Buckle, Richard. II. Title. III. Series.
GV1785.S58A3 1989   792.8'2'0924 [B]   88-9138
ISBN 0-916515-49-4

To
TAMARA KARSAVINA
whose dancing inspired me from the beginning
to
LYDIA LOPOKOVA
who brought kindliness and gaiety
into my professional life
and to
LEONIDE MASSINE
who taught me so much and who created
Le Sacre du printemps
I dedicate this book.
L. S.

CONTENTS

1	Childhood	1
2	With Russians in America	14
3	Pavlova	23
4	Nijinsky and Diaghilev	32
5	Fokine's Ballets	51
6	Early War Years	65
7	New Roles in Spain and America	81
8	Motherhood	94
9	Beam-ends	111
10	Post-war Triumphs in London	126
11	Second Love in Paris	144
12	*Le Sacre du printemps*	154
13	Without Massine	172
14	*The Sleeping Princess*	185
15	Departure and Return	196
16	The Nijinska Period	209
17	Return of Massine	226
18	An English Year	242
19	Illness	257
20	Beginning and Ending	271
	Index	281

ILLUSTRATIONS

Family Album
  With Mother, Father and Beatrice at Hastings
  Theatricals with Beatrice
  Aged sixteen*
  With Natasha at Monte Carlo†

Nijinsky and Karsavina in *Le Spectre de la rose* (Photo. Bert)

First Roles
  The Bacchanale in *Narcisse* (Photo. Art Baro: Barcelona)
  Papillon in *Carnaval* (Photo. Malcolm Arbuthnot)
  Apple woman in *Till Eulenspiegel*
  Ta-Hor in *Cléopâtre* (Photo. E. O. Hoppé)

Scrapbook
  1913. Nijinsky's wedding in Buenos Aires
  1915. The Cecchettis at Lausanne
  1916. Larionov, Diaghilev and Kremnev at San Sebastian
  1919. With Idzikovsky, Massine, Lopokova and
        Cecchetti, collecting for the Red Cross at the
        London Coliseum (Photo. News Illustration Co.)

As the Miller's Wife in *Le Tricorne*†

Les Femmes de bonne humeur
  Lopokova as Mariuccia*
  Tchernicheva as Constanza‡
  Idzikovsky as Battista*
  Woizikovsky as Niccolo (Photo. E. O. Hoppé)

Tchernicheva in *Pulcinella* against Picasso's set‡

ix

Massine in *Le Tricorne*

Woizikovsky in *Le Tricorne*

1920's Scrapbook

    1920. Chez Pasquier, Monte Carlo, with Antonova, Woizikovsky, Idzikovsky, Evina, Kremnev and Camishov

    1924. With Kochno in London†

    1925. On the Lido with Woizikovsky, Lifar and Diaghilev

    1929. With Woizikovsky at Vichy

As the Chosen Virgin in *Le Sacre du printemps*

Red Riding Hood in *The Sleeping Princess* with Mikolaichik (Stage Photo Company)

Columbine in *Carnaval* (Photo. Bragaglia)

The Doll in *Petroushka*‡

Chlöe in *Daphnis et Chlöe* in an old *Faune* costume (Photo. Numa Blanc)

Les Biches
    Woizikovsky
    As the Hostess

With Woizikovsky, Nijinska and Dolin in *Le Train bleu*‡

Massine in *Les Fâcheux* against Sert's décor for *Cimarosiana*‡

With Slavinsky, Lifar, Woizikovsky and Nemtchinova in *Les Matelots*‡

Gevergeva, Maikerska, Chamié, Tchernicheva, Sokolova, Soumarokova, Doubrovska and Danilova in *Zéphire et Flore*

With Lifar in *Barabau*†

In *Le Bal* (Photo. Antony)

Diaghilev. Painting by Elizabeth Polunin (Photo. Felix Fonteyn)

* Photo. Hana Studios   † Photo. Lenare   ‡ Photo. Sasha of London

ACKNOWLEDGEMENTS

The author and editor wish to express their gratitude to the following people:

Mr Peter Williams for permission to reproduce the Christopher Wood drawing used as a frontispiece and on the jacket; Mrs Whorwell and Mr Oleg Polunin for permission to reproduce their mother's oil painting of Diaghilev; Mr Nash, keeper of the Enthoven Collection, Victoria and Albert Museum, Miss Mary Clarke, Assistant Editor of *The Dancing Times*, and Mr Cyril Holness, the owner of Sasha's remarkable collection of negatives, for help with the photographic illustrations; Lady Juliet Duff, The Dowager Lady St. Just, Mrs Harold Bowen, Sister Sheriff, now Matron of the Lanherne Convalescent Home, Dawlish, M. Jean Hugo and M. Leon Woizikovsky for helpful information: Mr Mario Amaya for typing several versions of the book and making a number of suggestions; Mr Andrew Sykes and Mr Michael Jackson for aid with the Index.

Of the many reference books and books on the Diaghilev period which have been consulted, M. Kochno's *Le Ballot*, M. Grigoriev's *The Diaghilev Ballet, 1909–1929*, M. Lifar's *Serge Diaghilev*, Mr Haskell's *Diaghilev*, the late Mr Propert's *The Diaghilev Ballet: 1921–1929*, Mme Karsavina's *Theatre Street*, Mr Beaumont's *Complete Book of Ballets* and his *The Diaghilev Ballet in London* and M. Benois' *Reminiscences of the Russian Ballet* have proved most informative, useful for checking dates and helpful in arriving at a true version of disputed occurrences.

I

CHILDHOOD

Childhood in Leyton — The Such and Munnings families — Schooldays — Dancing to the barrel organ — Song and dance for the Conservative Party — Father's weakness — Stedman's Dancing Academy — Début at the Royal Court — Playing truant to see Pavlova — Lessons with Mordkin — A narrow escape — Summer at Bexhill — Engaged by the Imperial Russian Ballet.

Mother's parents lived at the Manor House, Leyton, Essex. The house was at the top of a hill, with a lily pond and enormous vine in the garden which impressed me as a girl. Leyton at the beginning of the century had not yet been swamped by London, and had a peculiar charm for a small child, being so near to the jolly street life of the East End, yet backing on the glades and ponds of Epping Forest.

My grandparents had a pony trap, a piano which I tried to play and a graphophone which thrilled me because I could dance to it. I suppose I remember this house on the hill so well because I loved it, but our own home is quite dim to me, though it must have been nearby.

Grandfather Henry Such owned a lot of property in Essex, and he gave each of his four daughters an Off-Licence as a wedding present. If well-run and in the right position, these were supposed to be gold-mines: anyway, there never seemed to be any shortage of money at home in those days.

Mother always wore lovely clothes; I adored watching her sail up the road, rustling with silk and taffeta petticoats. She had wavy chestnut hair, and when I was old enough I spent hours dressing it for her, copying the latest fashions from books. She used to have blouses sent from the shops in pretty green boxes for her to choose from, and she bought Paris hats at a shop called Broadman's (which still exists) in Stratford Broadway. My sister Beatrice and I had beautiful bonnets and Parisian lace pinafores for parties from the same shop. Our dolls were so perfectly dressed they were like real babies. I loved Mother, but I was always afraid of her.

At this time Father was articled clerk to a solicitor. He had the most exquisite writing I have ever seen, and excelled in Old English script. Completely untrained as a painter, he had a natural gift and loved to do water-colours. He did a set of Dickens characters, but what he liked to paint best were sailing ships— all out of his head—for most of the Munnings family had something to do with the sea.

Our branch of the Munnings family came from Lowestoft: they had been in Suffolk for generations. The first mention I have found was of a John Munnyngs in the church register of Bury St Edmunds for 1552, but my kinsman, Sir Alfred Munnings the painter, told me that all the Munnings are descended from two brothers who fought at Agincourt and were given land in East Anglia.

Grandfather Munnings and several of my uncles were sea captains. Some of these uncles were lost during the First World War. Good-looking Uncle Tom Munnings, however, was for some unknown reason at one time Mayor of Johannesburg, and died in South Africa. He caused a stir by bringing us home a stuffed crocodile on the top of a hansom cab.

Grandfather John Munnings was a real picture of a seaman, very small and broad, with one of those beards trimmed short all round the face and curly hair fluffing out from under his cap. He was a dear old boy when he was sober, but terrifying when he was tight, which was his usual state when Father and Mother took me to meet him at the docks. It must have been on one of these outings in the pony trap that I was first thrilled by seeing coster girls dancing in the street. Another thing I remember on an expedition to the docks was the sight of a string of Chinese

2

seamen walking barefoot in the gutter, each man holding onto the pigtail of the one in front.

My grandfather used to tell the story of how, the day after his wedding to Granny Henrietta, he sailed away to China. It took him two years to get there and back, and he was shipwrecked twice on the way; but on his arrival home my Uncle Jack was running about in petticoats. He would always comment at the end of this story, 'That's the way to do it, of course,' and I could never make out what he meant.

I stayed with the Munnings family in Suffolk for summer holidays when Grandfather was back from sea. He could never keep pace with his increasing children, some of whom were little older than me, or remember which was which. When we all assembled for dinner we had to show our hands to see if we had washed, and he used to hold a sort of roll call, rattling off the names in order of birth. He warned us that his hand weighed 'just a pound', and I was pretty scared of him. He snored so terribly I used to push things against the door at night in case he came to visit me. In later years he became a Trinity House pilot.

My mother had been brought up with a rod of iron, and she in her turn was very strict. I had to wash her pretty china and was caned if I broke any. As I grew older I was made to give up learning to play tennis on half holidays in order to scrub floors and do the washing. I boiled the clothes in a copper in the outhouse and lifted them out on a broomstick. There were many starched blouses, and petticoats to be ironed, and the rest of the washing went through a mangle. One day I had folded the handkerchiefs and was pushing them through the mangle while Mother turned the handle and the index finger of my right hand got caught. I was rushed to hospital.

There was an old gentleman who lived nearby called Mr Busby, who was very fond of me. He left me two pennies on a shelf every week and used to hide Mother's cane in the gutter round the roof of the outhouse. When he died his body was laid out in an open coffin in our first-floor drawing-room; afterwards whenever I went upstairs to my room, I used to peep through the door in terror to see if he was still there. It was in the drawing-room that I used to practise my piano, and I never really lost the feeling of Mr Busby lying in his coffin behind me.

At the age of seven I was sent off to join Beatrice at her school at Bexhill, but only spent two terms there. The discovery that we all had fleas in our hair was bad enough, but the reason I left the school was because I had scarlet fever. I was never allowed to return there, though Beatrice stayed on there for some time. Back at home, I went daily to have lessons in a Roman Catholic convent nearby. This must have been in 1910, because I remember Mother Xavier, beside whose desk I had to say my prayers every day, whispering to me, 'Have they caught Crippen yet?' I worked seriously at music and passed with honours several advanced examinations with the idea of becoming a pianist but I had already begun to dance.

It was outside public houses, mostly on Saturdays when the factories were closed, that I had seen girls dancing to a barrel-organ. They danced in fours or sixes, opposite each other, performing high kicks, *ronds de jambe* and splits—in fact the can-can. They also danced the cake-walk. These girls were just as good dancers of their type as the performers I saw later in cafés in Spain, and they bore a striking resemblance to them. They were attractive creatures, mostly dark like Gypsies, with kiss-curls stuck on their cheeks and foreheads, and little combs in their hair. Unlike the Spaniards, however, they wore no jewellery, only gold earrings and hats with feathers. Their skirts and their blouses with puffed sleeves were of every conceivable colour, but they had a preference for purple; over their shoulders there was always a little shawl. The skirts, with three or four flounces at the bottom, were worn over several frilled petticoats, and when these were lifted they revealed black stockings and button boots.

In Holy Week they didn't dance: they skipped. It was the custom to lower large beer-barrels from the drays into the cellars under public houses by lengths of thick cable; and during this week men used to hold these cables across the street to form gigantic skipping ropes. The weight of these must have been enormous, and there was an art in swinging them so as not to

4

hit the skippers as they jumped in and out. Old, young and middle-aged people joined in the skipping, and the coster-girls used to leap higher and higher over the rope, sometimes executing a wonderful side kick, beating the legs together. I longed to dance like those girls.

On certain days of the week an organ-grinder came to play in the street behind the garden wall of the Convent. Giving some excuse or other, I got permission to go home early. I would climb over the wall, so that the Mother Superior should not see from her sitting-room where I was going, and the organ man would greet me saying, 'Hello, Missy, got out all right again?' Then he would turn the handle while I danced. I had the time of my life, doing high kicks and jumps just like the coster-girls, completely forgetting the nuns on the other side of the wall, and oblivious of the passers by. When my friend had to move to another street I spent the rest of the afternoon on swings in a neighbouring park. After a few weeks of these little adventures a neighbour saw me dancing in my Convent uniform and reported me to Father.

Father did a lot of political work for the Conservative Party, and at election time our dogs wore blue and white coats. During the winter months Beatrice and I would sometimes perform at Conservative concerts organised by Father. We played the piano together and sang duets like *Tell Me, Pretty Maiden*. I arranged the dances at the end of these songs, and we had quite a repertoire. Beatrice was pretty, with long golden curls—at school she was known as 'Seven curls and a bit' because of the fluffy pieces on each side of her face—and she would always play the girl. I played the boy. I wasn't at all pretty and my hair was very straight, so it had to be put into curl rags. Just before the performances, after I had come back from school, I used to lay my head on a table while my mother pressed the rags into my hair with an iron. My boy's costume was black satin with a velvet cape and a three-cornered hat with ostrich feathers. It was hired separately for each occasion at a fee of half a guinea and kept in reserve at a costumier's shop in Petticoat Lane. We went to these functions either in a four-wheeler, or sometimes for a treat in a hansom-cab.

I remember going with my father and sister to sing and dance for a lot of old people in South London. We went on a funny little bus through the Blackwall tunnel, which only held four aside. It was pitch dark, lit only by an oil lamp hanging from the ceiling. One got in at a little door at the back, and when the bus was full the driver banged on the roof and pushed open a tiny flap, and we each handed up our tuppeny fares.

Many children have tragedies in their homes which affect the whole of their lives. Mine was the weakness for drink which Father inherited: this led to much unhappiness and the eventual break-up of our family life. My mother was a very religious woman; she went to church frequently during the week, as well as on Sundays. Father was often alone and made full use of these opportunities to drink to excess.

Week-end shopping in those days was very exciting, and mostly done in the evenings as the shops stayed open till past ten on Saturdays. Although it was a thrill to go on these expeditions with my mother there was always the dread of what was going to happen when we got home. There were frequently appalling scenes between my parents, and ever since this time I have had a horror of drunkenness. It was still more frightening to see Father steadily getting drunk when I was alone with him.

When the time came for Mother's return he would swallow neat vinegar. Although he 'took the pledge', he could never keep it. Sometimes he disappeared for days on end.

One awful evening I came home from my music lesson, knowing that Father had been drinking when I went out. When I opened the front door I could hear his voice, and I found him with Mother in the cellar. He had his hands round her throat. I kicked his shins with all my might as he had taught me to do if I were ever attacked by a man. Mother was only just able to murmur, 'Get a policeman. He's mad with drink!' I rushed out sobbing into the night and ran without knowing where I was going. When I saw a policeman I hadn't the courage to speak to him and tried to run past, but he caught me and said, 'Don't cry like that, gal. What's the trouble?' I said I had lost a shilling and didn't dare go home in case I was caned; and that good man gave me a shilling. When I plucked up courage to go home I found Mother sitting with a wet towel around her throat. She said that Mary Puddock, the servant girl, had run away earlier in the evening, and that Father had passed out in the cellar.

As I was by this time crazy to be a dancer and longed to be away from the unpleasant scenes as much as possible I persuaded my parents to allow me to go to the best dancing and dramatic school in England, Stedman's Academy in Great Windmill Street, off Shaftesbury Avenue. This building is now Jack Solomons' Gymnasium, where boxers weigh in before the big fights. I had for some time been practising high jumps over a tight skipping-rope, doing a *glissade* and a *grand jeté en tournant* as I went over the rope. It was at Stedman's that I really learned to jump.

In May, 1909, when I was having my first dancing lessons, Paris was seeing Diaghilev's Russian Ballet for the first time. Diaghilev was the son of a country gentleman and since his youth he had been interested in all forms of art. He had begun by editing an *avant garde* literary and artistic magazine, had organised a huge exhibition of Russian historical portraits in St Petersburg, had been attached to the Imperial theatres and had been associated with new developments in choreography and stage design. Turning westwards in 1903, he had exhibited Russian pictures in Paris, and he was the first to make known the splendour of Russian music to Western audiences. In 1908 he put on *Boris Godounov* in Paris, and in 1909 he introduced Russian ballet with opera at the Châtelet Theatre. Parisians were intoxicated by the new forms and colours of Benois and Bakst and by the superb dancing of Pavlova, Karsavina and Nijinsky in the ballets of Fokine. The movement had been launched which would transform stage production in Europe and America, make known such names as Stravinsky and Picasso, and give a new direction to the lives of a number of people throughout the world. One of these was to be mine: but at this time, I had never heard of Diaghilev.

The pupils of Stedman's Academy gave public displays; and at one of these, held at the Royal Court Theatre in Sloane Square,

I made my first appearance in the theatre, and received for it my first notice. About a ballet of fairy flowers a reviewer wrote: 'The Daisy was charmingly embodied by Miss Patricia Mutter and the responsibilities of the Butterfly, the Bee and Robin Red-breast were creditably borne by Miss Winifrede Browne, Miss Winifred Atwell and Miss Virginia Kynaston'; and of another number that 'Little Cora Poole-Goffin, a dainty maiden, danced to the evident enjoyment of herself and the audience'. The reviewer described me leading the Stedman Sextet in an Old English Country Dance and giving in *Mignon* 'a series of graceful and highly finished movements'. There was also a Tarantella in which I got so carried away that I cut my knuckles banging the tambourine, and there is blood on it to this day.

Of the girls who took part in that entertainment, Hilda Boot, later known as Butsova, became Pavlova's understudy; Cora Goffin became a famous Principal Boy and is now Mrs Emile Littler; and Hilda Munnings became Lydia Sokolova.

In 1910, when King Edward was dangerously ill gloom descended on our home. We were all loyal subjects. I can see my mother now, on the morning the King's death was announced, standing at the foot of my bed, crying and saying, 'Hilda, the King is dead'. We got up at 3 a.m. on the day of the funeral, and watched the procession from a point in the Mall not far from the Palace.

Together with other girls from Stedman's, I started my first professional engagement on Boxing Day, 1910, in the *corps de ballet* of *Alice in Wonderland* at the Savoy Theatre. We danced six matinées and were paid a pound a week. Dan Leno, Jr., was in the show, and there was a well-staged ballet. Hilda Boot, our principal dancer, came out of an oyster shell; and I was one of four lobsters, as well as being a jester. Every day as I left the house for the theatre my father used to throw an old shoe after me for luck. I would always say, 'Oh, really, Dad', and carry the shoe back to him, not understanding the significance of the gesture.

The treats I most looked forward to were visits to music-halls. A company of Red Indians came several years running to the

8

Hippodrome to take part in an amazing Wild West show. These men walked about London in all their feathers and war paint. The stalls were abolished and the whole ground floor became a battlefield, which in the second half of the show was transformed into a lake. Into this the Indian braves dived on horseback from a breathtaking height above the proscenium arch.

One of the excitements of those early days in Leyton and East London was to see the factory workers on their summer outings in 'Excursion Brakes'. These all-day 'Beanos' were great events, as there was so little entertainment in those days. Factories such as Crosse and Blackwell's, which stood where the Astoria Cinema now is, in the Tottenham Court Road, had hundreds of women workers who made pickles one day and jam the next—you could tell by the smell—and these were the sort of people who patronised the brakes. The brakes were long, high wagonettes harnessed with dray horses, driven four-in-hand. You climbed up steps at the back, and there were benches round three sides. The brakes had a canvas shade on top with a wavy fringe all round. The parties would start off in the morning, all on their best behaviour, trotting eastwards to Epping Forest or Southend. They would come back about half-past nine or ten in the evening, with a man seated beside the driver sounding fanfares on a silver horn. The horn-calls, the singing and the concertinas could be heard a long way off. There might be five or six or more brakes together. The horses would be going full pelt, the driver cracking his whip, all the men and women would be merry and singing at the top of their voices as each brake carried half-gallon or gallon stone jars of beer. But the beautiful thing was that the brakes were hung all round with coloured Chinese lanterns, which swung backwards and forwards as the revellers went by. Sometimes one of the lanterns would catch fire and be hastily pulled down and thrown on the road, while another was hung up in its place. If the party halted to rest their horses, boys would do cartwheels and hand-stands in the road to entertain them, calling up, 'Throw out yer rusty 'appence!' Coppers flew through the air and there was a scrum of boys as the Beano trotted off down the road.

Another pleasure was looking after our animals, which Mother taught me to love. At the time I left home we had seven Pomeranians which Mother bred, three cats, a large white Angora rabbit which had the run of the house, two parrots and a cockatoo, all of which talked, a chameleon which sat on a table to be fed with a spoon, a tortoise which followed us about, two canaries, a family of guinea pigs, chickens and two small owls. An old man walked from Orpington in Kent twice a week with fresh herbs and groundsel for the canaries.

I had been working at Stedman's Academy for about a year when Pavlova appeared with Mordkin at the Palace Theatre and had her first great success in England. Pavlova's peculiar genius made it hard for her to sink her individuality into an enterprise such as Diaghilev's new company, which was in the process of detaching itself from the Russian Imperial Theatres, and besides, she was out of sympathy with his experiments; so she formed with Michael Mordkin a small group of her own, and made appearances in London music-halls. She was the first Russian dancer that many of us in England had seen.

It was on Wednesdays and Saturdays that I went to Stedman's, and on those days Mother allowed me a shilling for my lunch and tea. A poached egg, tea and toast cost fivepence. On Wednesday afternoons, some of the girls used to go in the gallery at the Palace Theatre to see Pavlova and, sacrificing my lunch, I spent my shilling on a ticket instead and went with them. It was worth it.

There was a poster with a larger-than-life figure of Pavlova in the *Dying Swan* outside the theatre in Cambridge Circus; and hoping to be mistaken for a dancer like her, I used to stand waiting for my bus home at the corner of the Strand and Trafalgar Square in the third ballet position, reading a copy of the *Dancing Times*.

After going hungry two Wednesdays running, I pinched an extra sixpence from Mother's purse. This made me feel very guilty and I could not keep up the deception for long: besides I was longing to tell my family how wonderful Pavlova and Mordkin were, and I think they must have guessed from my excitement that I had been up to something. With tears and

confused emotions I owned up to the theft, and begged them to
see Pavlova dance so that they should understand how I longed
to follow in her footsteps. Mother said in her usual way, 'I *knew*
there was something going on'; but she and Father went to the
theatre and came home full of enthusiasm.

It was after this that Father was persuaded to write and ask
Mordkin if he would give me private lessons. Father agreed to
pay Mordkin's stiff fee of five guineas a lesson on condition that
I should be taught a solo dance. He had some idea that it would
be advantageous if I could say I had a dance especially arranged
for me by Mordkin. So the great day arrived and I reported at
Miss Phipps' Dancing School, Harrington Gardens, off Glou-
cester Road. I had five lessons, but I cannot say Mordkin taught
me anything I didn't know already—though he did arrange a
dance for me to Sidney Bayne's *Destiny Waltz*, which was very
commonplace.

Mordkin was a handsome and charming man, and I heard he
was much loved by all the Pavlova company. He was beautifully
built, and did strong character dances with scanty costumes to
show off his wonderful limbs. I remember one dance with a spear
and another with cymbals. He often had to give an encore, and
the audience went mad even at matinées. The company excelled
in rhapsodies and mazurkas—in these Helena Schmoltz and
Morosoff were terrific. The classical part of the programme consisted mostly of ensemble dances, Chopin waltzes and nocturnes.
Pavlova herself was at her greatest in those days and a profound
silence descended on the theatre when her music began. The
moment for me, though, was when Pavlova and Mordkin
danced the *Bacchanale* together.

While I was having lessons with Mordkin an advertisement
appeared in *The Stage* for a young character dancer with good
elevation. My father took me across from Stedman's to the
Pavilion for an audition. There we found a small company of
crashing, spinning, shouting Russians. They were a very rough
crowd, very badly dressed, a sort of circus act. The reason they
wanted someone urgently was that one of their girls was pregnant. They agreed to take me, and it was settled against my will

that I should leave for Germany with this awful troupe the next
Sunday, in four days' time. There was no Equity then to protect
artists, and these people could have abandoned me anywhere.
I was totally inexperienced and could never have stood up to
two shows a day of such a gruelling performance. It was criminal
to think of sending me. I begged, pleaded and wept, but my
parents had made up their minds that my chance had arrived.
When Sunday morning came, I locked my bedroom door and
threw the key out of the window. By the time it was found, the
Russians' train had left Victoria, and I was accused of base
ingratitude.

Father had once more forgotten that he had ever taken the
pledge. One evening he had a bad quarrel with Mother, and she
went up crying to bed. Father went to sleep downstairs. I was in
the drawing-room, doing some transposing. The house was
silent and it began to get dark. I heard my father's heavy footsteps
on the staircase, and held the door tight shut so that he shouldn't
come in to see me, but he passed and went on up the stairs.
Opening the door just a crack I saw in the fading light that he
held a carving knife. I screamed to Mother, who was in the room
above me, 'Lock the door! Quick! Lock the door!' Father was
completely bewildered. He turned round on me and shouted,
'Stop screaming at once. Are you mad?' Then, suddenly he
realised he had the carving knife in his hand. He staggered down
the stairs, hanging onto the banisters. After this he disappeared
for several days.

This episode coincided with a crisis in the affairs of Grandfather Such. He and Granny Such and various aunts came to
consult with Mother at this time. Financial difficulties were never
discussed in my presence, but I soon found out something was
wrong when Beatrice was brought back from School.

In spite of these troubles it was arranged for Mother, Beatrice
and me to go to Hastings for our summer holiday. With Mother
in a red bathing-gown and bloomers, we were dragged by a
stumbling horse over shingle and sand in our bathing-machine
down to the sea. We rocked about inside, peeping out of a
little round window. The horse would take us and the bathing-

machine into the water, then the attendants would remove him and let down the steps. With screams and pushes we climbed down into the icy English Channel, only to hang onto thick ropes attached to the bathing-machine and bob up and down. Beatrice and I really did better in the swimming pool, where we learned to dive singly and as a pair. In the evenings we either took sixpenny circular trips on top of an open tram-car or went for long country walks. That summer we lived happily from day to day, with no thought of the future.

My peaceful existence was interrupted by a telegram which summoned me to an audition at Miss Phipps' Dancing School. I heard later how disagreements between Pavlova and Mordkin had culminated in her slapping his face on the stage. They finished their season together at the Palace, but after that the company split in two. Most of the dancers, and certainly all the principals, joined Mordkin who was negotiating with Max Rabinoff (of St Petersburg, New York and London) for the first American season of Russian ballet. Mordkin had engaged six of Miss Phipps' English students, but ten days before the ballet was due to sail for New York one girl fell ill, and Mr Michael Mitchell, Mordkin's manager, sent for me. That was how I came to join what was called 'The All-Star Imperial Russian Ballet'.

Time was short, and I travelled up to London every day for rehearsals. One afternoon a few of us were taken down to Brixton to be photographed as a group in our ballet costumes. To make us look more numerous the photographer was told to join two prints together, one being in reverse, so that our faces occurred twice in the same picture.

From now on I was a professional, and at fifteen my youth was over. Although during the next few years I went back to my parents between engagements, it was under different circumstances and to a different home.

2

WITH RUSSIANS IN AMERICA

With Mordkin to America — The smell of New York —
Working with Russian dancers — On tour — The seductive
viola player — Doris Faithful's big feet and shabby luggage
— Stranded in New Orleans — The long trek home — Progress of technique.

I wonder what Diaghilev thought in 1911 when he heard that
Mordkin was taking a company off to America with the title of
'Imperial Russian Ballet'. It was a challenge to his supremacy;
yet as he was probably already confident in his mission as an
artistic pioneer he may have laughed at Mordkin's old-fashioned
company, knowing that his productions would have little value
except as a background to the brilliance of the star dancers.

Stars we certainly had—too many perhaps! Geltzer from
Moscow, Sedova from St Petersburg and Zambelli from Paris,
each wanting to top the bill. Dear Lydia Lopokova was also with
us at the beginning, but on the programme she was only listed
as 'ballerina': the two other Russian ladies had the rank of
'Prima Ballerina', and Zambelli was 'Première Danseuse Etoile'.
Mordkin had his hands full to control the warring temperaments
of his stars, and when he was taken ill with appendicitis on the
boat our tour seemed doomed to disaster.

I have always had a keen sense of smell. Although petrol is
the predominant smell nowadays in streets throughout the world,
even that cannot obliterate entirely the human and cooking smells
which are so distinct to me, and with closed eyes I could tell
whether I am in France or Italy, Germany or Spain. That ship,
the *President Lincoln*, in which we sailed for New York in the

14

autumn of 1911, just stank. It must have been a combination of German sauerkraut, fresh paint and the effects of the bad weather on the passengers.

My English companions in order of age were Sheila Courtenay, who was later with the Pavlova company; Rita Zalmani; Annie Broomhead, who later joined Diaghilev and became Bromova; Ethel Montague; Doris Faithful, who also joined Diaghilev; and Blanche James, who afterwards became a snake dancer. Mrs James, Blanche's mother, travelled with us as a sort of matron. She was a tiny little woman and quite ineffective.

I think I grew up on that journey. What with sea-sickness and home-sickness, I cried myself to sleep every night. That crossing was a crossing in more ways than one: I was leaving behind not only England but my childhood. From now on I had to fend for myself. Although I was so young and inexperienced, I was physically well developed and got the nickname of *Mammasha*, which means 'Little Mother'.

The excitement of passing the Statue of Liberty, seeing our first skyscrapers—dominated by the Woolworth building—and steaming slowly into New York Harbour, with the funny tub-shaped ferries crossing between the islands, made us forget the horrible smell of the ship, and we ran from side to side for fear of missing anything.

I soon found myself standing in the vast customs shed, where we were all divided up alphabetically and I had to queue under a letter M the size of a house. I listened to everyone around me speaking English with a strange accent, and was amazed by the number of black folk who seemed to inhabit this new world.

The business manager of our show had lists of places to stay at with their different prices, and he helped us to find accommodation. Leaving our little trunks to be sent on to the theatre, we packed into a taxi and drove up Broadway. We couldn't stop exclaiming at everything: the tobacco stands, the big displays of candy and biscuits marked 'One Cent', '3¢' or '5¢', the Flatiron Building and the height of the other office buildings, which might be considered nothing nowadays, but which was unlike anything we had seen at home. The elevated railway we called the 'overhead underground'.

We were staying, two to a bedroom, in a little *pension* on 52nd Street, which was very well run by a Frenchwoman married to an American. It was a brownstone house, identical with all its neighbours on both sides of the long, straight, gloomy street. It was different from London houses in that a steep flight of steps went up to the front door from the pavement. The dining-room was a small but very clean room in the semi-basement under these steps. We were well set up for morning rehearsals for we were given a good breakfast before we went to work, something hot as well as grapefruit or cornflakes, neither of which I had ever eaten before and which I found delicious. The Frenchwoman cooked us a very good dinner, but we had our lunch at Child's. We'd never seen anything like that vast crowded restaurant before. At Child's they cooked buckwheat cakes in the window. Buckwheat cakes and maple syrup—these for me were the smell of New York.

My home-sickness disappeared with all these new experiences, but it was replaced by another worry. I began to doubt whether I was really a good enough dancer to be able to cope with my work in the ballet company. After all, I had so little experience, and was only there by a fluke.

I was scared stiff when I went to our first rehearsal. An elevator took us to the top of the building, and there was a further staircase beyond that which led into the centre of an enormous loft. When we had all assembled, the trap-door was shut down over the staircase. In that high room in New York I was shut into my new life among dancers. I looked around at all the famous people among whom I was to work.

Katerina Geltzer was considered, after Pavlova, the great ballerina of her day, and she used to dance *Giselle* in our company. My memory tells me that she was not very pretty, but highly neurotic and excitable. In fact, I used to think she must be slightly mad to act as she did on the stage. Sedova was a sweet and gentle woman. Zambelli was the Italian-born star of the Paris Opera: she had made a guest appearance at the Mariinsky Theatre in

16

St Petersburg at the beginning of the century and was the last foreigner to do so.

Lydia Lopokova had not the appearance or physique of a classical dancer, but, to everyone's astonishment, whatever she attempted came off: she was always sure and her elevation was terrific.

What I have always liked about the dancing of Russians is the *manner* in which they jump. On the stage I tried to do it their way. The secret is to travel *through* the air, not *up* into it. I learned that if one refuses to allow the body to sense any weight lightness can become a habit. I loved the sensation of flying through the air.

I think that in a way Helena Schmoltz must have been my first inspiration when I saw her leading the rhapsodies and mazurkas with Morosoff in Pavlova's company. She was so blonde, elegant and attractive; and now that she had joined our company as first character dancer I felt all the more that she was the kind of artist I should like to be. How I hoped that I might one day dance like her! I loved the turn of her hands and her trim way of clicking her heels together. Like me, she never excelled to a high degree in classical work: she could do anything easily if it had a character element, as I could. Standing for ages trying to do a perfect arabesque, and all the other detailed polishing of classical technique, bored me. I wanted to express myself individually and in various moods—to do something *exciting*. It was Schmoltz who started me off.

My first sight of the Metropolitan Opera House left me speechless. The Russians, who had danced in St Petersburg and Moscow, were naturally not as impressed as we English girls were to find ourselves on such a big stage and in so splendid a theatre. I know of no other sensation so exciting to a dancer as that of suddenly having a space to express herself with freedom of movement.

The 'Imperial Russian Ballet' appeared for a couple of weeks at the Metropolitan with great success. Our repertoire consisted of *Giselle*, *Coppélia* and a *divertissement* called *Russian Wedding*, in which we wore beautiful costumes covered in pearls, and which was fun to dance. It was not until we went on tour that the discontent in the company became obvious. The ballerinas quarrelled about when to perform and when not to perform, according to the size of the town. Geltzer was the first to leave; and Zambelli soon followed her.

We English girls were paid three pounds a week. This proved desperate poverty, and we gradually grew out of all our clothes. Our parents sent us warm clothes for the icy New York winter, but by the time they arrived we were touring the south in the broiling heat of spring. On tour we enjoyed sightseeing when we got the chance, which is more than can be said of the Russians and Poles, whose only idea was to play poker at every possible opportunity.

In Boston I chiefly remember the Mother Church of the Christian Scientists, because we lived in rooms nearby. Philadelphia had the most colossal back-stage I have ever seen. Doors that opened on to the street were so high and wide that lorries, seeming to take up no room at all, could drive straight onto the stage. The set was rigged up in what seemed to be a tiny space in the middle of this vast area. On our way into Denver, Colorado, we were stuck in a snow drift and the train was followed by wolves. In Denver there was a fair where I saw a cow with two heads, and there was a booth with two little girls joined together at the stomach. I went and talked to them every day the three days we were there.

I developed a passion for the viola player in our orchestra, who was Italian and good-looking. In Little Rock, Arkansas, he took me for a ride in an open carriage and we drove to a pretty house with a balcony entrance on the outskirts of the town. I thought we were visiting someone he knew, but we were shown into a bedroom. I made a scene, rushed out of the house and demanded to be taken home at once.

In our special train I slept two in a bunk with Doris Faithful, head to toe. Doris grew almost visibly, and her feet were enormous. Her black button boots got so down at heel that they would not stand up on their own and were not safe to walk in as she kept slipping off the kerb.

Our little English group was pretty shabby compared with the attractive Polish dancers, who had seen more of the world. We had just one suitcase each and they all had names: mine was called Harriet. Doris Faithful had a very awkward, large, green, square fibre suitcase, which had been given her when she left home. This was known as 'Doris-grip', because the only way she could carry it was clasped tightly with both hands in front of her. Whenever we got a room to sleep in as a change from the train, she used to make me furious by her habit of opening the lock of this bag and emptying all her rubbish on the bed. As Doris grew bigger and more of her clothes wore out, so there was more room in 'Doris-grip', and it became a dumping-ground for all our surplus possessions. Eventually the men in the orchestra began to make a joke of the old green suitcase: it came in for some rough treatment, became a wreck and had to be tied up with string.

We English girls put a few cents together and bought a neat little wicker affair for Doris as a surprise. One night after the show we all collected in my room, where the old wreck was laid out on the bed with candles stuck all round it. We lit the candles, one of the girls dressed up as a clergyman and we held a funeral service for 'Doris-grip'. After this, we had a lovely time jumping on it and tearing it to bits. Doris sat on the floor in floods of tears, moaning 'What shall I do? What *will* my Mother say?' Then we brought out the new case, held a christening service over it, sprinkled it with water and named it 'Little Willie'.

Back in New York for a second short season, which was less of a success because some of our best artists had left us, I had another chance to look round the city. There were very few shops on Fifth Avenue then, and some of the houses had walled gardens in front. Central Park did not impress me at all: it was not a patch on Hyde Park. There were not many motor cars. Our theatre baggage and trunks would be picked up by long flat lorries drawn by horses. On this visit I was allowed to sit in the flies at the Metropolitan to look down on two marionette-like figures who were Tetrazzini and Caruso, singing *Aïda*. I also saw somebody walk across Times Square on a tightrope holding an open paper parasol.

When our manager Rabinoff decided to take the remains of our company out on the road again, it was Volinin who spoke up for the underpaid English and got our salaries increased by $25 a month. Sedova stayed with us until shortly after the second New York season: when she left the company was led by Schmoltz and Volinin. They were very much in love, and they danced beautifully together in *Coppélia*.

Our increase in salary did not really leave us much better off, as we now seldom slept on a train and had to pay for lodgings. The tour went from bad to worse. We played in some strange towns. At one southern college town, the hotel was only half-built and we slept with no roof over us. Some of the dancers stayed the night in the depot station waiting-room round an old pot-belly stove. The theatre was tiny and we dressed in corners under the stage in full view of the musicians. The footlights were gas jets, and when the curtain went up we found there wasn't a white face in the audience.

New Orleans was different from anywhere else, a mixture of France and England, with its wrought-iron balconies, twisted streets and trees everywhere. We had become so disorganised by this time and had been having such bad houses, that all the Russians and Poles decided to return to New York with what money they had, and so did the company's manager. Nobody thought of saying a word to the English girls, and one day when we arrived at the theatre for the evening's performance we found a notice posted up saying the engagement was cancelled.

Stranded in the Deep South with no money or prospects, we spent our days on the doorstep of the English Consul. He was no help at all, and could get no information from the offices of Mr Rabinoff in New York. The hotel manager, however, was kind to us and gave us all our meals free, so that for the ten days we were stuck in New Orleans we ate better than we had for weeks. In the end it was the local authorities who got things moving: they communicated with the New York police, and Rabinoff was forced to send for us. So one day a horse-drawn lorry came round to the door of the hotel. Our trunks were flung on to it and us on top of them.

We travelled back to New York on a tiny cargo boat, which was more than primitive. Our cabins opened onto the one and only saloon, where we had our meals, and they were so small that we had to go in, undress and get into our narrow bunks one at a time. Except for the benches we sat on to eat there were no seats of any sort. Huddled together in the evenings around that saloon, in our shabby old clothes, beneath a great swinging oil lamp, we were like characters in a Charlie Chaplin film. Luckily for us the weather held, for we were over a week on that boat.

When we got back to New York we deliberately parked ourselves, regardless of our bedraggled state, in one of the best hotels—much to the amusement of the bell-hops. To spur Rabinoff into action we sat on the steps of his office in relays throughout the day. The treatment worked. We got warning at breakfast time one morning that we were off. Three taxis drew up, with a van for our luggage, and we were hustled in, disregarding nasty remarks from the bell-hops who received no tips. We were rushed to the docks, and as we arrived alongside the *Lapland* the gangway was just being pulled up. In response to our shouts and screams they let it down again and we ran full pelt on board, our trunks and suitcases being flung onto the ship behind us. We hadn't a pennypiece between us, but kind Mr Mitchell, Rabinoff's representative, emptied his pockets of what he had and flung handfuls of money onto the deck as we were moving from the quay. We travelled back to England in style—that is to say, second class, and eating three square meals a day instead of just the ice cream, toast and coffee which had become our staple diet during the long tour. I arrived at Dover in March, 1912, having danced in a hundred and twenty towns in seven months.

One of the things I had learned in America was how to dance the Polish mazurka correctly. Unless the rhythms of this subtle and exciting dance are mastered from the very start they are almost impossible for an outsider to assimilate, and I was lucky to have had the chance of learning the mazurka from Poles when I was very young.

While I had been away my parents had moved to a new house

in East London, as Father had found a new job and wanted to be near his work; and Beatrice was training to be a nurse. My Grandfather Such, however, had got into money difficulties and sold all his property in the Leyton neighbourhood, including the dear old Manor House where I had been happy as a child.

3

PAVLOVA

The glamour of Pavlova — Lessons at Ivy House — How
Pavlova took a call — Her shoes and tricks of balance —
Encouragement from Sheraiev — With Kosloff at the
Coliseum — Vienna and Budapest — An audition with
Diaghilev.

Pavlova had bought herself a house in the northern outskirts
of London; and Mr Mitchell arranged that she should interview
a few of the English girls who had been with Mordkin in America,
with the idea that she should give us lessons. When I took the
train to Golders Green I could hardly believe that I was going to
meet the most famous dancer in the world, whom I had admired
from afar in the gallery at the Palace Theatre.

Golders Green was lovely in those days. From the station you
walked up the hill, which had huge trees on both sides. There
was no traffic: it was a country lane. When I entered Ivy House
that hot summer day, everything seemed so cool, white and shady.
The French windows were wide open with sun blinds pulled
down over them. There were big vases of flowers, and perfume
everywhere. The studio was awe-inspiring and seemed to me
almost sacred. It was the centre of the house: not quite square,
two storeys high, and with a gallery running round it. Off this
gallery with its pretty railing, white doors led to Madame's bedroom, boudoir and bathroom. Below, was the *barre*. On the
opposite side to the front door, windows opened onto the
garden, and round the room there hung several life-size paintings
of Pavlova in her most famous roles. Although the sun poured in
at the upper windows, down below there was a sense of coolness
which I shall always associate with Pavlova.

C

On that first day when we went to her house she gave us a wonderful welcome, and had iced fruit drinks brought to us in her drawing-room. I am afraid we were quite speechless, overwhelmed by the beauty of the house and by the glamour of Pavlova.

It was impossible when one met Pavlova like this in her own environment to believe the stories one had heard of her tantrums and hysteria, yet some of them must have been true. Perhaps even her scenes were part of an act, because in my limited acquaintance with this remarkable woman I could see that the only time she wasn't acting was when she was asleep. I never saw her asleep. I wish I had.

In the house she was always dressed in draperies, and seemed never to be alone, because there was always a swain in attendance to kiss her hand and tell her how beautiful she was, or to drape her silks and chiffons as she sat down. After tapping at the door timidly, one of these admirers would enter the room at her bidding, approach her with the utmost reverence, click his heels together, accept her outstretched hand, linger as long as possible over kissing it, then, with deep devotion in his eyes, would bring a bunch of her favourite flowers from behind his back with the left hand and whisper 'Anna Pavlova'. She then would kiss the gentleman on each cheek, fondle the flowers and thank him with such ecstasy that you would think she had never been given flowers before.

Pavlova had a profound understanding of the value of receiving graciously. She brought this to a fine art. Being the wonderful dancer that she was, it was rare for her to give anything less than a perfect performance. However, on an evening when she had danced less well than usual I have seen her work the audience up into tumultuous appreciation merely by the way she behaved with her bouquets. Accepting them with a charm which is rarely seen on any stage, she would press the flowers to her body, moving first one hand and then the other as she almost cuddled them. She would bend deeply from the waist, bowing to various parts of the house, give a brilliant turn of the head and shoulders, then run off, with head thrown back to reveal the line of her neck, taking the longest possible route to the wings. This picture she gave of herself, moving so delicately and swiftly with the flowers, was only the beginning. Before she had taken two curtain calls people had entirely forgotten her earlier performance in watching another important and exquisite aspect of Pavlova's art. They loved every movement she made during those curtain calls, and applauded accordingly. I've seen several dancers try to copy this amazing feat of Pavlova's, but they have never succeeded. She was the only one who has been able to build up applause from nothing.

In later years, when I travelled with Pavlova's company, I realised that there was a curious atmosphere of constraint among her dancers, and that nobody ever appeared quite at ease. The artists never seemed sure of themselves or of her: they were always anticipating the next move a little fearfully.

If some unforeseen incident occurred during a performance Pavlova could become in a flash extremely angry, and she would grumble quite audibly while dancing. Once during a ballet in which she had to pass between two lines of kneeling girls she saw a foot projecting too far, which might conceivably have tripped her up, though it did not. She ordered the curtain to be lowered and told her stage manager, Pianovsky, to inform the conductor that the ballet would start again from the beginning.

Pavlova had one trick of balance, the secret of which I discovered later in the following way. Our shoes were always made by Niccolini in Milan, and as Pavlova's feet were much smaller than mine I was surprised to learn that my shoes were made on her last. It is almost impossible to dance in ballet shoes just as they come from the maker, as they have to be adjusted to the individual foot. No two dancers 'fix' their ballet shoes in the same way, and whenever I see a new pair 'done up' ready for a girl to wear I invariably look to see what she has done to make them comfortable. Pavlova had a secret method entirely her own. Taking shoes which were made somewhat too large for her, she would insert an extra support of thin leather or cork in the forward part of the shoe, but some distance from the tip. Then, soaking them in water she would tread down the padded points as far as the support. When they were dry she cut a slit in the rear edge of the point and inserted a plait of tape. Finally, she would darn all over and round the point in the normal way. She thus contrived for herself solid platforms on which to balance.

Her shoes, however, were only part of the method which enabled her to hold an *arabesque* for so long. Watching her, you would close your eyes and think, 'She can't possibly still be there when I open them again', but she was. She would keep this up for ages, then suddenly do a couple of pirouettes and go flitting away. I asked her how she did it. Pavlova told me that as soon as she took the position, either an *attitude* or an *arabesque*, she would start to concentrate. From the point of the toe which rested on the ground she would think her way through the ankle—to the calf—to the knee—to the thigh—to the waist—to the breast—to the head—through the arm—to the tips of her fingers; and when she had finished this controlling thought-process it was time to move on.

I was always fascinated by the perfection of Pavlova's costumes: they were so exquisitely made. Those with tu-tus—that is, short stiffened ballet skirts—were works of art; they were constructed with such skill, the weight so nicely calculated and the cut so exact, with their layers of tulle, their sequins, ribbons or feathers for adornment, that they never wilted or changed their shape during a performance. Between performances they were as carefully groomed as their owner. Costumes like The Swan and The Butterfly had a specially prepared basket on the principle of an old-fashioned hat box. This basket was lined and padded, and was large enough for these costumes to be laid out flat and pinned on the sides, bottom and top, so that five dresses could be carried without any harm coming to them.

Pavlova was immaculate on and off the stage, with never a hair out of place. At home she wore pastel colours to show off her sleek dark hair. Her hats often had ospreys drooping round the brim to soften her face. The way she used her hands or placed her feet with their great arched insteps all combined to produce an impression of art. She always wore flowers, which became her better than mink.

One day during that summer of 1912 she took two of us with her into her aviary of tropical birds. It was very high, with a rounded top. She walked straight into it through double doors and stood with her arms outstretched. The many-coloured birds showed no fear and behaved as if she was one of them. She then took us to the lake at the bottom of her garden where she knelt down and called to her pet swan. The bird came to her immediately, and she folded her arms round its neck and talked to it gently. The swan's mate, meanwhile, remained watching nearby in absolute stillness.

The first day that we went to her house we had our practice clothes with us and were given a class in her superb studio. After that we came regularly for several weeks. Our main schooling and character lessons were from Sheraiev, who had been a famous teacher in Russia, but Cloustine gave us a few classes too.

One day Sheraiev said to me, 'Wait after class. I will speak with you.' I was terrified. After dressing, I went back to the studio prepared to receive my dismissal, while the other girls left the house intrigued by the mystery. Seeing by my face that I was scared, Sheraiev put his arm round my shoulder and said, 'Don't be frightened. I want to tell you to concentrate on character dancing and to learn as much as you can from the Russians. If you work very hard I think you stand a chance of being a good dancer.' His English was not as clear as that, but this was the gist of what he told me. I was so thrilled I ran all the way down the hill from Ivy House to Golders Green station to get home with the news as soon as possible. I didn't even stop to have the usual drink of milk in the dairy, although I was very thirsty, for fear the other girls whom I knew to be waiting inquisitively would ask me what the old man had said. When I got home, bursting with the news, my family showed so little interest in what Sheraiev had told me that I ran upstairs and had a good cry. However, I knew that a maestro like Sheriaev would not have bothered to single me out and say what he did unless he meant it: so I worked hard.

During the autumn of 1912, a troupe of Russian dancers, headed by Theodore Kosloff, appeared on the bill of the Coliseum music-hall. Kosloff and his wife Baldina had taken part in Dia-ghilev's famous first Paris season in May, 1909, but like Pavlova and Mordkin, they had decided to break away and form their own little company. At the Coliseum they were dancing a version of *Scheherazade* twice daily; and it is a proof of the profound impression that Russian music and the new ballets of Diaghilev had made on the Western European public, that within two years of the first production at the Paris Opéra of Fokine's *Scheherazade* with Bakst's *décor*, when Rimsky Korsakov's score was first heard outside Russia, an arrangement of this work should have reached the music-halls.

Together with several other girls who had been working with Pavlova, I was given an audition by Kosloff and accepted for his company. Baldina, Theodore Kosloff, and his brother Alexis were a very strong team. Theodore was not unlike Fokine in his manner of dancing, and obviously from the same school. Alexis was a first-rate comic character dancer, excellent as the Eunuch in *Scheherazade*. Our *Scheherazade* was quite different from Fokine's, as I was to discover later; and Baldina, being an 'old-fashioned' ballerina, danced Zobeide on her points—a procedure which would certainly have horrified Fokine. She had an unusual gift: she could sit in a box and record the movements of a classical ballet in some secret notation of her own.

Baldina had started dancing very soon after the birth of a baby, and before we had given many performances at the Coli-seum she heard that her little girl, who was being cared for at Bournemouth, had developed meningitis. The child was so seriously ill that her mother was sent for, but Baldina was afraid of breaking her contract with Oswald Stoll. Something had to be done, so the Kosloffs decided to let me go on in her place. I had one rehearsal between the shows and another the next morning. I was not unlike Baldina in appearance, but her costume was too big and I had to be padded out. With her wig, head-dress and make-up I might have been Baldina herself—except for the dancing.

It was certainly exciting to be dancing a ballerina's part at the London Coliseum at the age of sixteen, and I was shaking like a

leaf with stage-fright. Theodore, who played the Negro, was
very helpful all the time I danced with him, but as soon as I was
on my own in the tragic scene at the end I nearly went to pieces.
At the supreme moment when the unfaithful Zobeide pleads with
her husband the Shah for forgiveness before committing suicide
at his feet, I got carried away. Clutching furiously at the Shah,
I accidentally grabbed hold of his beard and was horrified to see
it part company with his face. I let go quickly, thinking I had
pulled it off, but it was on elastic and snapped back, not under his
chin but over his mouth. Needless to say I lost no time in stab-
bing myself and falling dead before him in an apologetic attitude.

An Austrian tour was arranged for the Kosloff company.
Just before the end of our four-week season at the Coliseum, I
was called to the manager's office and told that as I should be
dancing a Hungarian *czardas* with Alexis on the tour I would be
given an extra pound a week, making my salary five pounds in
all, but that on no account was I to let anyone know this. Almost
immediately after this, the dancers who were to get only four
pounds a week on tour decided to strike. When they said to me,
'You're with us, of course,' I was in a real dilemma. I had not
the wisdom to agree, but feeling that after my rise in salary
loyalty to the management came first, without asking anyone's
advice I refused to join them. I was sent to Coventry and called
a 'blackleg'. This made me so miserable that I cried when I
told my family, who made it worse when they explained that I
should have stood by the company. The strike was a failure and
the salaries remained at four pounds. The whole time we were
away I was hardly happy except when we were on the stage,
because of that wretched extra pound which I was afraid to
spend. We must have been away five weeks, because I know I
saved five pounds. Whether somebody got to know of this money
which was burning holes wherever I put it, I do not know; but
on the day we started for home my handbag was stolen and I
arrived back without a pennypiece in my pocket.

In Budapest I was nervous of dancing the *czardas*, the Hun-
garians' own national dance, and even Alexis was a bit apprehensive too. But we must have been quite good as we had to

give an encore and repeat the *czardas* at every performance in the city.

When we came back to the Coliseum for a two weeks' return date, London was talking of nothing but the Diaghilev Ballet, and I heard for the first time about Nijinsky and his phenomenal elevation. It was said that in *Le Spectre de la rose* when he leaped through the window, he would hang suspended in the air. How I should have laughed if anyone had told me that one day I should dance with Nijinsky in that very ballet.

The Diaghilev Ballet had paid its first visit to London during the Coronation season of 1911. This visit had been followed by another later in the same year, while I was in America, and by a third during the summer of 1912. After Pavlova quarrelled with Mordkin she had rejoined Diaghilev briefly for his autumn season in 1911, and London audiences had the advantage over Paris in enjoying the never-to-be-repeated experience of seeing Pavlova and Nijinsky together in *Giselle*. From then on Pavlova was to go her own way again, and Diaghilev was to continue on his appointed mission of creating new stars and new masterpieces. Londoners had been given the opportunity to lose themselves in the romanticism of Fokine's *Les Sylphides* and *Le Spectre de la rose*, and to be stirred by the passionate revelry of his *Scheherazade* and *Prince Igor*. They had also heard in *L'Oiseau de Feu* and *Petroushka* the music of Diaghilev's greatest discovery, Igor Stravinsky. London had, in fact, experienced the theatrical revolution initiated by Diaghilev, Benois, Bakst and Fokine, and though still gasping for breath, had failed to be shocked either by the eroticism or the unclassical choreography of Nijinsky's own first ballet *L'Après-midi d'un faune*. Now, early in 1913, the Diaghilev ballet were once more in London.

There were a few Russian men in the Kosloff company, and one of these was Nicolas Zverev, a cheerful young man whom we called 'Percy Greensocks', because he always wore green in class; another was his friend Tarasoff. These two heard from friends in the Diaghilev company that they had a few vacancies, and were told that if Diaghilev was approached carefully he might give us an audition. I knew later that Diaghilev had a low opinion of what London could produce in the way of dancers, and I do not suppose that he really entertained the possibility of engaging us: nevertheless, it was arranged that four of us girls, with Zverev and Tarasoff, should be given an audition to show our ability, if any, at the awful hour of ten o'clock on a Monday morning. And so I came to the greatest ordeal of my life up-to-date.

We changed into practice dress, and stupidly put on brand new ballet shoes. We had to face a committee more terrifying than any first-night audience: they sat with their backs to the towering safety curtain on the stage of the Royal Opera House, Covent Garden. Diaghilev, of course, was there, and Nijinsky, Maestro and Madame Cecchetti and Grigoriev. We had no music, and nothing arranged. We girls lined ourselves up to do some of our dances from *Scheherazade*. Just as we started I caught my uncomfortable shoe in something, and down I went with a crash. The stage was slippery and my feet had not got used to the shoes. Before we finished I had gone down three times. At last Diaghilev suggested that Cecchetti should give us some classroom steps to do, and with these I got on better. I cannot remember how the other girls danced, but Zverev jumped and did his *entrechats* and *pirouettes* splendidly, which seemed to save the situation. Still, we hadn't much hope as we crawled out of Covent Garden and down Henrietta Street to the Coliseum.

That same evening during our performance we got the news that five of us had been accepted; Anna Broomhead (later Bromova), Doris Faithful, Zverev, Tarasoff and myself. It fell to Tarasoff, who had arranged the secret audition, to tell poor Theodore Kosloff that he was losing us. Theodore was very sad, but stuck a photograph of himself in my autograph book, and cut a strand of beads off his costume to give me as a souvenir; and Alexis did the same. We completed our contract with them, dancing in Harrogate and Cheltenham. There we said good-bye to a company we had grown fond of and with whom we had been happy. I was to join Diaghilev in Monte Carlo at a salary of thirty pounds a month.

31

4

NIJINSKY AND DIAGHILEV

First impressions of Monte Carlo and the Diaghilev ballet — Learning the repertoire — *Le Dieu bleu* — Diaghilev and Nijinsky — *l'Après-midi d'un faune* — *Jeux* — Rehearsals for *Le Sacre du printemps* — Its rowdy first night in Paris — Russian singers in Paris and London — Pay-day at Drury Lane — Chaliapin gets slapped — Romola de Pulszka, Marie Rambert and Nijinsky at rehearsals — Cecchetti's prize — The voyage to South America — Nijinsky's wedding — His dismissal by Diaghilev.

Monte Carlo had not been popularised in 1913: nobody dreamed of bathing on the south coast of France in those days, and the summer sun had not yet come into fashion. Between December and April, however, it was the haunt of the smartest society of Europe and America. French and English aristocrats, Russian Grand Dukes, Indian Maharajahs and American emperors of commerce stayed at the Hôtel de Paris and gambled at the ornate Casino, surrounded by exotic gardens and perched on its rock above the sea. To entertain this rich and exclusive public, the management of the Casino provided the best opera that money could buy, and the spring season of 1913 was the third in succession for which the Diaghilev Ballet had been engaged to introduce some variety in the bill-of-fare.

We five arrived in Monte Carlo completely exhausted. Nevertheless, tired as we were, the journey from Marseilles onwards had been one continuous exclamation mark. 'Did you see that?' 'Just look at the colour of those flowers growing out of the wall!' 'Here's another lovely little bay!' and so on. It was so strange to get out at the railway station of Monte Carlo right beside that marvellous blue sea. I didn't think there could be anything more beautiful in the world. We were lucky because Tarasoff had written to one of his friends in the ballet to book us lodgings, and we had two pleasant apartments in the same street, at the top of a hill above the gardens. Our rehearsal room and the theatre where we were to perform were both part of the Casino building.

My first impression of the company was one of richness and profusion. There seemed to be such an abundance of everything, whether of ballet shoes and costumes or of the hats, shoes and gloves which the dancers wore in private life. We three English girls felt so dowdy in our blouses and skirts. Most of the girls were exceedingly pretty, particularly the Polish ones. Women all had long hair in those days, and most of the company were dark; but Olga Kokhlova had glorious dark auburn hair. I was one of the few blondes in the company.

Every day began with Maestro Cecchetti's class at nine o'clock. An Italian, he was very small and very short-tempered, though he usually had a twinkle in his eye. He spoke a fantastic language of his own, part French, part Russian and part Italian, which took several weeks to understand.

For class we wore white tu-tus and pink silk tights, but for the rehearsal which followed immediately, we wore *crêpe-de-chine* dresses which took three and a half metres of material to make. They were caught in with one bit of elastic under the breast and another around the thigh, and they fell in pretty draperies just below the knee. Although there was a lot of stuff in them, they were easy to move in and as we all had them made in different colours we must have been a wonderful sight. Rehearsals were conducted by Serge Grigoriev, our *régisseur* or stage manager. He was about thirty, and to us English girls he seemed tall and terrifying. He had a perpetually worried look and seldom smiled, though, when something amused him, he would let out a short, loud laugh. Not understanding much of what he said, I had the feeling that he was usually complaining: but no doubt Diaghilev was always complaining to *him*, and it was his job to pass on the comments and reprimands of his employer. When we failed to understand some explanation, he grew impatient and began to shout, covering us with a shower of spit. Being nervous, I never knew whether to wipe it off or leave it.

Men and women in the ballet were divided into groups according to size. The tall men were called 'men', the short ones 'boys'; while the female dancers were either 'women' or 'girls'. Doris Faithful, whose feet used to stick into my face on the American tour, was put with the group of tall women, which included Piltz and Tchernicheva, Grigoriev's wife; while I was put with the shrimps. I got pushed around a good deal at first, not knowing any of the ballets and speaking no Russian, and the Polish girls used to get annoyed with me and shove me about the stage, saying, 'Poooosh, Meeess.'

We were all called by our surnames, like boys at school. At first I was 'Munings'; later in the year I became 'Muningsova'. The only person in the company who could speak fluent English to us was Marie Rambert, but our chief character dancer, Adolf Bolm, could speak a little. We liked him as he was always ready to encourage us or to translate. There was no doubt about it, I had to do something about learning Russian. Gradually I began to pick up odd phrases. When, during rehearsals, Grigoriev would say '*Esho ras*' we did the same thing over again: when he said '*Snachalla*' we started again from the beginning. Learning a few words like this by association, I soon began to give the impression of knowing more Russian than I did.

We only had morning coffee at our lodgings, and ate our other meals at a delicious, cheap little restaurant. There was a man in the *corps de ballet* called Gaudin, half-Russian and half-French. He was a poor dancer and obviously a misfit in the company, but he was kind and useful at running errands. He collected money from us during rehearsals and went to Rumpelmayer's, the cake shop on the right of the garden. He would bring us fruit and cold drinks and piles of those attractive paper boxes of cakes tied together in pyramids. We worked like blacks and were always hungry or thirsty, so Gaudin was worth his weight in gold.

When our rehearsals finished, the great crowd of our company would pour down the alleyway onto the terrace and mingle with the smart visitors. On the terraces outside the Casino between eleven and one, or between five and seven, one could see a real fashion parade. It was the custom then to wear dresses in the morning, suits or costumes in the afternoon, and of course evening dress or semi-evening dress at night. The air seemed always to be impregnated with perfume, either from the women or from the flowers. Our dancers held their own with the fashionable visitors: they were as well suited to showing off the lovely French clothes as if they had been models. I was particularly surprised at the beauty of their shoes. Back in England we had somehow never bothered much about shoes, but theirs seemed like works of art.

It was very rare for afternoon rehearsals to be called when there was a performance in the evening, unless a new production was receiving special attention or an understudy had to be tried out. Diaghilev knew it was essential to have a certain amount of rest, as well as time to look after tu-tus, rehearsal dresses, tights and shoes; and the Russians still stuck to the traditional working hours of the Imperial Theatres. However, there was so much for me to learn that I used to work a great deal in the afternoons, and life was pretty hectic.

The season was about to begin when we arrived at Monte Carlo, and there were so many ballets for me to learn in a hurry that my head was in a whirl. Very often I would get through a ballet quite well the first time I danced it, then make a mess of it the second. I had to learn to fill my part in the *corps de ballet* of *Cléopâtre*, *Scheherazade*, *Prince Igor*, *Thamar*, *l'Oiseau de feu* and *Petroushka*. I was taught the part of a Polovtsian girl in *Prince Igor* while the overture was being played: there just had not been time to teach me. Luckily I picked up steps quickly.

There was one Fokine ballet, though, that we were not allowed to take part in until we had been in the company at least six months and had watched it frequently: this was *Les Sylphides*. Endless pains were always taken with this lovely work, and every performance of it had to be an absolutely perfect unity. Every girl who danced in that ballet was chosen not only for her grace, but also for her ability to move in unison with her fellow

35

artists. From the time of its first performance in Paris during Diaghilev's first season in 1909, *Les Sylphides* was never for long out of the repertoire, and although he easily got tired of nearly every other ballet, Diaghilev never lost interest in *Les Sylphides*: his company danced it until the year of his death. When we were allowed to appear in it we felt as if we had been give a special promotion, even though we had no solos.

One Fokine work in which I danced was destined to have very few performances before it was dropped for ever. *Le Dieu bleu* may not have been much of a ballet, but it was surely one of the most impressive spectacles designed by Bakst. The set was a great orange cliff and nearly every person on the stage was made up in varying shades of grey, green or brown. Nelidova was lily-white and Nijinsky as the god was plasticine blue all over. Bakst's original design shows Nijinsky in the role as he was first revealed in the ballet, at the top of a flight of wide steps at the back of the stage, seated on a throne with legs crossed, holding a flower. The whole company was massed round the stage, making various eastern gestures. There were a number of supers, including five little boys, who wore much more elaborate and glamorous costumes than the dancers. Some of their head-dresses were of white lace or net on gigantic wire frames about three feet high. The predominating colour of the costumes was white and most of the women wore bell-shaped skirts lined with a very heavy material. Karsavina had rather a thankless part with one solo, which she danced beautifully, manœuvring her hands and feet into the exotic positions Fokine had invented for her.

In *Le Dieu bleu* there were two dances that struck me particularly. One was performed by our three tall beauties, each carrying a stuffed peacock. They held these magnificent birds by their stiffened claws, allowing the long tail to fall over their shoulders or float in the air, and grouped themselves in lovely poses. The colour of the peacocks' tails was wonderful against their naked midriffs and white veils. Seraphine Astafieva danced in the middle, between Tchernicheva and Piltz; and although these girls were very tall, the peacocks' tails were so long that when the birds were perched on their shoulders they would still trail on the ground. The peacocks had a special container to be carried in when we travelled.

The other was the dance of the dervishes. Their costumes were made entirely of white ropes, about a thumb's thickness. Besides the ropes which formed the skirts, there were more attached to their caps, which hung down to about knee-length. The ropes were dead white, and the men's bodies were dark greyish-brown. As the dancers spun faster and faster at the end of their dance, they presented an extraordinary picture of whizzing white discs. It is amazing to think that Cocteau was responsible for this scenario as far back as 1911.

Following the triumphant Paris season of 1909, Diaghilev could at first only hold his seasons during the spring and summer, when the dancers he employed were on leave from the Russian Imperial Theatres; but in 1911 Diaghilev had engineered the dismissal of Nijinsky from the Marinsky Theatre in St Petersburg, thus securing the full-time services of the greatest living male dancer. From then on Diaghilev was his own master, guaranteeing full employment to a large company. Those dancers who were unwilling to leave the security of the Imperial Theatres to dance for him were replaced by others from Poland and elsewhere: but Diaghilev continued to engage stars, such as Karsavina, from the Imperial Theatres during their periods of leave.

Diaghilev loved Nijinsky; and he was incapable of loving anyone without trying to educate him and bring out all his latent possibilities. While Nijinsky's physical gifts were well developed before he met Diaghilev, the interpretive powers which later made him as great an actor as he was a dancer increased enormously under the latter's influence. Diaghilev never having been a dancer, could not invent dances, although he knew how to suggest the form and style they should take; and it would obviously be an ideal arrangement, both personally and artistically, if his chosen friend could be trained to interpret for him choreographically the ideas which were for ever bubbling in his head. It was during the year before I joined the company that Diaghilev, with a will-power and devotion which showed themselves in the form of infinite patience and forbearance, had set about turning Nijinsky into a choreographer—the first of several he was to create. Fokine, whose 'return to nature' in choreography had been one of the reasons for the renaissance in Russian ballet, but who had never really seen eye to eye with Diaghilev, left the company.

Nijinsky, however, was an awkward instrument: what gifts he had were instinctive. He was not incapable of inspiration, but reasoning and systematic organisation of his thoughts were beyond him. In 1912 his first ballet, *L'Après-midi d'un faune*, though it lasted only eight minutes, required an incredible number of rehearsals; and Stravinsky has recorded in his autobiography that when the time came to work with Nijinsky on *Le Sacre du printemps*, he had to teach the young choreographer 'the rudiments of music: the values of each note . . . time, speed, rhythm and so on'.

When I joined the ballet in April, 1913, Nijinsky was sole *maître de ballet*. His *Faune* was in the current repertory; his *Jeux* and *Sacre* were in rehearsal, and Diaghilev must have been happy watching over the birth, however difficult, of the new experimental works. There was every reason to believe that the company would continue with the divine Nijinsky as principal dancer and the rather less divine Nijinsky as choreographer for many years to come.

In appearance Nijinsky was himself like a faun—a wild creature who had been trapped by society and was always ill at ease. When addressed, he turned his head furtively, looking as if he might suddenly butt you in the stomach. He moved on the balls of his feet, and his nervous energy found an outlet in fidgeting: when he sat down he twisted his fingers or played with his shoes. He hardly spoke to anyone, and seemed to exist on a different plane. Before dancing he was even more withdrawn, like a bewitched soul. I used to watch him practising his wonderful jumps in the first position, flickering his hands; I had never seen anyone like him before.

When Diaghilev came for the first time to one of our rehearsals

I was scared stiff. His presence was awe-inspiring and he radiated self-assurance, like royalty. Tall and heavy, with a little moustache and a monocle, he advanced into the room, followed by a group of friends. Everyone who was seated stood up, and silence fell. With Grigoriev following discreetly a yard or two behind, he passed through the crowd of dancers, stopping here and there to exchange a greeting. Any male dancer to whom he spoke would click his heels together and bow.

Diaghilev then sat down, and we three English girls were summoned before him. Cowed by his majestic personality, I felt like a naughty school-child. Mim Rambert came to our rescue and translated his words. He told us that we should have to work very hard to improve our standard of dancing, and that we must take great care to do everything Maestro Cecchetti told us. We were glad when the time came for us to lose ourselves once more in the crowd. Diaghilev spoke quietly and deliberately, and during all the years I knew him I seldom heard him raise his voice.

At the start of our season when we were assembled on the stage before the performance, Diaghilev would wander on, looking magnificent in tails. He knew his appearance was impressive and he behaved accordingly. He would look for creases in the scenery, make sure the lighting was correct, mumble a few words to Nijinsky or Karsavina, ignoring the rest of us, give Grigoriev the word to begin, and go through the pass door into the front of the house. Carefully shaved and scented, his hair touched up with black dye, except for a white streak left on one side, he looked incredibly distinguished and I felt proud to have him as my director. This feeling of pride in Diaghilev never left me in later years, even when I knew he had holes in the soles of his shoes. Yet grand as he was, we always addressed him in the Russian fashion by his own first name and his father's, 'Sergei Pavlovitch'.

L'Après-midi d'un faune was an animated Greek frieze performed in profile to the dream-like music of Debussy. The story is very simple: a faun, idling in the afternoon sun, is surprised by some nymphs. When he tries to make love to one of them she is

frightened and runs away, so he consoles himself with a scarf
she has dropped. I heard that Nijinsky had had great trouble,
when first working out the ballet, in explaining his ideas to the
dancers. The girls were too highly trained in the turned-out
movements of classical ballet to be able to switch easily to the
angular turned-in movements, which were all done in straight
lines as if the dancers were sliding in parallel grooves.

I was soon cast for one of the nymphs in *Faune*. To have to
learn this curious new style of dancing in addition to all the other
roles I had to study was really the last straw. Nijinsky used to
stand in front of me, picking his thumbs and staring at me
through half-closed eyes. Then, turning to Mim, he would
ask, 'Does she understand?' One day he came up to me during
rehearsal and said, with Mim interpreting, 'You must try to
walk between the bars of the music and sense the rhythm which
is implied.' I went dizzy; clutching my head, I burst into tears,
ran off the stage and collapsed. I must have had a slight breakdown from nervous strain, but I was away from the theatre for
only twenty-four hours, for I was keen to keep my place in the
ballet, and determined to show all the Russian and Polish girls
that I could do as well as they did. None of them thought the
tubby little English girl could make the grade.

Once back at rehearsals I began to enjoy my work more than
ever. After watching the *Faune* in performance, I could hardly
wait to have another try at dancing in it. To be allowed to take
part in the *Faune* was an honour. The dancers had to be musical
as well as rhythmical and it was necessary to relax and hear the
music as a whole; it had to trickle through your consciousness,
and the sensation approached the divine. One walked and moved
quite gently in a rhythm that crossed over the beats given by the
conductor. At every entrance one made—and there were several
—one began to count, taking the count from another dancer
who was coming off. For every lift of the hand or head there was
a corresponding sound in the score. It was most ingeniously
thought out. I do not know how much of this Nijinsky did
himself, but he must have had enormous help from the composer.
In order to preserve the patterns of the frieze, you had to keep

your hands and arms flat in profile: to do this it was necessary to relax the hand and arm, for if you forced or tightened the gesture, the wrist fell back and the straight line from elbow to fingers was lost.

Nijinsky as the Faun was thrilling. Although his movements were absolutely restrained, they were virile and powerful, and the manner in which he caressed and carried the nymph's veil was so animal that one expected to see him run up the side of the hill with it in his mouth. There was an unforgettable moment just before his final amorous descent upon the scarf when he knelt on one knee on top of the hill, with his other leg stretched out behind him. Suddenly he threw back his head, opened his mouth and silently laughed. It was superb acting.

Jeux, which Nijinsky was also rehearsing at Monte Carlo, was all about tennis, and it must have been the first ballet inspired by the modern craze for sport. There were just three dancers, Nijinsky, Karsavina and Schollar. The set was a moonlit garden designed by Bakst and the music by Debussy was specially commissioned. It started with a ball bouncing onto the stage; the three dancers followed it, carrying tennis rackets; the boy flirted first with one girl, then the other, then with both at once. Another ball bounced onto the stage, they all ran after it and the ballet was over. *Jeux* had some pretty and original groupings, but there wasn't much to it. Nijinsky's idea must have been to turn his dancers into puppets by inventing a stiff and angular choreography, and to suggest that in the twentieth century love was just another game, like tennis. The novelty of *Jeux* was that it was danced on three-quarter-point: that is to say, the dancers neither stood on their points as in classical ballet, nor on the ball of the foot, but half-way between. Instead of wearing the usual padded toe-shoes, the girls and Nijinsky had slippers which were just slightly hardened at the tips. It was not really very effective, as it looked as if they were trying to dance on their points and not doing it properly. Bakst's conception of a modern sporting costume proved too comic at the last moment; so Nijinsky wore a white shirt with rolled-up sleeves and white tennis trousers which were stylised by cutting them short and sewing them

41

right round the calf, while the women wore white jumpers with simple skirts by Paquin.

Far more important than *Jeux* was the other ballet upon which Nijinsky was then working. *Le Sacre du printemps*, with its revolutionary score by Stravinsky, was destined to be a landmark in the history of modern music. It was born from the new cult of the primitive. Nowadays we all know the story of how Gauguin's dream of noble savagery drove him off to the South Sea Islands, and we have been told that it was Picasso's fascination for Negro sculpture which led him, in 1907, to paint the first cubist picture, but in 1913 no one had imagined a primitive *ballet*. In *L'Oiseau de feu* and *Petroushka*, both commissioned by Diaghilev, the young Stravinsky had said all he had to say for the time being about Holy Russia: now he 'looked back to some dark epoch at the beginning of time, to a land without a name, where a people of no nationality celebrated fearful rites to appease an unknown god'. To express the dread, hope and frenzy of these brutish folk, Stravinsky made a music whose rhythms, trembling, pulsing, flickering, thudding and crashing with a maniac piston beat, registered their animal emotions.

When I arrived in Monte Carlo the first of the two scenes in *Sacre* had already been arranged, and the English girls were merely fitted into the finale of that scene. This was complete chaos. We had to run about more or less *ad lib*, and stamp to various rhythms. We were really allotted no definite place on the stage, and the curtain came down on a stampede of humanity.

Marie Rambert had been especially engaged by Diaghilev to assist with the production of this ballet. Having studied eurythmics with Dalcroze, she was able to help Nijinsky and the other dancers with Stravinsky's complicated rhythms. In previous ballets we had always been able to dance to a melody: in *Sacre* we had to dance to counts far more complicated than in *Faune*. I think this was easier for me than for some of the other dancers, because my musical studies had been quite advanced. Some of the girls used to be running round with little bits of paper in their hands, in a panic, quarrelling with each other about whose count was right and whose wrong.

In the first scene I remember a group of Ancients with long beards and hair, who stood huddled together, shaking and trembling as if they were dying with fear. The second scene, with the sacrifice of the Chosen Virgin, began with all the female dancers standing in a large circle facing outward, the Chosen One among them. We all had our toes pointing inwards, the right elbow resting on the left fist, and the right fist supporting the head which was leant sideways. As the ring began to move round, at certain counts the whole group would rise on tip-toe, dropping their right hands to their sides and jerking their heads to the left. When one circuit of the stage had been completed, every other girl would leap out of the ring, then back again.

The dance Nijinsky arranged for Piltz in the principal role was nothing like as strenuous, either mentally or physically, as the one I danced in the later Massine version, but it was effective all the same. Her dance was divided into sections, and knowing how difficult the phrasing is, I can see how much easier this was for her. Having the sequence of her movements interrupted by passages of ensemble dancing, she could simply begin every time with a new series of counts. (I only had two short breaks, when some steps to which I used to count five were echoed by the *corps de ballet*.) At the end of her dance, Piltz was lifted, lying full-length, onto the shoulders of the tallest men in the company; then as the music crashed to a close, they raised her to the full height of their upstretched arms and ran with her off the stage. This was a very impressive scene.

The new ballet was first given during our Paris season, which followed that of Monte Carlo. A lot has been written about the hubbub which greeted the first performance of *Le Sacre du printemps* at the Champs-Elysées Theatre on May 29, 1913, and I am certain that not one of the dancers present will ever forget that occasion. The shouting and whistling in the audience began almost as soon as the music, and by the time the curtain went up, we were pretty scared. Grigoriev wrote in his book *The Diaghilev Ballet 1909–1929* that 'the dancers . . . were quite unmoved and even amused by this unprecedented commotion'. I can only say that I, for one, was not amused at all.

Sacre is quite a long ballet, and a very noisy one; but the uproar in the audience made it hard for us to hear even this music. We were all terrified that we were doing the fourth, fifth or sixth steps, while somebody else was doing the second; and Nijinsky was in the wings stamping and trying to count for different groups all at once. We could see Diaghilev too, walking up and down, holding his head. We must have been a lovely picture for the audience, racing round, jumping, turning, and wondering when the whole thing was going to collapse. The first scene ended with a burst of whistling from the front of the house, and we were extremely glad when the curtain came down. But we still had to change our costumes for Act Two, which was more difficult, if anything, than the first.

Anyone who has taken part in either version of *Le Sacre du printemps*, must remember the heat on the stage while it was being danced, even in the winter. I do not know whether it was our wigs, or the smell of our hot flannel costumes, which were a brilliant red in the first Act and white in the second, or the fact that there were so many of us packed together, or excitement, or fear, but we generated heat like a furnace; and at the end of the ballet there can have been none of the forty-odd dancers who was not soaking.

The great season which opened the newly built Théâtre des Champs-Elysées, by an arrangement Diaghilev had made with the famous French impresario Gabriel Astruc, was one not only of Russian ballet but also of Russian Opera, with Chaliapin in *Khovanschchina* and *Boris Godounov*. A day or two after we arrived in Paris, trainloads of singers began to arrive from Russia. Most of these people had never before been in Western Europe, and quite a number of the men wore their national costume—Russian shirts and baggy trousers tucked into their boots. As some of them had beards as well, they appeared to have stepped straight off the stage. When they walked down the street people thought they were an advertisement for the Russian Opera and Ballet, and Diaghilev very soon gave orders that they were to wear ordinary suits.

From Paris the Diaghilev Ballet went to London, opening at

the end of June; and for the first time the company danced at the Theatre Royal, Drury Lane. Here too I made my first appearance with them in my home town. The London season, which Sir Joseph Beecham presented with his son Thomas conducting, was, like the Paris one, a combination of ballet and opera. How strange that London audiences should have first heard Stravinsky's *Sacre du printemps* and Moussorgsky's tremendous operas written forty years earlier, in the course of the same season! It was possible to see Nijinsky in *Le Spectre de la rose* one night and to hear Chaliapin in *Boris Godounov* the next.

Diaghilev had already made his name with the London public as an impresario of ballet, and now that he had the enterprise to bring them such glorious productions of opera as well, he was recognised as one of the wonders of the theatrical world. There were nearly a hundred and twenty singers and dancers involved in this unique season. I found it hard to believe that I was dancing on that historic stage where I had seen Dan Leno and Herbert Campbell in pantomime as a child.

Every pay-day—that is, once a fortnight—we would line up in the green room behind the stage at Drury Lane, and Grigoriev would be sitting there at a table, with piles of golden sovereigns and half-sovereigns, silver crowns, half-crowns, shillings, sixpences and threepenny pieces. In those days, salaries in the Diaghilev ballet were calculated in French francs, and it cannot have been easy for Grigoriev to work out the sums due to different artists. It was quite a sight to see our company, all so elegantly dressed, lining up to receive those piles of gold and silver, and signing the ledger. Even I, with my fifteen gold sovereigns, plus a little silver, would feel as rich as Croesus as I walked out into the sunshine of Russell Street.

One day I came into the wings on my way out of the theatre and stopped to stare at Chaliapin, who was waiting to make his entrance in one of the operas. There was no one else near us except three stage-hands. I stood gazing with admiration and wonder at that magnificent figure. Under his make-up for *Boris*, which was world-famous, you could not imagine Chaliapin's own face at all. I was wondering how he could possibly sing through all that paint and hair, when one of the men from the chorus walked straight up to him, mumbled something in Russian and struck him a great whack across the face. I was so shocked I nearly called out; and one of the stage-hands said, 'Blimey, see that?' Chaliapin lifted up both his arms, puffed himself out like some gigantic bird, looking as if he were about to burst—then, at that precise moment, he got his music cue. He advanced with enormous strides onto the stage and let out a note loud enough for ten men. I left the theatre without delay in case I was roped in as a witness, but if there was a sequel I never heard of it.

I saw very little of my family at this time although I was living at home. I got back from the theatre after everybody was in bed, and left before eight in the morning to be in time for class. Classes were held at the Territorial Drill Hall in Chenies Street, off Tottenham Court Road. They always began at nine o'clock, and woe betide anyone who was late. We would arrive to find Maestro Cecchetti watering the floor and whistling an unidentifiable tune. He had a funny way of breaking into a whistle as he was talking to you.

Diaghilev allowed several painters and sculptors to watch these classes. Among them were Laura Knight and Una Troubridge, whose head of Nijinsky as the Faun—the only sculpture of him except Rodin's little sketch ever done from life—I was to find in a junk-shop forty years later. Nijinsky was certainly the main target of these artists, and sometimes when he worked privately with Cecchetti during the lunch hour they were allowed to stay and sketch. There was one girl who was always sitting, watching in silence, and we were surprised to find that she was allowed to join in our classes with Cecchetti. As she was not a regular member of our company this was exceptional. We learned that she was the daughter of a famous Hungarian actress. Diaghilev, who never let pass an opportunity to make up to influential people, had allowed her to study with us, although she was not really a dancer. Her name was Romola de Pulszka. She spoke English and used to come and sit in the *corps de ballet* dressing-room and talk to me.

46

Nijinsky, I noticed, even though he was always surrounded by people, seemed always to be alone; he was incapable of mixing in any way. If he spoke at all it was to somebody with whom he was dancing, and then he would talk softly and shyly, without looking at the person, and move away as quickly as possible. Before working, Nijinsky used to walk about a lot on the tips of his toes. He would move a few steps to the right, then a few to the left, holding his hands up in a curious characteristic way with the backs touching his cheeks, his head tilted downward. He used to do a lot of jumps in the first position, gradually jumping higher and higher, then lower in a *diminuendo*. This is a very good way to practise jumping, and I have always copied it. The one person who never hesitated to talk to Nijinsky was Mim Rambert. She had been such a great help during the *Sacre* rehearsals that he had got used to her, and she was never embarrassed by his stand-offish manner. She spoke to him mostly in Polish, I think, and seemed never to miss an opportunity of getting him to talk. I have often thought that if Mim had been given the chance she could have done more than anyone else to keep him sane and happy.

For the final class before we broke up for the holidays, we were ordered by Cecchetti to wear our best clothes. Tu-tus, tights and shoes, everything had to be new or clean, and it was not easy for us all to change into our ironed and fluffed-up ballet skirts, crowded together in the dirty little dressing-room down a steep flight of stairs under the stage in the Drill Hall. The whole company was assembled, and Cecchetti gave us a terrific class, with lots of lovely jumping, which I always enjoyed in that huge room. At the end of it Maestro went up on the stage and said, in his own special mixture of Italian, French and Russian, 'I will now tell you who in my opinion has made the most progress during the year. I am going to give her a prize.' There was a dead silence.

All the soloists had gathered near the stage and I was standing at the back. When Cecchetti said, 'Eeda', I thought I was being reprimanded for mopping my purple, sweaty face. But once again he called, 'Eeda!' and added, 'Come up here and receive your first prize for good work.' My legs trembled as I moved through the crowd and up the steps to the stage in a profound silence. All those Russians and Poles had been working like blacks for nine months and it was the English girl who walked off with the coveted prize—a signed photograph of the Maestro in a silver frame. I think even Diaghilev and Grigoriev had a shock.

Our next engagement was in South America. Some of the dancers could not see the point in going across half the world to appear before a lot of supposed barbarians. Most of the Russians and Poles were pretty ignorant, and probably thought South Americans had two heads or hung from the trees by their feet. Diaghilev was terrified of the sea, so we were not really surprised to hear he would not be with us on tour: on the other hand it was strange to think of Nijinsky travelling without him. Diaghilev's place was taken by his associate, Baron Gunzburg; and since our conductor, Monteux, refused to go, he was replaced by M. René Baton. We heard that Romola de Pulszka was to be allowed to travel with us and to walk on in small parts with the ballet.

We sailed from Southampton on the *Avon* in the middle of August, 1913. I shared a cabin with Marie Rambert. It was very hot on the crossing, which took twenty-one days, but nothing would deter Mim from doing a complete class every morning on her own, and however hot it got she went religiously through her movements in our cabin every day.

Romola de Pulszka was travelling first-class, having presumably paid for her ticket herself, which was strange if she was seriously trying to become a member of the *corps de ballet*. Although, apart from Nijinsky and a few of the principals, we all travelled second-class, after a few days at sea we were allowed to mingle with the big noises on the upper deck. We noticed that Nijinsky was spending a good deal of time with Romola. I suppose it was the first time since he came from Russia that he had found himself without the constant companionship of Diaghilev. As we sailed further south, some of the company became apprehensive about this flirtation, about which there was less and less concealment.

48

After our stop at Rio, Baron Gunzburg gave a dinner on the ship to announce the engagement of Nijinsky and Romola. We all guessed that Romola had prevailed on Gunzburg, who was a friend of hers, to help her organise this affair, and a ring had presumably been bought at Rio. The rest of us thought it was tragic and dreaded Diaghilev's reactions.

Only a few chosen ones went to the wedding in Buenos Aires, but we all were invited to the reception afterwards at the hotel where Nijinsky and Romola were staying. It was an extremely awkward occasion, for there was not a single person present— except possibly Gunzburg, who was either blind or mad—who could honestly congratulate bride or groom. I was only a minor member of the *corps de ballet* without any special knowledge of what went on behind the scenes, but I know there was not one of us who would not have stopped the wedding if he had had the means.

Nijinsky just smiled and picked his fingers, while Romola looked as pleased with herself as was possible in the circumstances; she must have sensed our disapproval. I think they were both as worried and uncomfortable as we were. Surely someone must have talked to Nijinsky about the future and tried to make him see sense. Perhaps Mim did: I never knew.

Romola had never really been one of us, and she obviously had no intention of discussing her affairs. From the time we had sailed from Southampton she grew more remote, keeping her scheme to herself. After the wedding, she was completely aloof, never came near our dressing-rooms, and soon gave up dancing her little bits in the company as well.

Our South American tour was a success with the public, but in the course of it Nijinsky became more and more difficult. Apparently Romola had been looking into his contract. It seems that, as a mere formality, he had one in which Diaghilev agreed to pay him an enormous sum of money; but as Diaghilev had always given him all the comfort and luxury he could possibly want, besides paying his expenses, this contract had never really been fulfilled. One night when we were back in Rio, Nijinsky refused to appear. This was a serious matter and a breach of his agreement. Later, when we got back to Europe and were going on holiday, we heard that he had received a telegram dismissing him from the company. Although the pretext was his refusal to appear that night in Rio de Janeiro, his marriage was obviously the real reason.

So Nijinsky found himself with a wife to support and nowhere to dance. His whole world had collapsed around him. Now that he had quarrelled with the Imperial Theatres there was no other company he could join—for Pavlova would never have put up with another genius as great or greater than herself in her troupe. Diaghilev had not only seen to it that Nijinsky should always appear to the most perfect advantage in glorious productions, with the backing of a fine *corps de ballet*, but he had also poured into him the fruit of all his knowledge and experience, and turned him into a creator of ballets. Now it was all over.

5

FOKINE'S BALLETS

Fokine rejoins the Russian Ballet — Fokine and Karsavina
in *Le Spectre de la rose* — Rehearsals of *Daphnis et Chloë* — The
beauty, art and industry of Karsavina — *Scheherazade* —
Nicolas Kremnev shows interest — The arrival of Massine —
Les Papillons and *Midas* — Strauss's *La Légende de Joseph* —
Stravinsky's *Le Rossignol* — The novel production of *Coq d'or*
— Dancing *Prince Igor* with a chorus — Pre-war London —
'Have you seen the Russians?'

New ballets had to be created to satisfy the appetite of a public
that was coming to expect from Diaghilev an annual crop of
new sensations; and with Nijinsky gone, there seemed to be no
alternative but the re-engagement of Fokine.

When Michael Fokine succeeded the ancient Marius Petipa
as *maître de ballet* at the Mariinsky Theatre in 1908, the reforms
he instituted had seemed as revolutionary to the conservative
balletomanes of St Petersburg as the innovations of Nijinsky were
to appear to Parisian audiences in 1912. Like Nijinsky, a product
of the Imperial School, but unlike him, a man of wide culture,
Fokine who was ten years older, had been inspired to introduce
a new 'naturalness' into the spectacles presented at the Czar's
court. His belief in the dramatic possibilities of ballet made him
anxious to renounce irrelevant displays of virtuosity; his study and
practice of the art of painting enraptured him with the idea of
'local colour'; and his knowledge of music convinced him that
the made-to-measure marches and waltzes of the traditional
ballet were out-of-date. The visit of Isadora Duncan to St
Petersburg in 1905 demonstrated the expressive possibilities of

a freer type of movement, and Diaghilev's ventures in Western Europe had finally given him the opportunity to put his theories into practice with a freedom which would have been impossible at the Mariinsky. A ballet like *Scheherazade*, arranged to a symphonic poem by Rimsky Korsakov, with a blazing set by the 'easel painter' Bakst—and a story, moreover, about an orgy with Negroes in a Shah's harem—would have been unthinkable at the Imperial court.

In Nijinsky and Karsavina Fokine found the ideal interpreters of his new works: both were as remarkable for their acting as for their dancing ability. Fokine had, in fact, loved Karsavina in his youth, but she had married someone else and he had married another dancer, an exotic beauty who was known as Vera Fokina.

If Fokine had been a reformer in his day, he was not a man like Diaghilev whose mind would always remain open to new ideas in painting and music. He had not taken too readily to the early scores of Stravinsky, and he had been shocked by Nijinsky's choreographic experiments. His return to Diaghilev was, no doubt, a convenience to them both, but it must have seemed doubtful to those in the know whether he would for long continue to work peaceably in the company. Fokine came back not only as choreographer but as principal dancer.

We reassembled in Prague after a short holiday which followed our return from South America, and it was grand to be back and to start work again. Several of the old company had chosen to stay in Russia, but others had been engaged in their place: and soon after our arrival, the great Fokine joined us. It was fascinating to be rehearsed by him in his own ballets with which I was already familiar and to see him working out the new ones.

I enjoyed watching Fokine dance, and I loved to see him with Karsavina in *Le Spectre de la rose*. It was an entirely different sensation from watching Nijinsky. Nijinsky had been such a myth, and he had that miraculous elevation, so that one was dazzled by his performance and never thought of analysing or criticising it. Fokine danced with a complete understanding of the music and of the steps he had invented to go with it. Nijinsky had been sexless—an elfin thing. Fokine dancing with Karsavina was very much the lover. When the beautiful Karsavina danced *Le Spectre* with Nijinsky, she seemed to show a certain detachment, as if he was merely a dream to her, and when he floated out of the window she really woke up. When she danced the same ballet with Fokine there seemed to be a secret affinity between them. I used to say to myself, 'He loves her. I know he does.' When he leaned over her as she slept in her chair and brushed her forehead with a kiss, just before his exit leap, you could almost hear him think, 'Wake up and remember me.'

In Fokine's *Daphnis et Chloë*, I had my first experience of dancing a ballet with bare feet. This gave me a strange sensation of nakedness, like walking in public in a nightgown. The music which Ravel had written to order for Diaghilev had glorious moments, and yet the work on the whole never quite came off. Whether this was because the structure of the score was fundamentally undramatic, or because the story was not particularly interesting, I do not know. There is something futile about the character of Daphnis: after all, when Chloë is captured by pirates he doesn't even rescue her, but just falls flat on his back and waits for a god to do all the dirty work.

We had very attractive hair-styles in that ballet: the hair was built upwards at the back of the head and wound round with strips of coloured material which allowed a pony-tail of curls to tumble out of the top. Our dresses, as in all the Grecian ballets, were made of a fine flannel or cashmere, and Bakst's patterns were painted on this material.

One day when Fokine was rehearsing *Daphnis* he called Maikerska, with whom I was always paired off, and myself. He said he wanted to make a new arrangement of the Dance of the Seven Veils, and he didn't know which of us to choose for it. I was very excited because I had been in the ballet under a year, and to be called for a solo part was something extraordinary. We learned the new dance, and the day of the dress rehearsal arrived. It was not an easy dance, as one had to wear a number of veils, one on top of the other, and then perform a sort of strip-tease. Maikerska had been in the ballet longer than I had, so she was given the first chance. Half-way through she got into a muddle with the veils. Fokine stopped the orchestra and asked what she had done. She replied in an agitated voice, but he shouted, 'Get on with it.' Foolishly she answered back, and Fokine, who could be very sulky and bad-tempered, got angry. 'Get off the stage,' he called, 'and give the veils to the English girl.' The veils were put on me, and I had to go out and do the dance. I managed to get through it somehow; then Maikerska was given another chance. Fokine did not know which of us to choose; and I think it was the first time in the history of the Diaghilev ballet that any part was shared alternately between two dancers as a regular arrangement.

I loved the calm of Karsavina's Chloë in the first act, and the relaxed way she lay on the ground watching Daphnis dance for her. What a contrast to Act Two when she was the Pirates' captive! The passion and despair she put into her gestures, writhing and fighting with the ropes which bound her, had an effect which I can only compare with a thunderstorm.

Fokine danced Daphnis with gentleness, and I am sure he enjoyed doing it. It is difficult to compare him with Nijinsky in this role. I never knew if Nijinsky genuinely loved dancing and lost himself in the pleasure of movement: although I watched him closely many times he never showed by excitement or by a sparkle in his eye that he had been carried away by the exhilaration of the dance. Of course his technique, speed and elevation were miraculous, and to praise Fokine is not to belittle Nijinsky. Fokine had a fine-proportioned and elegant figure, which Nijinsky had not; he was a good-looking man and he danced with full understanding of what he wanted to convey.

Tamara Karsavina was one of the rare dancers who gripped your attention whether you were watching her from the stage, from the wings or from the front of the house. I could not bear to miss any movement she made, and was sometimes so reluctant to stop watching her from the wings when I should have been changing my costume, that I was nearly late for my entrance. She made so deep an impression on me that I have been able in later years to describe to her minute details of her costumes and head-dresses in various roles which she had quite forgotten. Besides being an exceptionally beautiful and fascinating woman, she had a sublime stage presence, so no wonder that a novice like myself was overwhelmed. She never appeared to be nervous, or if she was she concealed it admirably. She talked very little to anybody, and seemed entirely given up to her work in the theatre. Never by any chance did she miss going through the full daily Cecchetti class. (He had one class for each day of the week, and this never varied throughout the year except for the one terrible day when a whole class was done on point.) I have sat at the back of the stage in a corner and watched Karsavina doing a class by herself in semi-darkness. For over an hour she would work away in a grubby white tunic, with a bit of green stuff tied round her middle. She rarely left out the tiniest exercise and would correct herself as she went along. By the end she would be soaked through, with the green dye coming off all over her tunic. In performance she was just as thorough, and besides dancing so perfectly she would display the full marvel of her graciousness and charm.

I cannot remember any ballet of Fokine's in which Karsavina did not fulfil her part to the uttermost. I think of her beauty as Echo in *Narcisse* as she reflected Nijinsky's movements; of her extraordinary simplicity in *Le Pavillon d'Armide*. In *Thamar* her baleful majesty was unforgettable, and I admired her light and tidy foot-work when she danced with the visiting stranger whom she was to love and kill. Nobody has ever surpassed her in *Les Sylphides*: but of all the ballets she danced with Nijinsky, perhaps nothing was better than their teamwork in *Carnaval*, for his technique and her beauty showed to such wonderful advantage in this ballet. The speed of his mischievous head movements and of his twinkling feet and hands was matched by that of her pointed toes as she ran hither and thither with her swaying white crinoline painted with cherries, looking so pretty and gay.

When Karsavina danced *Scheherazade* she wore a charming but rather simple costume, mostly peacock blue with pearls, and a tulle skirt over tight little trousers. She had bare feet and an osprey in her head-dress. As Zobeide she looked so relaxed and at home on the cushions with her husband, the Shah, that when Nijinsky as the Negro came bounding out of his door at the back, painted and colourful, and danced like some beautiful animal, rocking from side to side, longing to ravish the lady of the house, you really felt she had done a dreadful thing in ordering the locked door to be opened. Nijinsky was very exciting, but rather mad, and therefore frightening: Karsavina was so distinguished, and danced so freely and so simply, that it was startling to see her paired with this savage.

The ballet worked up to an orgy, and to dance in it was so exciting that you found yourself throwing your arms and body around in a frenzy. At the moment when the Shah reappeared downstage from the prompt corner, I really felt terrified, and ashamed to have taken part in turning his home into a mad-house, which had been as peaceful as a lily pond when he went away. What with Bakst's scenery, his gorgeous costumes, the Wives in their pink and green, the vivid cushions, the flight of steps, the Bacchanalian entrance of the *corps de ballet* carrying enormous plates of fruit above their heads, the Negroes—six black and six dark-grey—this ballet made a sensation unlike any other.

In later years when Luba Tchernicheva succeeded Karsavina as Zobeide, and Massine took over from Nijinsky and Fokine, the whole atmosphere changed. It was tense and exciting, but lacked the abandon that made you feel you were part of the drama. I liked Leonide Massine as the Negro immensely. He dropped the madness, and did the thing more as an exotic captive. He was a great partner to Luba. They were of the same generation and if only she could have relaxed and really let herself go, they would no doubt have been the greatest couple of recent times. Luba wore a thickish costume, with trousers of a flimsy material, open in the front and clasped here and there with pearls. She had to have rather heavy-looking shoes with a good heel, because on her head she wore a magnificent white hat with two beautiful ostrich feathers. But she had so much on that it impeded her dancing, and although she acted superbly, I some-times felt she should have followed her Shah to the wars in a gorgeous palanquin, and left us to get on with the party. How-ever, the scene of her death used to bring tears to my eyes.

When Massine left the company in 1921, Leon Woizikovsky danced the Negro. He was never an actor; his talent was for genuine dancing. At the end of the ballet when he is struck with a sword, he did a most wonderful leap. He ran across the front of the stage and did the *grand jeté* as Fokine had planned it, but he somehow contrived to fall on the side of his neck, threw his legs in the air, seemed to spin on the top of his head and then collapse. He could never explain how he did it, and we could never work out by watching him how it was done.

I have no doubt that Rimsky Korsakov's music for *Scheherazade* was the most moving that we danced to. It never failed to create a tense atmosphere on stage, long before the curtain went up. It was a ballet that every dancer enjoyed, which is rare indeed. Ever since this ballet had first been given, Diaghilev had omitted the third movement, playing the first over twice. Fokine must have insisted that the third movement should be restored when-ever Vera Fokina was to dance *Scheherazade* with him, because it was only danced when she was performing. He had certainly made a superb arrangement to a particular passage in a minor key—a *pas de deux* for the two principals, with the other Wives and Negroes joining in. It was a splendid sight, with all the women being carried about and put down again in varied poses. However, this extra movement upset the time schedules of performances and I believe Diaghilev thought it disturbed the balance of the ballet.

The first male character dancer in our company was Nicolas Kremnev: and since he was short, he was also leader of the 'boys'. He had been trained in St Petersburg by the celebrated teacher Nicolas Legat. His technique for character dancing was amazing, and he could perform all kinds of stunts, such as doing *entrechat-six* with his knees, his feet sticking out sideways, and landing from a jump with his body low on the ground, then springing into the air without a pause. In *Le Pavillon d'Armide* he performed astonishing feats as the chief Jester, wearing a costume hung all over with tinkling bells. Fokine took advantage of his strange gifts and arranged grotesque solos especially for him. He was tight-limbed, small and almost ugly in appearance, but fascinating to watch and I used to stand and stare whenever he was dancing, trying to find out how he did his tricks. Being more than a little pleased with himself, he must have noticed me watching him, and he soon started talking to me. As my Russian at that time was mostly limited to words which were useful for my work, and his English was practically non-existent, we spoke mostly in French; neither of us was very fluent, but somehow we managed.

Kremnev told me his father was a veterinary surgeon who looked after the bay horses at the Imperial Court. His mother, who was given to drinking too much, created jealous scenes and made such an exhibition of herself in public, that his father was finally driven to commit suicide. The fact that we each had a difficult parent seemed to be a bond of sympathy between us.

When I was first being courted by Kola Kremnev people used to say to me, 'You be careful. He has a bad temper.' They could have saved their breath, because not only was I very flattered to be escorted everywhere by a *premier danseur*, but it was the first time in my life that I had ever been petted or had received any special attention. My suitcase was carried for me whenever we travelled and everything was done to make me comfortable. It was nice to think of oneself as grown-up with an admirer, like the other couples in the company. I began to enjoy life immensely.

It was during these early months of 1914, while we were touring Germany, having a wonderful time, happy to be working with Fokine on his new ballets, and meeting with success everywhere, that we heard that Nijinsky had raised the money to put on a season of his own at the Palace Theatre in London. He was giving several ballets to which he had no right, and we heard the production and performances were poor. Those two weeks were the last time Nijinsky ever attempted to dance without Diaghilev's great organisation behind him; his talent alone was not enough to guarantee success. The failure of his venture was undoubtedly a great shock to him, and this as well as the responsibilities of married life which he did not understand at all, began to cause his mind to slip away.

Fokine's new ballets in 1914 were not all up to the standard of his old ones. *Les Papillons* was meant to be a sequel to *Carnaval*, but it was a stupid ballet. Pierrot put a lighted candle on the ground, and we all danced around it until the principal dancer, usually Mme Karsavina, got her wings singed, then Pierrot caught her, blew the candle out and handed it to someone off-stage. Of all the new works *Les Papillons* was the only one that had its first performance at Monte Carlo, where we went at the conclusion of our German tour: the others were all reserved for Paris.

I have never in my life been able to dance on my points in new ballet shoes without first breaking them in. For the dress rehearsal of *Les Papillons* I foolishly put on new shoes, and these were so desperately uncomfortable I couldn't feel my feet at all. As I couldn't understand what was being said I did not know which parts of the ballet were supposed to be done on point. Right in the middle of some runs Fokine stopped the rehearsal and shouted, 'Why English girl not on points?' While the whole company waited for me, with Fokine calling from the front of the house, I ran to a fireman's bucket and stuck each foot in turn into the water. This made the whole difference in softening up my shoes, and for the rest of my dancing career a fireman's bucket was always my best friend.

Fokine was also rehearsing a short ballet called *Midas* to the music of Steinberg. I could never really understand what this ballet was about, it was all so vague; it was supposed to be funny Greek, but it never seemed funny. Karsavina, I remember, looked like a little girl in a short tunic with one side of her bodice cut away to reveal a breast, bare except for a piece of net. As Midas, Bolm was unconsciously the comic relief. He had a great wig with curly hair which made his nose look bigger than ever, and at a given moment he had to press a spring to release two horns or ears on either side of it. These wretched things, which looked like bananas, did not work simultaneously: one would pop up some time after the other and make him jump. The ballet was not up to the Fokine standard and *Midas* soon fell by the wayside.

Diaghilev set great store by Fokine's new ballet *La Légende de Joseph*, because the illustrious Richard Strauss had consented to provide a score. The ballet was to have a set by the fashionable painter-decorator Jose-Maria Sert, husband of Diaghilev's dearest friend, Misia; a gorgeous affair with twisted baroque columns, flights of steps and a palm tree, all black and gold. Bakst had been told to design costumes suggestive of the rich fabrics in the pictures of Veronese. Potiphar's wife, a mimed role, was to be played by Maria Kuznetzova, a statuesque and handsome opera singer.

Diaghilev thought Fokine was too old to play the youthful Joseph, the part which should have been Nijinsky's, and during the previous winter in Russia he had found a young man whom he now destined for the role. Diaghilev had spotted Leonide Massine's handsome face in the *corps de ballet* of the Bolshoi Theatre, Moscow, and had dissuaded the boy from giving up ballet to become an actor. Although his figure was not without defects, he was soon to give proof of a quick intelligence and a capacity for hard work. His first appearance on stage with the Diaghilev Ballet was during our German tour in the small role of the Street Watchman in *Petroushka*, and I distinctly remember the day Massine arrived from Russia to join us on tour, looking remarkably like a medical student. A room had been booked for him at our hotel, and Diaghilev asked Kremnev and myself to look after him. We took him home after the first performance and he had supper with us. He was the same age as myself; thin, shy and quietly spoken. Coming fresh to the company as he did, he must have been very scared. His eyes were so enormous that they seemed to swamp his little pale face, yet when he looked at you they remained completely blank, as if there was a shutter at the back of them. (Nijinsky's eyes were fearsome and furtive: he could not look at you without blinking, and would soon look away.) Massine would stare straight at you, but his eyes never smiled. It was a strange sensation to realise that there was no way of telling what thoughts were in his head. From the first we all found him fascinating. In *La Légende de Joseph* Massine was given the part of the young Joseph, who, after resisting the advances of Potiphar's Wife and being denounced by her to her husband, is rescued from a cauldron of boiling oil by a convenient angel. There was very little acting in the part, it was strictly a dancing one, but as Massine was not then a very powerful dancer Fokine cut down his movements to a minimum and the part of Joseph was much reduced. Massine wore a diminutive white tunic, which amounted to almost nothing at all, and he looked rather touching.

As a spectacle *Joseph* was staggering. A large rostrum ran across the whole back of the stage, and on this there was a long table round which the big groups and spectacular effects took place. The costumes were magnificent, particularly those of Potiphar's Wife. She moved about on high gilded clogs, attended by servants, two of whom had a couple of honey-coloured wolfhounds on white leads. Nearly everything in the ballet was some shade of gold, except for Massine's white tunic. I was one of six slaves in a dance for three tall girls and three short ones. The ballet on the whole was not exciting, and it was not given for long.

Diaghilev had prepared two other ambitious works for his Paris season, both of which were to involve singers as well as dancers. The first of these, Stravinsky's short opera *Le Rossignol* based on Hans Andersen's story of 'The Emperor and the Nightingale', was not an unqualified success. As Fokine had his hands full, Diaghilev had sent to Russia for Boris Romanoff to do the choreography for *Le Rossignol*. His dances were simple and old-fashioned, combining well with the delicate, pretty designs of Benois, but Stravinsky's music was in those days considered modern and difficult. I cannot remember much about the work and it made no great impression on me, but I remember we girls ran around the stage dressed as Chinese, with little lanterns on sticks. These were supposed to light, but some did and some didn't, which made us giggle a lot and the whole effect was a failure.

The one undoubted triumph of the 1914 season in Paris was *Coq d'or*. For the perennial problem of how to present opera so that the audience should not be disillusioned by the unromantic appearance of singers—the best so often being fat and forty—Diaghilev found a solution so simple that it seems incredible no one had thought of it before. His idea was to have the singers on either side of the stage, seated on several tiers of raised benches, all dressed identically, while in the centre the action was danced and mimed by members of the ballet. It was a brilliantly successful method of production.

Coq d'or was a satire on monarchy in terms of a comic fairy tale. It seems easy, in the light of after events, to see in King Dodon the unfortunate spoon-fed Czar; in the beautiful Queen of Shemakhan, who turns out to be an evil enchantress, the Czarina whose counsels hastened the fall of her husband's Empire; and in the Astrologer the monk Rasputin, who made fools of them all.

Sinister undercurrents and prophetic forebodings went for nothing with the enchanted public of *le tout Paris*, who listened joyfully to Rimsky-Korsakov's languid melodies (one of which at least was to become a household favourite as *Hymn to the Sun*) and blinked at the blinding reds and yellows of Gontcharova's set. Natalie Gontcharova and her husband, Larionov, were two Moscow painters who were to prove devoted friends of Diaghilev and the Ballets Russes. The sets and dresses for *Coq d'or* were inspired by Russian peasant art, but had undergone the influence of the cubism of Paris. Gontcharova and Larionov had started a private art movement of their own called *Rayonnisme*, a name which might be translated as 'dazzle'; and the colours of *Coq d'or* were dazzling indeed. In an interview with a Paris journalist Diaghilev described how he had found his new designer in Moscow painting pictures on the foreheads of people in cafés. We loved the clothes Mme Gontcharova designed for us because they were comfortable to dance in, and made us feel we were looking our best. It was also enjoyable to dance to the accompaniment of fine singers, although this had its drawbacks. With two distinct volumes of sound on either side of the stage, the music in the orchestra pit, which we were supposed to follow, was reduced to an almost inaudible background. Karsavina, of course, did not have the same trouble, as her lovely dances were arranged to the soprano's solos. As a rule she rarely smiled when she was dancing, but in *Coq d'or* she appeared very gay, and smiled a lot, so I think she must have enjoyed dancing the Queen of Shemakhan.

In the first act I was one of the old King's maids or nurses. When he climbed up on to his great wooden bed to enjoy an afternoon's snooze, we stood close together with our backs to it, half asleep, moving our feet in and out; then circled round the bed flicking and flapping with long coloured handkerchiefs at imaginary flies, the King occasionally waking to swat one also. This dance was very cleverly arranged: having started quietly, it gradually built up into a lively episode and brought laughter and applause at the end.

The singers wore long-coated, dark red costumes which were bulky and not really very becoming, but they were designed for comfort and with the idea of not detracting from the dancers. The steps they sat on were very large, so that they were comfortable and had plenty of room.

As in the previous year, the London season followed that of Paris, and again Diaghilev presented a combination of ballet and opera, with Chaliapin singing *Boris Godounov*, *Ivan the Terrible* and *Prince Igor*.

Fokine's glorious Polovtsian dances in the second act of *Prince Igor*, with the whole chorus singing at the same time, were even more difficult than dancing to the songs in *Coq d'or*, but they were an unforgettable experience. The audience during this great scene often became as excited as the dancers, but they could not know what the artists on the stage were going through. The hubbub was unbelievable. As the ballet nears its climax there is a passage in which the chorus sing single accompanying notes for quite a long time and the orchestra is playing the melody full blast. When the dancers are near the footlights they hear the tune, but when they move upstage all they hear are single notes coming out of a lot of mouths. Meanwhile, the poor singers cannot hear the orchestra and the dancers are blocking their view of the conductor. As the ballet nears its end the dancers always begin to giggle and shout, and when the curtain falls to frenzied applause the stage is always in complete pandemonium.

That last pre-war London season was memorable for me in many ways. I was in love with Kremnev and proud to have a fiancé. I knew I had made progress as a dancer and that there was a place, and perhaps even a future, for me in the Russian Ballet. The London season in 1914 was one of unique gaiety and splendour. The same devoted public came to see us every night, and it was made up of all the smartest and most brilliant people in Society. Lady Ripon, Diaghilev's great friend and the first patroness of the Russian Ballet, rarely missed a performance; and Chaliapin's dressing-room would be crowded with interesting people and well-known beauties. Karsavina was at the peak of her career and nearly everyone was in love with her. The Aga Khan sent her an enormous basket of roses every night, which must have cost a fortune, and she would look at him with those huge dark eyes and say, 'But deeer Aga, how vairy kind you are, vairy kind indeed.' It was an exciting and wonderful sight to see the auditorium at Drury Lane packed every night with such a brilliant crowd; each performance was like a Gala, and on the last night the audience applauded for so long that Sir Joseph Beecham came before the curtain and asked them to go home.

Our company had its own glamour; the grandeur and elegance of those Russians and Poles would be a revelation to dancers today. The girls got their clothes from the best dressmakers; the men wore top-hats and morning coats, with beige or grey waistcoats and spats. Vladimirov, our principal male dancer that season, had a little Chinese valet who trotted after him everywhere he went. The Diaghilev Ballet was surrounded in mystery. We were never allowed to go to parties or to be seen anywhere except on the stage, and we became a kind of myth. Wherever you went, you would hear people saying, 'Have you seen the Russians? Have you seen the Russians?'

When we broke up for our summer holidays we little thought that it would be five years before we danced in London again.

6

EARLY WAR YEARS

War — The Company scattered — With Kremnev in music-
halls — The Ballet reassembles in Lausanne — Munnings
into Sokolova — Kremnev's jealousy — *Soleil de Nuit* —
Red Cross Galas in Geneva and Paris — With Diaghilev in
the United States — The charm of Lopokova — Dancing in
Cléopâtre — Massine's abortive flirtation — Hazards of touring — Nijinsky rejoins at the Metropolitan — Dancing the
Bacchanal in *Narcisse* — Back to Europe with horses.

War broke out in August, 1914, while we were all on holiday:
most of the dancers, being Russian or Polish, had returned to
their homes, but Kola Kremnev and I were in London. We had
no work and we did not know how to go about finding any.
I lived at home with my parents, but Kola was stranded. Money
was scarce at that time, for my grandparents had died, leaving
very little. Kola had lodgings in Bedford Place, Bloomsbury, in
a boarding house where the food was as meagre as our finances.
It was about this time that I began to study Russian in earnest,
and I learned not only to speak it properly but to write the old
script. We used to do our exercises every morning at Chandos
Hall in Maiden Lane, in a dirty basement room. It was here we
met for the first time and made friends with a young Pole called
Stanislas Idzikovsky, whom we both thought had the makings
of a remarkable dancer.

Hunting for work, we called on agents and managers whom
we had heard might be interested in us, but war conditions were
bad, and no one was very venturesome. We felt we might have
more future on the music-halls, but we had nothing suitable for an

act. Our first shot at work was to assist at a big gala matinée in aid of unemployed artists, which took place at the Gaiety Theatre in Aldwych. Idzikovsky and I danced the Harlequin and Columbine scene from *Carnaval*, with Kola in his old part as Pantalon. We spent what money we had in getting costumes and wigs and buying music, but after the show, although my father wrote letters galore to the organisers, we never so much as got our expenses paid—so there were three unemployed artists at least who did not benefit by the performance.

There was a Mr Rosen in London at that time, a well-known Russian singer, who taught singing and ran Russian choirs. He got together about twenty singers, and Kola and I danced while they sang. We were engaged at the London Pavilion for some weeks and had such a success that we were offered bookings in several other music-halls, which meant doing three shows a night and five on Saturdays. We thought nothing of starting the evening at Streatham, for instance, then going by private bus to the London Pavilion in Piccadilly and returning to Streatham for the last show there. This work lasted for some time, so I got to know another side of the theatre world.

Our engagement ended just as Annette Kellerman, the Australian swimmer and dancer, came to London, advertised as 'The Living Venus'. Postcards were sold with her photograph and measurements on one side and on the reverse a picture of the Venus de Milo with her measurements. According to the postcard there was only half an inch difference. Annette danced on her points quite well for such a tall woman, and in her act she did a kind of strip-tease, at the end of which she would dive into a tank, clad in white all-over tights. Rita Zalmani, one of my original Imperial Russian Ballet friends, was with me as a principal nymph in a little ballet which we performed round the tank. After all, we had to eat.

Kola and I put together several numbers; and at last I danced the *Destiny Waltz* solo which Mordkin had taught me years before, altered and made more complicated. We made quite a name for our act, and were engaged to reappear at the London Pavilion.

After this we were offered an even better contract at the New Oxford music-hall, which stood where Lyons' Corner House now is, at the corner of Oxford Street and Tottenham Court Road. Until recently you could still read high up on the building —the words 'The New Oxford'. Daisy Dormer, one of the great music-hall stars of the day, was topping the bill, and as dressing space was so limited she agreed to let me share her dressing-room. Daisy was a sweet person, and taught me to make the best wet-white I have ever come across. Lubov Tchernicheva, to whom I later passed on the recipe, used it to whiten her body for *Cléopâtre*.

At the end of our first week at the Oxford, when our salary was brought down to us in the dressing-room on Saturday night, there came a note from the management offering a further week's engagement. But far more exciting was the cable which arrived at the same time. Diaghilev wanted us to join him in Lausanne with a salary of four hundred Swiss francs a month. Everyone was to receive the same amount, which was just enough to pay the bill in a modest hotel or *pension*. We were so thrilled that we did not even consider accepting our extra week's engagement, but packed up, kissed Daisy good-bye, got our papers through with all speed and left for Lausanne the very next weekend.

In 1915 few people thought the war would be a long one, and it might have seemed understandable if Diaghilev had bided his time and allowed his Ballet to fall into abeyance. However, he had good reasons for reassembling whatever company he could and continuing work. Apart from the need of money, there was the importance of keeping the repertoire alive and preventing his company from being forgotten by the public; above all, he was brimming over with ideas, and in Massine, he thought he had found a wonderful instrument for expressing them. Despite the warring countries around him, Diaghilev succeeded in assembling the nucleus of a new company at his base in Switzerland. This he could probably not have achieved without the help of the indomitable Grigoriev, who in order to join Diaghilev, travelled from Russia through Finland, Sweden, Norway, England and

France, and after a week, was sent all the way back again by this devious route to recruit new dancers.

Diaghilev had signed a contract with Otto Kahn for a North American tour to begin early in 1916; and one of his chief pre-occupations at this time was to secure the release of Nijinsky from internment in Austria so that he might fulfil the conditions of the contract, which stipulated Nijinsky's appearance with the Ballet. In the meanwhile, classes and rehearsals went ahead, and, under the eye of the painter Larionov, whose interests extended to all branches of the theatre, Massine was making his first experiments in choreography. Larionov and his wife Gontcharova shared Diaghilev's passion for exploring new forms in art. Together with Stravinsky and a new-found friend, the brilliant Swiss conductor, Ansermet, they now became members of Diaghilev's artistic council. At different periods of his life, Diaghilev was surrounded by different groups of friends with whom he used to discuss his projects and talk over the ideas which were subsequently imparted to his choreographer of the moment. From the first days of the Russian Ballet, it had always been hard to attribute the true authorship of a work, although on the programmes credit would usually be given to an individual member of the group, and this was to remain true until the end of Diaghilev's life. Whatever part he played in its conception, Diaghilev himself was never mentioned on the programme as the author of a ballet. Of the earlier committee, only Bakst remained, Benois and Fokine having returned to Russia.

During the past nine months in London, Kola had taught me to speak Russian quite fluently, and in Lausanne, where the company was so much smaller than before and we all lived on rather more intimate terms, Diaghilev was much surprised to discover this. Soon after our arrival he realised I had been working so hard and had made such progress that he decided to give me solo roles to learn. The first was Papillon in *Carnaval*: it was not easy for me to follow Nijinska in this. One day Diaghilev told me that he had included my pictures with those of other principals and soloists sent to the States for the advance publicity of our tour. He said 'I have signed your photographs myself with the name Lydia Sokolova, and I hope you will live up to the name of Sokolova, as it is that of a great dancer in Russia. Please forget from now on that you have ever been anything but Russian.' So that was the end of Hilda Munnings and Muningsova. The Russian Ballet had a new soloist.

Of all the years we travelled with Diaghilev, those six months in Switzerland were the happiest, and I believe if he had been asked later he would have said the same. Kola and I lived in a Swiss-German inn in the suburb of La Rosez on the hillside, a short distance out of Lausanne. I had a room with a balcony overlooking vineyards, orchards and the Lake of Geneva.

Diaghilev rented a beautiful villa called Belle Rive, right on the lake's edge. His food was brought in daily from an hotel, as he couldn't afford a staff. Massine was there, under the protective wing. He was always very polite to me in a formal way, and was the only person who ever addressed me in the correct Russian style with my own name and my father's—Lydia Fredericksovna. I, of course, called him Leonide Feodorovitch.

Soon after we arrived Massine began work on his first ballet, a curious experimental affair without music called *Liturgie*, based on the story of Christ. It consisted of a series of short scenes, and every dancer, whether a soloist or not, had to count silently to various rhythms. But as more and more dancers arrived and our prospects improved, *Liturgie* was abandoned and we started work in earnest.

The company now consisted of a few old friends such as Tchernicheva, Massine, Gavrilov, Kremnev and myself, with the addition of Idzikovsky from London, whose audition Kola had arranged with Grigoriev when he was passing through on one of his long journeys to or from Russia, and a number of newcomers enlisted in Russia and Poland. There were three pairs of sisters, of which one of each were to become well known: Vera and Lida Nemchinova, Maria and Gala Shabelska, Luba and Nura Soumarokova. Drobetsky had somehow crossed Germany to Poland and had brought back several men, who were allowed out of the country on the pretence of going to Switzerland for a tuberculosis cure: these included Woizikovsky and Slavinsky, both of whom later distinguished themselves. So, during those happy days of work and preparation in beautiful surroundings, we often used to arrive in class to find an unfamiliar face, young and fresh, excited at the prospect of a new life. One day, I remember dear Maestro Cecchetti made up the only dance he ever arranged during all the years he taught us. It was a frightful little hopping affair to *Moment musical*. He just *could not* invent a dance.

Before the war, when we girls had all worn those loose-draped garments for rehearsals in different pastel colours, I had struck out a line of my own by having mine made in black. Diaghilev must have remembered this, because he came into class one day and announced that since it was more than ever difficult under war conditions to get nice material and keep things clean, all the girls in the ballet should wear black tunics in rehearsal, they were also to be shortened and simplified. From the point of view of allowing the choreographer to see more clearly the patterns he had invented, this was an improvement, and it is possible the idea may have come from Massine.

Leonide Feodorovitch now began to prepare his ballet *Soleil de Nuit* to music from *The Snowmaiden* by Rimsky Korsakov. This was a simple but delightful work, with sets and dresses in the Russian peasant style by Gontcharova and Larionov. We became very attached to these two painters, and of all the designers we ever worked with they remained our dearest friends. Vladimir Polunin, who painted so many of Diaghilev's subsequent sets for him, and his wife Elizabeth, who did a portrait of me, were two other painters with us at the time.

Diaghilev often had to set off for Paris to raise more money from his friends there to pay for everything we needed—from food to ballet shoes. Everything was short in those days, and we had difficulty in getting the make-up and shoes we needed. Before the war we had always been given a very generous allowance of shoes—a new pair every four days, with pink satin ribbons to sew onto them: those lavish times were never to return. We always knew when Diaghilev had been successful after one of his Paris trips, because Massine would be wearing another sapphire ring on his little finger. Massine, like Nijinsky, collected several of these, but whereas Nijinsky's had been set in gold, Massine's were set in platinum. I am sure Diaghilev was very happy at this time, living in his spacious villa by the lake, with its marble floors and masses of greenery and flowers, and with Massine developing into a brilliant choreographer under his eye.

It was a happy time for all of us, exciting, friendly and expectant: but for me there was one fly in the ointment—it was at Lausanne that Kola started his jealous scenes. A friend of his called Svetlov had come from Russia to join the new company. Svetlov was a most annoying person: he had a stupid habit of treating the simplest remark as if it had a double meaning, usually of a vulgar kind. As he got to know me better, his jokes became more familiar, until Kola, with whom I was very much in love, began to accuse me of flirting with his friend. One day Kola let fly, and there was an awful brawl. I began to remember the warnings I had been given when our friendship began in Germany. All the same, nothing on earth could really spoil the pleasure of being in love, of being back with Diaghilev, of having interesting work to do in that pretty place, of having learnt Russian and of having become Lydia Sokolova.

At last the Diaghilev Ballet danced again in public. We gave a gala matinée at Geneva in aid of the Red Cross on December 20, 1915. I danced Papillon in *Carnaval* and was one of the girls in Massine's first completed ballet *Soleil de Nuit*.

It was fun to dance *Soleil de Nuit*, which had no plot, but was just a number of dances strung together. Although the costumes were vivid in colour and wonderful to look at, they were appallingly uncomfortable. All our abandon and zest for dancing was nipped in the bud. We had horrible thick pads tied around our waists, then there were tight heavy costumes on top of them. The tall, mitre-shaped Russian head-dresses, once they had slipped slightly to one side, just refused to stand up straight again. All this was a pity, because if our movements had been less hampered we could have danced with as much enthusiasm as we did in *Prince Igor*. The boys had a delightful number led by Kremnev as principal character dancer. They carried pigs' bladders

F

on the end of sticks which they banged on the ground as they made their entrance one behind the other, performing eccentric jumps. This was a kind of buffoon dance, and in his solo as another kind of buffoon, Massine wearing clappers on his hands painted with great sun symbols, performed all those eccentric jumps he liked so much. This ballet gave us an opportunity of sampling the nature of Massine's invention, and we approved.

On December 29 we travelled to Paris to give another performance in aid of the French Red Cross—the second and last appearance of the Diaghilev Ballet in public during 1915. *Soleil de Nuit* was repeated and enthusiastically received.

Nothing but the desperate extremes of war could have made Diaghilev go to America. For one thing he was terrified of the crossing; for another, I am sure he was a confirmed European, doubtful if the New World had much to teach him or if it would be capable of appreciating the refinements of his repertory. He had admired the novelty of rag-time, the cake-walk, and Negro spirituals, but the day had not yet come when he could imagine his ballet borrowing subjects from the popular American art forms of vaudeville or cinema. The sum of Diaghilev's knowledge of the arts in America would not have been enough in normal times to lure him on a ten-day voyage—even though Fanny Elssler, Patti and Bernhardt had blazed the trail. The state of society in the great republic probably filled him with some misgivings. Being a liberal Russian aristocrat, he undoubtedly felt that the Americans had a right to their belief in the equality of man—so long as slavery was abolished in name only and the lower classes knew their place.

But the war was on. Diaghilev and most of his company were expatriate subjects of the Czar. England and France were too closely engaged to sustain expensive seasons of Russian Ballet, while the United States were still serene in their isolation. So Diaghilev set off at the head of his company, full of gloomy forebodings, for the 'Land of the Free'.

On January 1, 1916, we sailed from Bordeaux for the United States. It was rough and bitterly cold, and we had the usual boat-drills. Diaghilev kept his lifebelt always near at hand and hardly left his cabin. As we neared New York it got very foggy.

Suddenly sirens sounded, foghorns blew full blast and poor Diaghilev thought the end had come. He rushed with Massine to his allotted lifeboat, lifebelt and all, only to discover we were just passing the Statue of Liberty.

It was strange to think I had the advantage over the entire Diaghilev company in having been to America before. I could feel superior in knowing my way about New York and teaching the Russians how to use dollars, quarters, dimes and nickels. My return to New York was under very different circumstances from my first visit. I had solo parts to dance and I had become a Russian. My first thought was to run out and see if Child's was still there, with its buckwheat cakes: of course they were, smell and all. I found I loved America again.

Lydia Lopokova now joined us as a principal dancer. She had been in America ever since our tour in 1912 with the so-called Imperial Russian Ballet. Before that she had danced with Diaghilev during his second Paris season, when, young as she was, she had taken over the role of the Firebird from Karsavina. Lydia had grown up a bit since I had seen her last, and her dancing was stronger, but in other ways she was little changed. We were a new company, rather serious, and only just settling down together, most of our very young dancers being unsure of themselves, in awe of Grigoriev and frightened of Diaghilev; and Lydia brought a touch of gaiety into our rather heavy atmosphere.

In all the years of my friendship with Lydia Lopokova, I have never known her say or do an unkind thing either in the theatre or out of it. She was sweet to everybody, never jealous and never coveting another dancer's roles; but she always seemed to be hopping off somewhere, and obviously valued her private life as much as her life in ballet. She had a quick brain and was very witty, and her best friends were often intellectuals. Although she danced so much with us from that time on, and was one of Massine's most treasured artists, she never sold her soul to Diaghilev, fond of him as she was.

In 1916 I did not get to know her well because she was working so hard, rehearsing the repertory and learning the new dance

Massine created for her in *Soleil de Nuit*. No one who ever interpreted this solo after her did it so well—but this must be true of any part she created in a Massine ballet. She brought so much out in this simple and attractive dance, changing from slow to quick and lifting her shoulders as she sped around the stage. She could switch on such a plaintive air, just by walking towards the public with her hand outstretched. Lydia had a remarkable sense of sincerity, but always with a suspicion of naughtiness. In later years Vera Nemchinova looked delightful in this dance and performed it extremely well, as did Shura Danilova, but neither had the poignancy and humour of Lydia.

On the stage, as well as off, Lydia Lopokova was full of surprises. She had not the appearance or physique of a classical dancer, but to one's astonishment whatever she attempted came off. Few dancers have performed with such assurance or flown through the air as she did. Lydia had tiny strong feet, little hands and short arms. She had no idea of hairdressing and wore very little make-up on the stage—what there was was usually still there next morning—but when she stood looking up at Big Serge (which was what she called Diaghilev), with her screwed-up little bun of hair, the tip of her nose quivering, and an expression between laughter and tears, I defy anybody to say she wasn't worth her weight in gold.

We opened on January 17 at the Century Theatre, which was small and attractive and reminded me of a London theatre, although Diaghilev probably thought it was not big or grand enough for his company. Perhaps I liked the Century because it was the first theatre, excepting the two galas in Geneva and Paris, where I performed and was billed as a solo dancer.

I enormously enjoyed dancing Ta-Hor in *Cléopâtre*: it was a wonderful sensation to be left entirely alone to act a dramatic part on a large stage. This was my first big role, and I danced it with our most famous male dancers. The story concerns the slave girl, Ta-Hor, who loses her lover, Amoun, to Cleopatra. After one night of love the handsome Amoun is condemned to death, and Ta-Hor pleads for his life in vain. Adolf Bolm was very fine as Amoun, being tall and of somewhat Eastern appearance.

Flora Revalles had joined us in Switzerland to play our dramatic roles. She was a great friend of Ansermet, our new conductor, but she was not really a dancer. She was tall, good-looking and charming, but I remember her less for her performance in *Cléopâtre* than because she had a baby alligator which she carried round in a basket. When we went on tour after New York, she used to nurse it on her lap in the train, but it grew very fast and eventually bit her in no uncertain fashion, so she left it with a zoo.

After Bolm, I was to dance Ta-Hor in *Cléopâtre* with Massine, which was a thrilling experience, as, like most of the girls, I had secretly fallen for him. My heart ached for just one tiny spark of understanding in his eyes, but however much I made love to him on the stage, I never once penetrated that frozen stare. Luba Tchernicheva, who succeeded Revalles as Cleopatra, may have had more success than I did. She had the most wonderful, quivering brown velvet eyes with yellow flecks in them. She and I had an exciting moment of drama in the ballet when she won my lover from me: I then felt the full force of her eyes. Luba and I were great friends for many years and I loved her dearly.

There was one young woman in our company who was always in love with someone, and as she was very attractive the someone was usually in love with her. Diaghilev had a name for her which might be roughly translated as 'Hotpants'. There were signs that she and Leonide Massine were mutually attracted; in fact, the silent but ardent flirtation was obvious to the whole company. For anyone to flirt with Massine was against all the rules, and to those who had lived through the Nijinsky episode the situation was truly alarming. The finale of this little romance was played in Washington, D.C., while we were on tour following our fortnight at the Century Theatre.

We were invited to a party at the Russian Embassy in aid of the Russian Red Cross. We performed several dances in the middle of the ballroom, including that of the nursemaids from *Petroushka*, and afterwards we joined in the ballroom dancing. There was a terrific crush, and my partner saw a little room which was empty, so he guided me through the door. Almost immediately we were followed by Massine and his would-be girl-friend. We were all laughing and flirting and having a wonderful time, when to our horror we saw Diaghilev standing in the doorway, a champagne bottle under his arm and glasses in his hand. We froze. He had seen enough; he turned and walked away. The following morning a message came round via the bush telegraph —that is by Vassili, Diaghilev's servant and spy—that anybody who interfered with the peace of the company by disturbing Massine in his work would be expelled immediately. Leonide and the lady did not speak to each other for many a day after that. As for the rest of us, any girl who valued her position in the company was careful to steer clear of Massine.

We visited sixteen towns on our tour, sometimes sleeping on the train or, when we were stopping more than one night in a town, at hotels. The travelling was so luxurious compared with my last tour of the States that I did not mind it at all. For one thing I had a bed to myself.

One night we had a narrow escape. We were all on a special train, the orchestra, electricians and wardrobe hands, as well as some leading supers we took round with us to rehearse the local ones we had to engage wherever we went. Our train had been held up on the journey because of fog and a cow on the line. We woke up to realise we were going at enormous speed and that the train was rocking like a boat as it tore along. Then we gradually came to a standstill. Suddenly we heard a terrific roar and the clanging of a bell as an express roared past us. Apparently being behind schedule, we only just had time to pull into a loop-line before the express came along, and we missed crashing into it by a matter of seconds.

When we returned to New York, we opened on April 3 at the Metropolitan Opera House. After moving heaven and earth to get Nijinsky out of Austria, Diaghilev had finally enlisted the aid of the King of Spain. The King's efforts had been successful, and Nijinsky was expected to join us in time for our second New York season. In fact, he only arrived the day after our opening, and as we needed to rehearse with the new company, he did not appear in public until a week later.

The critic for the New York *Evening Sun* reported my performance as Ta-Hor in *Cléopâtre* at the matinée of the second day of our season: 'Another *Lydia*, this time La Sokolova in the role of maid forlorn, strangely recalled Pavlova in pose, person, action and gesture.' This was odd as it never occurred to me that I bore any resemblance to Pavlova. Of Nijinsky, who had arrived that morning and whom he saw sitting in a box the same evening, this critic wrote, 'the dark little man, exquisitely groomed in dead black, with a lustreless top hat, sat among the subscribers with his fair-haired wife, observed of all observers. While watching his old companions, the "choreographic Caruso" hadn't a word to say. But in his first American interviews on coming ashore earlier in the day, Nijinsky declared that, having kept up constant practice on the European liner, he was in the pink of condition, and he looked it. That calm exterior of Slavic temperament suggested smothered fires. The most famous male dancer in the world has been a long time coming to New York. Now he is here, he won't have to show himself as he had feared, in a music-hall "sandwiched between performing dogs and acrobats". Instead the greatest Lyric Theatre on Earth waits for him, yawns for him.'

Nijinsky's dancing, however, had deteriorated: he had grown heavier and looked very sad. We felt sorry for him, and of course it must have been awkward for Massine and himself to be in the same company. Diaghilev and Massine were staying at the Ritz, Nijinsky and Romola at the Claridge. When Otto Kahn insisted on Nijinsky's dancing with us, he could not really have understood the calamity of his previous dismissal. Nijinsky's experiences since his marriage had obviously affected him greatly, and he already showed signs of abnormality. He never spoke a word to anyone and picked his fingers more than ever.

A letter I wrote home at this time (Sunday, April 9, 1916) gave news of my French bulldog, of Kremnev, Nijinsky, President Wilson, presents received on my recent birthday and my progress in the ballet. '. . . there is so much to tell you. First I think about Beckie, poor little girl, she is in the hospital with distemper . . . her eyes got the white film over them and she

wouldn't leave me a second so I knew it was best to give her to
the Doctor. It's a beautiful place and is costing 75 cts. a day. . . .
Next about my birthday. It was the jolliest I had for a long time.
I had Beat's letter on the very day, and on my breakfast table
there was an enormous bunch of roses just as they are given on
the stage, with ribbon as well, from Kremnev. He also gave me
a beautiful opening camera, the very latest style, and a silk handbag, and in the evening, two bottles of wine and some chocolate
to take to the girls who were most awfully good to me. My
greatest girl friend, a Polish girl, gave me a powder box, a shoe
horn, a soap box and a looking-glass in that very heavy imitation
ivory. Hilda Bewicke gave me a clock and a hairpin tray in the
same stuff; another one gave me a white frame and another, a
box of soap and perfume. They were so sweet, too, they all gave
them at different times so that I was receiving presents all day,
even when I went to the theatre at night. . . . I am now rehearsing
another solo part of Nijinska's, the Bacchanale in *Narcisse* a dance
quite alone. It goes on next week. . . . Nijinsky is here and is
making a lot of fuss—won't appear without tons of money,
saying in the papers horrid things about the ballet. You know
just how they always turn around on those who make their
names for them. But I think it is settled that he is to dance on
Wednesday. I forgot to tell you that when we were in Washington
we danced after the performance for the Ambassador (Russian)
at a ball. . . . We drank champagne and got home at four o'clock. . . .
President Wilson and his wife were introduced to us on the
stage. . . . In one of the towns Diaghilev introduced me to an
American Ambassador going to Petrograd, as his first dancer. . . .
I think the season will be breaking up on the first of May . . .
we shall all be glad as we are simply dead beat. When you think
we have been at it hard for nine months. It's snowing hard and
I am still wearing my fur coat. I've been to the Cinema to see
the fight between Willard and Moran. . . . I expect I shall be
going to a place called Atlantic City for the holiday as it's only
three hours from here. We played an evening there, but it poured
with rain all day long and we ran from one cinema to another. . . .
Yesterday Bolm was unable to dance *Petroushka* and so Kremnev

rehearsed half an hour before performance and did the principal part. It wanted some pluck, as there is a whole scene of his own, but everything went off all right. We have heard Diaghilev wants to give Bolm the slip now that Nijinsky's here, and so any part of his that Nijinsky won't do, Kremnev will get . . . the dressers at the Metropolitan say we are worked to death, and that the American girls wouldn't come near the theatre. . . .'

My dear Kola by this time, however, had grown so possessive that scenes of jealousy after the extra drink became a part of my life. Although I was still in love with him, I began to long for a little more freedom.

I was chosen to follow Bronislava Nijinska in *Narcisse* (and eventually other Fokine ballets) because I was strong, with a good elevation, and above all because I had powers of endurance. When I was cast as the Bacchante in *Narcisse*, I was frightened not only of the dance itself, but of the entrance I had to make. I had to wait for my cue in the top wing, holding the hands of two Satyrs; and we made a very fast entrance. Supporting me on either side, the men ran right round the stage, while I bent backwards as far as possible and kicked my legs in the air. They dragged me past the footlights before flinging me away to begin my Bacchanale. As it was impossible to see where I was going I had to rely entirely on my supporters, and I should never have been surprised to find myself flying into the orchestra pit. The Bacchanale was long, repetitive and difficult, with endless jumps and a lot of spinning on the same spot. It was in learning this dance that I picked up the knack of counting my jumps on my fingers. I wore a dress of thick cashmere and a long, hot, red wig, with my own hair, which was thick and heavy, underneath it. In addition I had a wide cashmere scarf fitted to my wrists and hanging down three-quarters of a yard on either side. In my hands I carried a cup and jug. I was laden.

Before sailing for Europe on May 6, we heard that a new tour had been signed with Otto Kahn for the autumn. Kahn had once more insisted on Nijinsky heading the company. But because of their differences, Nijinsky had refused to appear again in America unless Diaghilev remained in Europe and handed over the direction of the company to him. Everyone except Kahn, Nijinsky and Romola realised that this was madness: but we understood that Diaghilev was hard-pressed to find engagements to keep us going in wartime, and that he had no option in the matter.

The trip back to Cadiz on the *Dante Alighieri* would have been a pleasant one if it had not been for the horses. We had watched these poor creatures being loaded on board. Those for the top decks were driven up the gangway with sticks, but the wretched beasts for the holds were lowered by cranes, their eyes bulging with terror. Stalls had been made with wooden poles to pass between the horses' legs which prevented them from rolling about or lying down. There were canvas tubes from the holds to the deck to give them a little air. They screamed all night, and every day some were thrown over the side, dead. The boats were down all the way, and we were so laden with ammunition and horses, that you could have stepped off the deck straight into the sea. It was very hot, the water was calm, and at night we had a brilliant moon. I watched huge turtles and creatures like sea-serpents, as the ship split the clear water. To avoid submarines we steered a course near the Azores. We carried a cow and a calf on the top deck: the cow was milked for the first-class passengers, then the calf was killed for food during the last few days at sea. It took ten days to cross the Atlantic in 1916, and that was a trip I shall never forget.

7

NEW ROLES IN SPAIN AND AMERICA

First visit to Madrid — *Las Meniñas* and the dwarf — Lying
to King Alfonso — The company's second North American
tour — Nijinsky gives trouble — *Till Eulenspiegel* — The
disciples of Tolstoi — Dancing *Le Spectre* with Nijinsky.

When we arrived at Cadiz in May, 1916, we were excited to be
seeing Spain for the first time, but our landing was marked by a
disaster. The Spaniards unloading our baggage and properties
dropped the scenery of *Thamar* into the sea, and that was the
end of Bakst's magnificent décor.

Everything in Madrid seemed new and exciting. One of our
first surprises was the system of night watchmen. Returning to
our lodgings on the first evening we found ourselves shut out.
We banged on the door and shouted, all to no avail. Then we
noticed somebody arriving at the house opposite. He clapped
his hands several times, whereupon out of the shadows there
arrived the watchman laden with keys. We realised that in every
street or block there was one of these men who would have to
let us in at whatever time of night we came home.

I was amazed to find Madrid so small. There wasn't even a
hairdresser's shop. We all had long hair in those days and mine
was difficult to wash: being very thick as well as long and blonde
it needed special care. I made enquiries and found the lady who
dressed hair at the Court. I went to her tiny house and she
washed my hair there.

Although we started work an hour later in the morning, we
found it trying not to begin our performance before ten o'clock
at night, by which time we were often tired out. The change of

81

diet presented problems too: Spanish food was very rich and always served in enormous helpings. The neighbourhood where I lived was noisy at night, with sellers of lottery tickets crying out, and late homecomers clapping their hands for the night-watchman; these and the friendly mosquitoes disturbed our night's rest.

We all loved Spain, however, and it was a thrill for me to be called 'Señorita' for the first time. The Spanish women always wore black, with little lace mantillas on their heads in the day-time. Ladies never walked, and when they drove out were accompanied by a duenna. I used to watch them going by in their carriages when they took the evening air in the park, and think how fascinating and mysterious they were. We did not perform every night so we were able to visit the cafés and enjoy the dancing, singing and guitar playing.

The royal family were our friends from the first night onwards. King Alfonso loved the ballet, and was our most enthusiastic supporter. Queen Ena was so lovely we used to take it in turns to peep at her round the drop curtain.

Kola was enjoying the Spanish wine, and the chief result of this was an increase in his possessive behaviour towards me. He thought nothing of locking me into my room while he went to the theatre or to drink with his friends.

Being in Spain naturally inspired Diaghilev and his *entourage* to create a Spanish ballet. Dear Gontcharova and Larionov had joined us in Spain, and it seems that to them—or at least to Larionov—must be given most of the credit for the invention of *Las Meniñas*.

This short work, arranged by Massine to the melancholy music of Fauré's *Pavane*, could be regarded as a homage to Velasquez, a gracious tribute by the Russian Ballet, as it were, to the glorious past of Spain. There were only two couples and a dwarf, and the women wore exaggerated versions of the dresses and coiffures in which Velasquez painted his doll-like Infantas. Because he was Spanish and available at the moment, José-Maria Sert was given the task of designing these elaborate costumes, but it is hard to believe that Diaghilev had much admiration for the work of this splendiferous *pasticheur*, who was less a painter than a fashionable decorator on a monstrous scale. However, Sert could not go far wrong with the example of Velasquez before him. Sert's wife, Misia Godebska, besides being an admirable pianist, beloved by Renoir and Vuillard, was Diaghilev's most intimate friend; and this also probably influenced Diaghilev in his employment of Sert as a designer. There can be no doubt that *Las Meniñas* was a charming trifle.

We enjoyed a long holiday at a delightful sandy place on the north coast of Spain, near the frontier, called Fontarrabia. (It was here that I saw Leon Woizikovsky save Tariat, a French boy we had in the company, from drowning in a rough sea.) From there we went on to San Sebastian, where Larionov, Massine and Diaghilev put the finishing touches to *Las Meniñas* and where it had its first performance on August 21. The dancers were Massine, Novak, Kokhlova and myself, with Antonova as the dwarf.

Diaghilev and Larionov were always keen to try something novel and while the ballet was in preparation they found a real dwarf. There were several troupes of these dwarfs in Spain, but this one worked on his own. We were invited to Diaghilev's hotel bedroom to meet him, and there was a conference. The little man sat for a while, trying to understand what the talk— partly in Russian, partly in Spanish—was all about. Then he got bored, slipped off the chair onto his tiny legs, grabbed a lot of cherries from a dish, filled his mouth with as many as it could hold, and began prancing up and down the room, shooting out the stones at everybody in sight. It was a panic. Larionov always stuttered when he got nervous, and Diaghilev kept saying, 'Get rid of the little brute' over and over again, and Larionov couldn't think how to manage this in Spanish. At length we got him out of the room. Sert was greatly relieved to hear the experiment had been a failure.

After this it was decided to make Antonova play the part. She was small, and with clever padding and a wonderful make-up —false nose, cheeks stuffed with cotton wool, and a built-up shoulder—she was very good indeed.

For the part Antonova had a stuffed parrot fixed to her shoulder which she stroked and pretended to be talking to, while she peeped at the two couples making love in the garden. As she watched, she had to laugh in a sinister way and mimic our gestures, then when she finally left the stage she conveyed in mime that she was going off to start a campaign of scandal in the Court.

Our dresses were enormous: the hoops stuck out twice the length of our arms and the wigs were twice the width of our shoulders. The iron-framed hoop cut into my shins and made them bleed. Those costumes were so big they would not get into the dressing-rooms, so we had to put them on with our wigs in the wings; and they were so heavy that when you turned round, you had to do it very carefully all in one piece. My dress was deep purple velvet and gold, with a wig of dark-brown ringlets. Massine, my partner, had a wine-red velvet suit. Olga Kokhlova's dress was pink and silver, and she wore a blonde wig. I really loved that little ballet and enjoyed every minute of it, although the weight we had to carry was terrific.

From San Sebastian we went to Bilbao, where the King and Queen came to visit the Spanish fleet, and we were invited to give a gala performance. The King was apparently delighted with his first sight of our Spanish ballet, and he sent round bouquets for Olga Kokhlova and myself. Grigoriev tried to switch my bouquet to his wife, but I wasn't giving it up for anything and I held on to it. I still have the King's card with my name on it.

During the interval the principal dancers were taken by Diaghilev to be presented to the King and Queen in their apartments, and on this awful occasion I was obliged to tell a lie to His Most Catholic Majesty. There were five of us, Lopokova, Tchernicheva, Idzikovsky, Woizikovsky and myself. Going up the stairs, Diaghilev said to me 'Hilda, don't mention your nationality. I have just told the King all my artists are Russian.' (My Russian friends always called me 'eelda', Lydia being a more common name in their country, but my English friends call me Lydia, which I prefer.) We went through several small rooms into a bigger reception room with a parquet floor. Tchernicheva, being our famous beauty, went up first to be presented to the Queen; she was followed by Lopokova, our ballerina, and her partner, Idzikovsky. The rest of us were taken to the King. Everyone conversed with the Royal couple in French, but Diaghilev, no doubt thinking my French would give me away as being English, said to King Alfonso, 'You can speak to her in English', which he did. On my replying to some question, the King remarked, 'But surely you are English?' Remembering Diaghilev's warning, I replied, 'No, Your Majesty, I was brought from Russia at an early age and educated in England.' I knew he didn't believe me and as he would not let the subject alone I began to feel very uncomfortable.

I went on to be presented to the Queen, and while I was making my curtsy, I saw to my horror the impression of Idzikovsky's red lips on her beautiful, long, white gloves. At the same moment I heard Lopokova saying to the King in a clear voice full of affection and enthusiasm, 'Yes, isn't she wonderful? She's the only English artist we have in the company.' If ever I was thankful for a thick make-up, I was that night. I felt the blood rushing to the roots of my hair. Lydia, of course, was quite unaware of her blunder.

But our troubles didn't stop there. As we were backing out of the presence, Woizikovsky, like a bull in a china shop in the big Russian boots he was wearing for the next ballet, kicked something over with his heel. It turned out to be a huge backgammon box, the lid of which flew open, scattering draughts all over the parquet. There we stood, King, Queen, naval officers, Diaghilev and six desperate artists, all watching those wretched discs spinning and rattling in every direction across the highly polished floor. Not knowing what to do, but anxious to rectify the damage, Woizikovsky made a dart across the room; but the King came to his rescue and patted him on the shoulder, saying in English, 'Never mind about that, old boy.' We beat as dignified a retreat as we could, and as soon as the Royal door was closed, we fairly hurtled down the stairs, knocking each other over in our haste to get away from the grinding teeth and black looks of poor Diaghilev.

We looked forward to our second American tour with apprehension. Not only was Diaghilev not to be with us—and we knew how essential his presence was, both from the artistic and social point of view—but the running of the company was to be entrusted to a man who would have been incapable of it at the best of times, and whom we now judged to be not quite right in the head. We had no confidence in Nijinsky; as a choreographer, whatever good ideas he might have, we knew he was helpless without Diaghilev or Bakst to guide him, while as a director he could not even begin to cope with the varied and incessant problems which beset a travelling company. What made matters worse, Nijinsky in his folly had insisted that Grigoriev should not accompany the ballet. After Diaghilev, Grigoriev was the most indispensable person: he not only knew how to get the company with all its baggage from one place to another, but he was responsible for paying the dancers, and also mounted every ballet on the stage and rehearsed it. Grigoriev understood each dancer's problems, and he knew by heart the whole repertoire of the Diaghilev Ballet. Above all, he had the gift of not losing his head in an emergency. The business side was to be entrusted to Drobetsky, Diaghilev's secretary, and to Barrocchi, who was by now married to Lopokova, while Kola Kremnev was to replace Grigoriev as *régisseur*. My gloomy forebodings were therefore not unmixed with pleasure at Kremnev's promotion.

So Diaghilev remained in Europe with Maestro and Mme Cecchetti, Grigoriev and several dancers, including some of the most interesting in the company: Massine, Tchernicheva (Grigoriev's wife); Woizikovsky and his girl friend, Antonova; Idzikovsky and *his* girl friend, the English Evina; Maria Shabelska, who was a very good dancer indeed; Kokhlova and Novak. By keeping this nucleus with him, Diaghilev made it possible for Massine to prepare a new work.

The rest of us set sail on September 8 from Bordeaux on a wild and stormy night. Outside the purser's office there was a notice warning passengers that the ship could be stopped by the Germans, and that any subjects of the Allied countries could then be removed as prisoners-of-war—a pretty idea to go to bed with!

We had a beastly crossing. It was rough and cold; moreover my sealskin coat had become impregnated with *Quelques Fleurs*, a very pungent scent, which made me sick whenever I put the coat on. From that time on I could never smell *Quelques Fleurs* without a feeling of nausea.

On our arrival in New York we found two new dancers had come to join us from Russia: Spessivtseva and Frohman. Margarita Frohman was a character soloist, sister to the tall and handsome man who had been one of the principals of the company when I first joined and who had danced in *Le Dieu bleu* with Karsavina. Olga Spessivtseva was one of the most beautiful dancers I have ever seen.

Kola Kremnev was quite confident that he would be able to cope with Nijinsky, but although I was in love with Kola, I saw his shortcomings all too clearly. He had absolutely no sense of proportion and no tact. Without pausing to think, he blundered impetuously into every situation, and when diplomacy was called for he lost his temper. In addition he was too much 'one of the boys' to be put in charge of the company: he was too lenient to his fellow artists and had no authority over them. To control a ballet company you have to be a tough leader, who can say no and mean it. Kremnev was the last person who should have been given a position of such responsibility.

As for the other bosses, Barrocchi who did the business, was a man quite outside the company, and who knew nothing about us. Drobetsky was one of the most ineffectual human beings I have ever met. He was the husband of Fanny Pflanz, one of our three tall beauties, and we had a standing joke about him always repeating the phrase, 'Oh, how I do not love fools.' So with this group of brilliant administrators, we began the trickiest engagement in the history of the Diaghilev Ballet.

Nijinsky made no effort to come and greet us. We didn't seem to belong to anybody. From the day of our arrival in New York we were at sixes and sevens, with no one to organise us; and it was frustrating not to get any work done. Nijinsky had formed the habit of not turning up for anything unless he was fetched, and Kola was driven to distraction rushing to the rehearsal room and then to Nijinsky's hotel and back again. Fitting a number of new dancers into our repertoire was no easy task: in this we missed Grigoriev's knowledge and experience. However, the old ballets were somehow rehearsed and put into shape.

According to his contract with Otto Kahn, Nijinsky was due to produce two new ballets during the three weeks' season at the Metropolitan, before the company went on tour; but *Till Eulenspiegel*, the first of the two new ones, proved such a problem for Nijinsky that *Mephisto Waltz*, the second, was abandoned.

Richard Strauss's symphonic poem *Till Eulenspiegel* was as German in its way as *Die Meistersinger* and no doubt there were some people at that time who thought the music an odd choice for the Russian Ballet in an America which was soon to abandon its neutrality; nevertheless the brilliant score, rich alike in colour and incident, was clearly cut out to be the basis of an effective ballet, and the legendary hero, a kind of Flemish Puck, was one to inspire a vivid characterisation in Nijinsky the dancer, who had brought Fokine's Harlequin to life. Unfortunately, Nijinsky the choreographer was no longer able—if he had ever been—to work out the details of the ballet unaided. He had some very good ideas, but there were long periods when his mind seemed not to function creatively. If he had not been obliged to act as artistic director of the company, if his private life had been without worries and, above all, if there had been plenty of time, perhaps he might have been able to create a fine ballet on his own. On the other hand, perhaps his mental breakdown was already too far advanced for such a thing to have been possible at this time. It is only fair to record that Nijinsky had only three weeks to work with the company between their arrival and the season's opening. Some choreographers can invent parts of a ballet without their dancers being present; some have no difficulty in creating a forty-minute ballet in three weeks, while for others such a thing would be out of the question. Two years later, Nijinsky, by then far advanced in mental illness, wrote in his diary: 'Once I created a ballet to music of Richard Strauss. . . . I was asked to do it in three weeks. I protested. . . . Otto Kahn . . . said he could not give me longer. . . . It was "taken out of the oven" too soon, and therefore was raw. The American public liked my raw ballet. It tasted good, as I cooked it very well. I did not like this ballet but said, "It is good."'

Till Eulenspiegel was to be a very big affair. Incidentally it was the only 'Diaghilev Ballet' which Diaghilev had no hand in and which he never saw. Nijinsky had found a clever young American designer called Robert Edmund Jones. We were all called together and told the synopsis of the ballet by Jones, while Nijinsky stood by, picking his fingers.

The medieval costumes were very fine: strong in colour and fantastically exaggerated. I remember the tall girls who wore the cone-shaped hats, had veils suspended from them which were so long that they trailed yards behind them on the stage, carrying out the line of their trains. Some of those costumes were so striking that I believe they alone might have made a success of the ballet, if only Diaghilev had been there to exercise control. The minimum of progress, however, was made with the rehearsals of *Till*. Nijinsky would appear and disappear. As ever he had great difficulty in explaining what he wanted, and sometimes it was clear that he did not know himself. As the day announced for the first performance drew near, we all became extremely nervous at the ballet's sketchy state; no proddings from Kola could make Nijinsky work faster or show signs of realising the seriousness of the situation. Whenever Kola reported to the management that the ballet was not nearly ready, Nijinsky and Romola would retort 'Nonsense! Of course it will be ready in time'.

Romola Nijinsky* in her life of her husband has several things to say about the production of *Till* which cannot pass without comment. She mentions Grigoriev as having been with the company, which of course he was not. She also complains of Monteux, our French *chef d'orchestre* coming to Nijinsky a few days before the opening of *Till* and refusing to conduct the German music of Strauss. Monteux, the dearest of all our conductors, and a wonderful one for dancers, was fed to the teeth with Nijinsky's bungling over *Till*, and if he used this excuse,

* *Nijinsky* (Gollancz, 1933).

89

which I suppose is not impossible, it was only because he was at his wits' end and anxious to disassociate himself from the fiasco. Romola also describes the artists of the ballet going on strike because they 'refused to dance to German music'. The reason for the strike was that we were exasperated by Nijinsky wasting hours at a time, and as the management would not listen to any of our complaints, we thought drastic action was necessary. She describes how Nijinsky sprained his ankle and had to rest, with the result that *Till* was postponed for a fortnight. No doubt, Nijinsky did sprain his ankle, but at the time we believed that this was only a delaying tactic on his part, since the ballet was quite incomplete and could never have opened on time.

After all these vicissitudes we managed to get the first act in good order, but we still had been given only a vague outline of the second.

At last the day of the first performance arrived. It was right at the end of the season, just over a month after our arrival in America, and the dress rehearsal was on the same morning.

I played the part of an apple-woman. When the curtain went up on the market-place, I was standing in the centre of the stage in a delightful peasant costume, hand-painted on canvas: I looked very German, with my boots and rosy cheeks. On my head was balanced a bundle full of painted apples held together by a string. Nijinsky as *Till* danced round the various market stalls, stealing things and playing with them. Then suddenly he jumped at me, pulled the string and sent my apples tumbling all over us both. He picked one up and ran away, eating it.

At the dress rehearsal we got through the first act pretty well. Nijinsky danced gaily and without concern for the future. At the end of it, though, we were terrified, because there was really no more ballet—just a few scrappy bits, under-rehearsed. At this point arguments broke out. Nijinsky and Romola got into a car, went back to their hotel and refused to see anyone. The dress rehearsal stopped in the middle.

Otto Kahn and the management of the Metropolitan were naturally aghast. Poor Kremnev, who was almost in tears, could only say, 'I tried to warn you, but you wouldn't believe me.' A conference was held, and the company was called together. It was explained to us that the theatre was sold out and that a postponement was out of the question. We were asked if we could possibly manage to pull the ballet through. So the remainder of the afternoon flew by as we did our best to piece together what we could and fill in the gaps. It was agreed to tell Nijinsky that everything was wonderful, that his ballet was fine and that he had nothing to worry about, so long as he knew what he was going to do himself in the second act. Perhaps that was the only time in ballet history when the dancers more or less improvised nearly half a ballet on its opening night. Naturally *Till* was not repeated in New York. Romola Nijinska describes a performance of it in San Francisco and implies that it was danced throughout our tour. If this was so, I have no recollection of it.

No chapters in Romola Nijinska's romanticised biography of her husband are more misleading than those describing this New York season and the American tour that followed. She puts into Vaslav's mouth long speeches which would have taken him a whole week to say, as he always spoke in monosyllables. Reading her descriptions, one would think that poor Nijinsky conversed and behaved as a normal person, which was quite untrue.

The coast-to-coast tour was booked, and there was no way of getting out of it: it seemed doomed to failure from the start. How we envied the group who were wintering happily with Diaghilev in Rome! Kola slept very little, and every night after the performance he would sit up for hours, writing to Grigoriev and Diaghilev a full account of the day's happenings, with descriptions of all the dreadful things that were going on. He never knew what was coming next. Kola begged the American management to place someone of their own in charge of the tour, so that he could concentrate on working with the company.

There were two men in the Ballet who were disciples of Tolstoy: Kostrovsky, an epileptic who used to preach equality, vegetarianism and goodness-knows-what to anybody who would listen to him, and my old friend Zverev, whom we used to call 'Percy Greensocks', but who was later to earn the nickname of 'Rasputin'. These two subjected Nijinsky to a course of Tolstoian philosophy. On long train journeys, Kostrovsky and Zverev would move into Nijinsky's compartment and settle down to their non-stop preaching: Romola was turned out. I think it might well have been their fanatical ideas that put the final touch to Nijinsky's confusion. Perhaps as a consequence of all this talk about equality and brotherhood, Vaslav began to change round as many of the principal roles as he could, often at very short notice; and it was during this alarming period that he decided I should dance Le Spectre de la rose with him.

To dance Spectre with Nijinsky was, of course, a special event for me. However hopeless he might be as a director of the company, he was still 'The God of the Dance', and it was an unimaginable honour to appear with him in a pas de deux. I ordered a lovely new dress for the great occasion; and I should have liked a few moments of peace before the ballet, to put on my make-up quietly and carefully. Unfortunately Le Spectre de la rose was preceded by Cléopâtre, in which I danced Ta-Hor. This meant I was covered all over in brown make-up, with a black wig stuck on my dirty brown face, and with filthy bare feet, after grovelling on the ground for over half an hour.

As soon as the applause for Cléopâtre seemed to have died down, I made a dash for my room. Tired and hot, I had to undo the thirty safety-pins with which my long, thick sash was fixed tightly around me. I was standing in a hot bath, scrubbing the brown make-up and dirt off my feet and legs, when the stage-manager flew into my dressing-room without stopping to knock. 'It's no good doing that,' he said, 'you'll have to come on again. The public won't stop until you've taken another call.' So on went my costume and wig, and half brown and half white, I came down again to take a curtain call, only to see Nijinsky fussing in the wings, ready for Spectre. It was too much to bear. How I got myself cleaned up or put on the new white make-up, with tights and ballet shoes, in order to open Spectre looking like a débutante radiant after her first ball, I simply do not know. It is the sort of thing that still happens to me in nightmares. All the same, I have a long press-cutting describing the enthusiasm of the audience that night.

Dancing *Spectre* with Nijinsky was very frightening. He was always doing something unexpected. He would throw me in the air and catch me as I came down, or take his hand away at the moment of support in an *arabesque*. If I had come off my point then, the picture and atmosphere would have been ruined. He also puffed and blew.

When Nijinsky gave his famous part of the Negro slave in *Scheherazade* to Zverev, and cast himself as the old Eunuch, it was really the last straw. On our arrival at some town where he was advertised to dance *Les Sylphides*, he refused to do so, saying that he would dance *Carnaval* instead. The set had been hung, the lighting was fixed, and everyone was dressed; then fifteen minutes before the overture, he made the announcement. There was only one thing to do. He was locked in his dressing-room with the wig and costume for *Les Sylphides*. Sure enough, he made up and dressed without any more argument, came quietly on stage and began to practise his usual jumps, while we formed the opening group. He took his place and danced as though he had never thought of anything else. It was a nerve-wracking few minutes for us all before the curtain went up.

In the course of this unfortunate tour we performed in Los Angeles. We were taken to visit the Hollywood studios, where we met Charlie Chaplin, to whom I talked about London, and where we also saw Flora Finch making a film in a hut.

In Chicago, Romola, fed-up with the Tolstoians, packed and left for New York. By then, the company was split into factions, nothing was danced properly any more, and the takings were getting less and less. The Metropolitan management at last realised what was going on, and the tour was cut short in Albany.

No ship could be found to accommodate the whole company, so we were divided up for the return journey to Europe. Kremnev and I travelled home in a party of ten on a dirty Spanish boat. Our diet throughout the voyage consisted mainly of beans, large round grey ones.

8

MOTHERHOOD

Expecting a baby — The spy — Diaghilev in Rome — Matrimonial trouble — Beginning of the great Massine period — *Les Femmes de bonne humeur* — Reactions to the Russian revolution — A tragedy in Naples — The new spirit in painting and music — *Parade* first performed in Paris — Let down by the family — More Nijinsky trouble — Back to South America — Birth of Natasha — Ordeals mental and physical.

For years I had been wondering if and when I should get married to Kola Kremnev. In Los Angeles, towards the end of the American tour, I found that I was going to have a baby, so the question of marriage was raised in earnest. Only then did Kola reveal to me that he was already married. His first wife was a Gypsy and he had not seen or heard of her for several years. The law in Russia at that time was that if a man had not seen his wife for three years, and could prove it, he was free to marry again. Kola was quite confident that if this was the law in Russia, no other country could possibly dare to legislate otherwise or interfere inconveniently with his private life. Pregnant or not, I refused to be rushed into anything, and I decided that before taking steps I should speak to Diaghilev.

It was a depressing journey on that Spanish ship. I whiled away the time trying to teach myself to sew and make baby clothes, and there was a kind woman on board who showed me how to knit. As we neared Europe a rumour went round the ship that we might be stopped by Germans and taken off as prisoners, so we asked the advice of the Captain. He suggested that we should all disembark at the first port of call, which was Cadiz, and this we agreed to do.

We had so little money on landing that we had to pool our resources to buy tickets for Madrid. Grigoriev was supposed to meet us near the French frontier, and take us to join Diaghilev in Rome, but we ran into him in Madrid, and were packed off into a north-bound train. On arrival at Hendaye we found there was an hour's difference in the time between Spain and France, and as we had just missed our connection we had to put up at an hotel opposite the station for the night.

After leaving my things at the hotel, I wandered across the road to watch the arrival and departure of people at the Franco-Spanish frontier. As I was standing in a doorway, looking at a crowd going through the customs, I saw the lady who had taught me to knit on the boat. She seemed to be in an awful state, because the men had emptied all her cases and were firing questions at her. I waved and called out, whereupon a soldier guarding the door asked me if I would like to go in and talk to her. In my innocence I said I would, and the soldier got permission. 'Just look at what they are doing to me,' she said. 'They've taken away my address book and all my papers.' At that moment, two soldiers asked for my passport, which I had left with Grigoriev. As I hadn't got one, I was arrested. They took me into a tiny room, where I found a French officer with a long beard and masses of gold braid. The two soldiers clapped their bayonets across the door, and I was informed that I was a prisoner. The officer cross-examined me about my friend. All I could say was that I had supposed she was American and that she had been very kind to me during the rough crossing. As none of my answers seemed to satisfy him I began to cry and I told him I was expecting a baby. In the end he felt sorry for me and sent for Grigoriev, who arrived, very indignant, with his famous black brief-case full of our passports and papers. He explained in his faulty French that I was a dancer. Eventually the officer revealed that my friend was a spy and that they had purposely diverted some of the ship's passengers to this route in order to catch her. He still wouldn't believe that I didn't really know her, but he accepted Grigoriev's written word that he would be responsible for me until the end of the war, and let me go.

As soon as we arrived in Rome, Diaghilev came to the rehearsal room to greet us, but he was very glum and seemed to blame us for not having made more of a success of our tour. We felt guilty, although the disaster had been no fault of ours. Diaghilev was particularly annoyed with Kremnev for having failed to hold things together, and summoned him to render an account of our calamities at a private interview. When Kola had to tell him that I was pregnant Diaghilev was very angry.

I was sent for on the following day, and he saw me alone. He talked to me for a long time, saying that in his opinion there was only one thing to be done: I must have an operation and get rid of the baby. This, however, I refused to do. He tried to make me see how my career was in jeopardy, and that becoming a mother would complicate my whole life when it was essential to keep working in the difficult time of war. But I could not be persuaded; and the more he talked the more sure I was what a wonderful thing it would be to be a mother. Of course, I was terrified of Diaghilev and it was very hard to stand up to him in argument. I felt that nobody could ever have rejected his advice before, and at the same time I realised that I could not expect him to share my feelings. At last, seeing that he could not influence me, he gave in gracefully and said, 'Very well, we must get you married as soon as possible. Your parents will be horrified.' Then I had to tell him about Kola's Gypsy. When he recovered from this new revelation, he immediately began to take the same point of view as Kremnev; he was sure that Russian law would get us out of trouble, and he made an appointment to see the Russian Ambassador.

We got into a carriage, picked up Kremnev and drove to the Embassy. The Ambassador made it seem very easy: he agreed with Kola and Diaghilev that there was nothing in Russian law to prevent a marriage taking place, and forthwith they all began to draw up a contract. Feeling more helpless than ever with these three men against me, I kept insisting, 'Will this marriage be legal in England?' I was assured that since I was marrying a

Russian, Russian law was all I need worry about. Nevertheless, they seemed to think an English wedding might help, so I was bundled back into the waiting carriage and driven to the English church, but it was closed and the clergy were all on holiday. All this time Kola was as white as a sheet—furious and inclined to blame me for everything. Back into the carriage we got, and without the blessing of the Church and by Russian law I became, by a stroke of the pen, the second Mrs Nicolas Kremnev.

I could see that I should be no use on the forthcoming South American tour if I were unable to dance, so I wrote to my parents, telling them the whole story, asking if I could come home to have the baby.

The lucky group who had remained with Diaghilev in Rome had been far from idle. Massine had prepared new ballets. These works marked the beginning of a glorious period in the history of the Diaghilev company; for although the wanderers were destined to pass through several trials before the end of the war, Massine was now launched on a wave of masterly creation.

When the Russian Ballet had first come to Europe, what thrilled Parisian audiences was not that they danced ballet, but that they were so Russian. Classical ballet was not new to Paris: Russian exoticism was. Diaghilev, who in ballets like *L'Oiseau de feu* and *Petroushka* 'revealed Russia to itself and to the world' was by no means committed exclusively to the art of his own country—how could he be without degenerating into a mere purveyor of local colour, a hawker of peasant arts and crafts? He had loved Italian pictures, French furniture and German music almost as long as he had been reading Pushkin. The man who brought *Les Sylphides* and *Carnaval* back to France and Germany, did not reject the ideas of French poets like Vaudoyer, who suggested the theme of *Le Spectre* in 1911, or of Cocteau, whose scenario for *Le Dieu bleu* was realised in the following year. He commissioned scores from Debussy, Ravel and Strauss.

The new period which began in 1917, was a cosmopolitan one, for Massine's ballets were to take their subjects from several different countries, while they reflected artistically the diverse experiments of the school of Paris.

97

Les Femmes de bonne humeur, which Diaghilev called his Italian ballet, owed its existence to his enthusiasm for the music of Domenico Scarlatti. He and Massine played through the Neapolitan composer's five hundred sonatas before choosing the two dozen they needed for the ballet, the story of which they took from Goldoni's comedy in Venetian dialect, *Le Donne di buon' umore*. The selected pieces were then given to the Italian composer, Vincenzo Tommasini, to orchestrate. There was only one slow number in the ballet, so to match the rapid motion of Scarlatti's sewing-machine music, written for the harpsichord, Massine invented for his dancers the jerky, flickering movements of marionettes. Realising that something fantastic was required and anxious perhaps to keep pace with Diaghilev's pursuit of originality, Bakst suggested that in his set the buildings surrounding the little square should all curve inwards, as if reflected in a convex mirror. His first sketch—unique in its attempt to vie with the experiments of cubism—still exists: but Diaghilev decided after all to have his buildings rectilinear, while giving them a slight inward tilt, which was perhaps a feeble compromise, though it gave him the chance of announcing cryptically on the programme that in this décor Bakst had 'taken the first step towards the annihilation of stage perspective'. His costumes were rather elaborate eighteenth-century clothes in brilliant colour, and his characters wore grotesque make-up with curly noses and impossible eyebrows to emphasise their doll-like nature.

In my opinion *Les Femmes de bonne humeur*, which Massine had been able to produce during his long, peaceful sojourn in Rome, was the most perfect and complete ballet of its type ever invented. It was like a whole series of paintings imposed one upon the other: you could stop the ballet at any given moment and find you were looking at an entrancing composition. So ingeniously had Massine worked it all out that I do not think there was a single insignificant movement in it. Nothing could have been gayer or more fun to dance, and the costumes were a joy to wear. Bakst had made a detailed sketch for each artist's make-up, and whenever he was in the theatre he would himself paint a star, a crescent, or a sort of wiggle on our faces or chests.

Lydia Lopokova as Mariuccia, the maid who carries love letters and produces all the complications of the plot, was irresistible. If anyone could dart about the stage as swiftly or neatly as she did, nobody could ever imitate the witty way she used her head and shoulders, or the zest with which she threw herself into the action, as if every step was improvised on the spur of the moment and every situation was occurring for the first time.

In the roles of the two noblemen, Massine and Idzikovsky were well contrasted. Massine appeared so handsome, elegant and dashing, while Idzikovsky was so perfectly cast to type that it was impossible for another dancer to follow him and give satisfaction. His short legs in breeches and white stockings and his arched, pointed feet helped him to execute the high, staccato jumps which Massine had put into his solo, some of them done with one leg tucked under. With his laughing face and tilted nose, he looked like a real eighteenth-century caricature, and I think it was his best part.

Maestro Cecchetti, as the old Marquess, was in his element. Like many Italians, he was a born mime, and he adored the scene in which he flirted with Massine and Idzikovsky dressed up as women. The part of the vain and amorous old marchioness was portrayed by Mme Cecchetti in such a way that she seemed real.

The slow melancholy dance of Constanza, performed by Luba Tchernicheva, was one of the loveliest numbers Massine ever arranged. It was simple and pathetic, though tiring, as she hardly came off point at all. Floating about the stage in an ecstasy of languour and love, she swayed from side to side, and linked her little fingers, turning out her elbows at interesting angles. How superbly she did it, and how beautiful she looked in her wide-skirted red silk dress.

The performance of Leon Woizikovsky as the waiter taking an order for dinner, miming all the dishes, including spaghetti, and then serving the meal, was a masterpiece. But no scene was more memorable than that of Mariuccia's little dinner party for

the three men. How fascinating it was to watch them run in and
out of the house, fetching tablecloth, cutlery, glasses, carafe,
chicken, and stools, setting the table in front of your eyes on the
stage. Then, from the moment the meal began, there was no let-
up until they had all dined and each had danced a solo. Massine
was brilliant, jumping on and off his chair as he grew more excited
by the wine, and playing an imaginary guitar. One had the impression that this happy group of people really were getting
tipsy and enjoying an excellent meal. So wonderfully planned
and rehearsed was this episode that I have watched it a dozen
times without seeing it vary.

Each of the nine principal dancers in this ballet had a solo,
and all these dances were fitted together in a craftsman-like
manner. In the fugue of the finale every dancer made a separate
entrance from a different point, and all ran round and round each
other and in and out between the furniture. At the end everyone had to hold one of Massine's extraordinary poses while, roaring with laughter, they watched the old Marchioness rocking
about on the floor in misery at the loss of her wig.

Rome in 1917, before Mussolini had begun to excavate, was
more like Rome in the eighteenth century than like it is today.
Priests or seminarists as they walked in crocodile to and from
their colleges would call out personal remarks to us. One night
as I was walking home alone in the dark I was pounced on by
a tipsy monk. He was fat and horrid and as he folded his arms
round me he slobbered '*Mia bella biondina!*' I gave him the kick
with my knee which my father had taught me.

I was longing to see the sights of Rome, and the first things
that delighted me were the fountains. Kola and I stayed at a
dreary hotel near the Pantheon, but as we only slept there we
didn't mind. I enjoyed buying little baskets of figs with nuts, and
the flower stalls were beautiful.

Mme Cecchetti was very much to the fore at this time. Being
at home in Italy made her more than usually gay and sweet. She
sometimes gave us lessons, and I shall always be grateful to her
for teaching me the correct method of balance in the pure classical movements of the mazurka in *Les Sylphides*.

In February the first Russian revolution under the liberal Kerensky had taken place. As most of our company were Russian or Polish, this upheaval was to change not only their lives and those of their families, but the whole course of their country's history. At the time these big things happen people find them hard to interpret. The company did not know how the change of government would affect Russia or the course of the war, or even their own lives, and until they could interpret the events in a personal way they did not know whether the news was good or bad. Diaghilev, for example, who was twenty times better informed than any of his dancers, seemed to welcome the events of February with a kind of optimism. He had always been a liberal in politics, just as he was in artistic matters, and having foreseen that some change was coming, perhaps he believed this revolution was a change for the better; but in the spring of 1917, few could foresee the Bolshevik revolution or the excesses which were to follow. During our Rome season, determined not to be behind the times, Diaghilev substituted for the Russian national hymn, which would have been played at a certain Rea Cross gala, a tune which later became famous as *The Song of the Volga Boatmen* and Stravinsky sat up all night to orchestrate it.

We gave four performances in Rome at the Teatro Constanzi, and *Les Femmes de bonne humeur* was shown to the public for the first time on April 12, 1917, with great success. Another novelty of the season was the playing of Stravinsky's *Fireworks*—the first composition of his Diaghilev had ever heard—and while this was played in the orchestra-pit the stage was occupied by a construction which lit up, made by the futurist Balla.

From Rome we went to Naples, arriving on a fine sunny day, and were thrilled to see between the houses blue glimpses of Vesuvius, the bay and islands. Naples smelled of garlic, Macedonia cigarettes, olive oil which had been cooked in several times over, and inadequate sanitation.

We were rehearsing *Contes Russes*. I was one of the girls who hid under the huge spreading cloak of the Swan Princess, giving it the appearance of having a frame underneath it like a crinoline. At certain musical cues we had to emerge from under the cloak in pairs into a V-formation, then perform a clever dance with our hands. Evina was an expert on this number, which was complicated and quite hard to remember. One morning when we were practising this I began to feel very ill, and Grigoriev allowed me to drop out. Kola took me along a promenade which was separated from the sea only by a few rocks. The sea was rough and we watched a fishing-boat about two hundred yards off shore which was in trouble; it turned round and round, rocked from side to side and suddenly capsized. There were few people about, but two men jumped into the water. However, they could make no headway as the sea threw them back onto the rocks. A small boat was eventually launched, but it was so long before it could reach the overturned craft that of the four men who were brought in three were dead and the other was taken off to hospital. By this time a crowd had collected and there were women weeping and kneeling in prayer. I had never seen stark tragedy in real life before, and there was nothing I could do but stand and pray for the poor men. When we got back to our hotel I fell into a dead faint, and when I came to I found myself in bed. The proprietress of the hotel who was leaning over me, told me that she could read the signs—I was going to have a baby. If I had not been sure of this already I certainly could have had no doubts from then on, for I felt a movement like a bird fluttering inside me.

Diaghilev's enthusiasm for the new régime in Russia again manifested itself on our arrival in Paris. He arranged that in the final scene of *L'Oiseau de feu*, the dancer in the part of Prince Ivan Tsarevitch should carry a huge red flag. There were protests, however, and it was soon scrapped.

Besides *Les Femmes de bonne humeur*, another new ballet was given in Paris that spring, which had been prepared in Rome during the winter. *Parade* was the invention of the young French poet Jean Cocteau, and it introduced the painter Picasso and the composer Erik Satie to the ballet-going public. Diaghilev always liked to feel he was in touch with all that was new in music and painting. Sharper than most people to spot good quality in the work of young artists, he needed, nevertheless, someone to keep him informed of what was going on in the studios of Paris. This function Jean Cocteau was delighted to fulfil, as Boris Kochno did later.

Parade combined several novelties. Cubism was already ten years old, but *Parade* introduced it to the theatre public. Picasso was famous in a small circle, but *Parade* was his first work for the stage. Even Erik Satie, the eccentric composer of *Sept Morceaux en forme de poire*, was, in his fifties, only just being discovered. *Parade* was the first ballet to take its theme from the popular entertainments of the present day—the first of many to deal with the circus and the music-hall. It was also the first ballet to recognise the existence of the cinema. *Parade* discovered America.

It seemed doubtful whether transferring the experiment of cubism to the stage would be successful, but Cocteau was ready to try anything. He also appointed himself standard-bearer to the new school of musicians known as *Les Six*, which was supposed to have come into being through admiration for the work of Satie. Their aim was tuneful simplicity: claiming to be essentially French in spirit, they were against everything rich, heavy, pretentious or German. In *Parade* Cocteau arbitrarily associated the new painting and the new music, and brought both into the service of the Russian Ballet.

The scene of *Parade* was outside a booth on a fairground, in front of which performers came out to give a sample of their turns and lure the public inside. These turns—two acrobats on a tight-rope, a dancing horse, a Chinese conjuror, and a child prodigy in the form of an American girl who cranked up a car, used a typewriter, and imitated Charlie Chaplin—were punctuated by the altercations of rival managers, one American and one French. In lieu of costumes the managers wore eight-foot-high structures in wood and *papier-mâché*—cubist compositions by Picasso—in which skyscrapers, human features and fragments of clothing contrived to suggest their personalities, their backgrounds and their ruthless nature. These two monsters conversed partly in gesture, waving a stick, a contract, a pipe or a megaphone, partly percussively beating a tattoo with their feet. In this extraordinary way they conveyed a vivid picture of a business conference.

Into Satie's tuneful, jazzy score, which was a sort of crystallised popular music, Cocteau insisted on introducing the naturalistic sounds of shooting, of ships' sirens and of typewriters: those noises were intended to give mental prods to the public and to supply a third dimension, in the way that cubist painters used fragments of real newspaper as reminders of everyday triviality in their visions of a serene and ordered other-world.

Parade was so delightful that I am sure it would be a favourite if it could be done today. Massine was witty and grotesque as the Chinese conjuror, and his trick of swallowing an egg was as convincing as anything done by a member of the Magic Circle. As the two Acrobats on an imaginary tight-rope, Lopokova and Zverev in their blue and white all-over tights had an extraordinary charm, and Lydia put great zest into her circus *cabriole*. The old joke of two men playing the front and back legs of a horse had been often seen, but the men inside the horse in *Parade* were dancers which made all the difference: they never failed to arouse roars of laughter. The part of the American Girl was created by Maria Shabelska, but I took it over later when she left the company. It was lucky that the short, white-pleated shirt and blazer which the American Girl wore were easy to move in, because her entrance and exit were extremely difficult. These consisted of sixteen bars of music, and with each bar she had to jump with both feet straight out together in the front and almost touch her toes with her outstretched arms. This is hard enough to do on the same spot, but when it was a question of moving around a vast stage at full speed it was no mean feat. When it got to dancing rag-time in this part, whacking myself on the head and tripping myself up with the back foot in true Chaplin style, I began to enjoy myself.

Parade has been represented by people who have written about it as a mere stunt. This was not the case at all. The public always seemed to be most enthusiastic, and so was our company. You can always tell when the company approves of a ballet, because you will find a number of them watching it from the wings.

I was expecting to leave the Ballet in Paris and have my baby at home, but my parents wrote an angry letter, saying they could never forgive me for not being married in church and that they never wished to set eyes on my child. The shock was so great that I nearly lost the baby. Once again I had to appeal to Diaghilev for help. With great generosity he immediately gave permission for me to remain with the company and to be included in the list of passengers for the South American tour, as one of the staff. I wrote a violent letter to my parents, saying that I hoped we would be torpedoed on the way to South America, so that they would be able to wipe me off their slate for good and all.

From Paris we went to give a short season in Madrid. Although the baby was due in three months I carried on dancing all my parts. At this time Kola was drinking more and more, and the trying situation only made his temper worse.

The Spanish royal family constantly came to see us, and when we were not appearing on the stage at the Teatro Real, we danced in a small private theatre at the top of the building. This had a charming little stage, complete with footlights and spots, and the auditorium was a beautifully decorated square room. The Court did not sit in rows, but were scattered about in arm-chairs and sofas informally; and after dancing we went forward to meet them. I remember the King offering Diaghilev some sort of gift for us, but he refused it, saying that it was an honour for us to dance before the King, though perhaps a few signed photographs would be welcome. We got neither present nor pictures.

One night when I was dancing my difficult Bacchanale solo in *Narcisse*, with cup, jug and red wig, I started off with such abandon that I forgot to count the number of jumps on my fingers and finished several bars before the music, so that I had to improvise. This had never happened to me before. When I saw Grigoriev rushing towards my dressing-room, I tried to tell him how upset I was. He said he would have to fine me; but when he went on, 'Surely, you should know you have no right to leave off any part of your costume,' I realised that he had not noticed my miscalculation, while I had not noticed that I had gone onstage without that dreadful, heavy shawl.

Nijinsky had joined the company in Madrid. As a prisoner-of-war, released from Austria at the request of King Alfonso, he could only dance in neutral countries, of which Spain was one: and after the South American tour he had cabled to Grigoriev asking if he could join the company for their Spanish season. In spite of the report Diaghilev had received of Nijinsky's behaviour in North America, he agreed to take him back. This was not pure altruism, of course, since he knew the Spaniards would be eager to see him dance for the first time, and besides it was essential for him to send Nijinsky off with the Company on the forth-coming South American tour in order to fulfil his contract. Romola describes how charming Diaghilev was to herself and her husband when they arrived in Madrid: he put himself out to be so friendly that Nijinsky was enchanted at the prospect of a renewed artistic collaboration, and she herself fell completely under Diaghilev's spell. Naturally Diaghilev was more eager than anyone to see everything running smoothly and Nijinsky dancing at the top of his form again. However, Romola was really an outsider in the world of the ballet and she probably began to feel rather left out: this, and the fact that she had a naturally suspicious nature, soon led to further trouble. When she found that Kostrovsky and Zverev were back at their old tricks and were telling Nijinsky he ought to stop dancing and devote himself to tilling the soil, she leapt to the conclusion that the two fanatics were instigated by Diaghilev who, if he could not regain his former influence over Nijinsky, would rather put an end to his career as a dancer. This absurd idea could only have occurred to a woman who was herself undergoing severe mental stress.

According to Grigoriev in his annals of the Diaghilev Ballet, 'The experience of the American tour over which, however un-successfully, he had exercised complete control, had fostered illusions in him and his wife.' He could see from the success of Massine's new ballets that he was not indispensable to the com-pany, but he blamed Diaghilev for not giving him the same degree of publicity as he had enjoyed in the old days.

When the ballet moved to Barcelona, the Nijinskys attempted to run away. Diaghilev himself, who had had no warning that they planned to leave, averted this flight at the eleventh hour.

On finding a pile of Nijinsky's luggage in the entrance hall of the hotel, he sought the advice of the governor of the province. Under Spanish law, an artist billed to appear was obliged to do so; and Nijinsky was prevented by a police escort from leaving Barcelona.

We were thankful that Grigoriev was to be in charge of the South American tour, and it did not occur to any of us that he would find it just as hard to cope with Nijinsky and his moods as Kola had done in the United States: perhaps it did not occur to Grigoriev either. Diaghilev and Massine came to see us off on July 4, 1917, when we sailed from Barcelona on a lovely ship called the *Reina Victoria Eugenia*.

There was plenty of strong drink on the ship, and as Kola had no work or responsibilities he was drinking heavily nearly every evening. One day, after one of many public rows, he followed me down to the cabin and hit me so hard on the face that I had a bruise across my nose for several days. His unreasoning jealousy was rapidly growing worse and scenes were frequent.

It was very hot when we landed at Montevideo and there were few people about. I remember walking from the docks through quiet, wide streets. As we approached the residential quarter of the town we saw big flat-roofed buildings—they must have been blocks of apartments—with square openings in them which were shady balconies. The girls who were seated in these openings, getting what air they could, were ivory-skinned, with straight blonde hair, lovely big eyes and expressions of complete serenity. They were so beautiful it was impossible not to stand and stare.

After giving a few performances in Montevideo, we sailed down the coast to Rio de Janeiro, of which I have one unpleasant memory. I was wandering round the shops when I came across a large open one with no doors, only shutters to pull down at night. This shop was full of every kind of monkey in cages—marmosets, gibbons, and lovely little golden-haired lion monkeys. I was fascinated. A woman came up to me and said, 'Do you understand Spanish?' I said I did. She then went for me in no uncertain fashion. I could not imagine what I had done wrong, but I heard later that Brazilians considered it wrong for a pregnant

woman to look at a monkey. Calling me a wicked girl and
every other kind of name, she pushed me out of the shop; then,
while a crowd of spectators stared and giggled at me, she shouted,
'You will give birth to a baby with a monkey's face!' I burst into
tears and hurried away.

On the train journey from Rio to São Paulo we climbed higher
and higher into the mountains. They told us the engine was fed
with timber, so sparks were flying the whole time. At dusk
we were going through a tunnel when we saw flames and fragments of burning material flying past the windows. Part of the
train had obviously caught fire, and my friends were very concerned for me and anxious that in my condition I should be saved
from shocks. When the train pulled out of the tunnel, it drew up
and we found our scenery truck was blazing. The stupid people
had hitched the open truck next to the engine, where it was
inevitable that sparks would fall. We were miles up in the mountains and there was no sign of life. There was nothing for it but
for the artists to pull what they could out of the burning mass.
We lost the scenery of *Le Spectre* and *Cléopâtre*. Grigoriev had
travelled from Rio by car, so he had a nasty surprise when he
arrived at São Paulo and Kremnev broke the news to him.

The next morning I felt somewhat shaky, but went to the
theatre to teach another girl my difficult Bacchanale from *Narcisse*.
During that night I awoke with a strange feeling, but did not
realise my baby was on the way. I had had a full examination and
had been told that it could not be expected for two months.
Finally, I became so ill that Kola, with difficulty, managed to
wake the hotel people and call a doctor. An ambulance came, and
with sirens screaming, I was rushed to the most amazing maternity
hospital one could imagine. When we arrived Kola was in such a
state he kept repeating, 'No money to be spared!'—as though
we had masses instead of mighty little. The hospital people were
all jabbering Portuguese at the tops of their voices. It was
decided not to wait, but to operate at once without even examining me. We were all marched off to the operating theatre,
where they gave Kola a white coat and put me onto a sort of
combined table and chair. I was strapped down with leather

straps while the surgeon got out his knives and various instruments with the help of a nurse. I was then given chloroform and he got on with his butchery.

What they did to that poor child I cannot imagine. They used instruments on her head, leaving it a most peculiar shape and covered in sores. They cut the cord too short, so that for months she had a ruptured navel, and she weighed less than two kilos. I could not feed her and for the first week they kept her from me.

Natasha was born on September 1, 1917. Nothing was done for my wounds, and ten days later they were still so bad that Kola and I decided that it was better for me to escape from this nightmare hospital; so we packed and returned to the hotel. Before we left, the doctor and nurses said, 'You know that your child cannot live more than a few days. You had better leave her with us and we will see to her. Go away and forget.' Natasha weighed so little that I guessed that they would put her in an incinerator, so I took her with me.

At the hotel I tried to dress the wounds myself, but I couldn't manage it. Kola wanted to help, but at the first sight of them he fainted dead away on the floor.

The baby was so minute and thin, with her skinny little legs folded up crosswise, that I decided she must be swaddled, and got long strips of linen and bound her tiny legs together. I had to send to a toy shop for some doll's clothes. I had no idea what to do about her navel or her head, or how to feed her.

Meanwhile the ballet had left for Buenos Aires, and as we had only enough money to buy our way out of São Paulo we had to follow them immediately by ship. One day I was sitting on the deck of this horrid little vessel, trying to feed the baby with some form of powdered milk and crying quietly to myself with misery, when a young man came up and spoke to me in Spanish. He told me he was a medical student and asked to look at the baby. He explained that her navel was ruptured; he got sticking plaster and tied it tightly around her. Then he told me her head had eczema and instructed me what to do with it as soon as we landed. There was no doctor on board the ship and there were precious few medical supplies, but the student got what was necessary from the captain and dressed my wounds. I am sure that young man saved my daughter's life.

As Natasha was still alive when we arrived in Buenos Aires we decided to have her christened at once; so it was in the Russian Church in that South American capital, with Grigoriev as godfather and Mme Jasvinska as godmother, that my daughter received the name of Natalia Nicolaevna Kremnev.

It is not permitted for a mother to attend the baptism of her baby until a period of six weeks has passed after the birth. But a few words and *other things* were exchanged with the deacon, and I was allowed to watch the ceremony from a distance: it was endless. As the baby had to be submerged naked in the water, we had asked the deacon to have this warmed; she was so frail that I thought a chill might carry her off. When the time comes for this part of the service, the child is passed from one godparent to the other several times and then lowered into the water. To my horror she gasped and screamed, and from the third dipping my poor little baby emerged scarlet. The fool of a deacon had made the water much too hot, and I could do nothing about it because I wasn't supposed to be there at all. However, she survived yet another ordeal. We had a dinner party after the christening at which the priest and the deacon got very merry and were the life and soul of the party.

During all this time Grigoriev was having a taste of what it was like to cope with Nijinsky and his wife. Nijinsky pretended to put the ballet out of his mind and sometimes refused to dance what was advertised. He accused Grigoriev and others of plotting his death, and engaged a sort of bodyguard to protect him from imaginary attacks. It soon became evident that his mental condition was such that he ought to be prevented from dancing, in case he did something extraordinary on the stage. In fact, his last public appearance was at Buenos Aires on September 26, 1917.

9

BEAM-ENDS

Barcelona — A nurse for Natasha — Felix Fernandez —
Spanish Flu — Revolution in Lisbon — Lack of engagements
—Natasha left in Portugal — Tour of Spain — Bullfights —
Freak performance at Logroño — Felix versus the Gypsies
in Seville — From Barcelona to Lisbon to fetch Natasha —
Stranded in Madrid — Diaghilev on his beam-ends — His
kindness — Telegrams from London — An English en-
gagement at last — Paris in wartime.

On the return journey I had a difficult time feeding Natasha.
She could not digest powdered food and in a month had put
on only a very few ounces. The ship's doctor did what he could,
but he held out little hope that she would be alive when we
arrived in Barcelona. If she were, he advised me to go straight
to a maternity home.

Natasha survived the voyage, so I took her to a hospital run
by nuns. These women were very kind to me and gave me the
address of a young mother who would feed the baby. She worked
in a factory, so I went to her home in the evening, and found her
in two small rooms with her husband and child. The child was
eighteen months old, and stood by the side of his mother to be
fed while I talked to her. The woman's name was Felisa and she
was very beautiful. I showed her my dying baby, and she said
simply, 'Give her to me. She can have the other side.' It was
like seeing a starving puppy being fed. I could not stop my
tears.

Felisa undertook to come and look after Natasha on condition that she could bring her little boy with her, to which I

agreed. I discovered she was feeding her child with solid food as well as milk, and I was somewhat aghast to find he was not house-trained. (Luckily the floors in Spain are tiled.) We had to pay her quite a good salary, so it was essential that I got back to work. I was desperately out of practice, and it was rather worrying that my wounds had still not quite healed, but I was determined that Diaghilev should not be disappointed in me after his kindness in letting me travel to South America with the Ballet. I worked like a black in class, and was soon fit enough to start rehearsing Massine's latest work.

While he was in Italy Diaghilev had discovered the manuscript of some unknown piano pieces by Rossini. These enchanting tunes were supposed to have been written during the composer's old age, when he was living in Paris, to entertain the guests at his dinner parties; and Diaghilev had them orchestrated by Respighi. They were destined to become *La Boutique fantasque*. The dolls in this fantastic toyshop were to perform dances of various nations, and one of the first of these which Massine put into rehearsal was the Venetian Waltz for Gavrilov and myself. I still recall some steps from this waltz, although it was never performed, for Diaghilev soon decided it was too gentle a number with which to open the *divertissement* of dolls in the first scene of the ballet. It was scrapped in favour of a *tarantella*.

Our stay in Barcelona was quite a long one. We used to go to the cafés at night to watch local dancers. I was fascinated by the girls who would shake their shoulders at amazing speed, holding a little shawl across their naked breasts, letting it gradually slide down, then with a delicious movement twitching it up again and turning away so seductively that the audience would stamp and shout. Some of the men dancers, too, were magnificent.

No one watched these dancers more keenly than Leonide Massine, for while we had been away, he and Diaghilev had searched in many towns for a Spanish dancer around whom a ballet could be made. Unfortunately Flamenco dancers, however brilliant their technique, tend to rely on improvisation, and it is almost impossible to find one who can learn a dance and can be counted on to do the same steps two performances running.

Spanish 'flu was raging in Barcelona, but I never realised how serious it was until, calling one day at the English Consulate, I was told that all but two of the staff had died in a fortnight. However, with Felisa's feeding, my baby was getting stronger and putting on weight, and I decided I must persuade Felisa to leave her son and come with me to Madrid, where our next engagement was, to look after Natasha. This was arranged, but before leaving we had to ask Diaghilev for a sum of money to compensate her husband.

Poor Felisa had never left her family or her husband before, and on this journey—and indeed for weeks afterwards—I was obliged to listen to her wailing, 'Oi mi hombre, mi madre, mi padre. . . .' Shortly after our arrival she went down with 'flu. In Madrid the sickness had not only quietened the streets—it had emptied them; and the theatre attendances were very poor. As several of the company caught the germ, we were sometimes performing with only a skeleton cast.

It was in Madrid that we met Felix Fernandez. Diaghilev had first seen him dancing in a square in Seville, and had come to the conclusion that he was the most brilliant Spanish male dancer of his day. He was now dancing on the stage of a café in a back street of Madrid, where working people used to go. Diaghilev must have been in some doubt whether this fiery, ignorant boy would be able to work and fit in with his highly disciplined company, but he took the risk and engaged him.

The employment of Felix was the first step towards the realisation of the great Spanish ballet which Massine intended to create, though at that time neither Diaghilev nor Massine can have known exactly what form it would take. The essential was that Massine and the company should learn to perform Spanish steps in a Spanish way; and Massine in particular had to master the grammar of the Spanish dance before he could work out his choreography. At this stage Diaghilev and Massine probably saw Felix as the eventual star of their Spanish ballet, for if they had only needed a professor, it would surely have been more reasonable to engage an older man with experience of teaching. As Massine learned more of the secrets of this very special art and grew more sure of himself, and as poor Felix's unstable nature became apparent, so, I suppose, they gradually came to visualise Massine as the hero of the ballet. One thing is certain: Felix joined the company in the confident expectation that Diaghilev intended to make him a world-famous star.

Four days before the Ballet were due to leave Madrid for their first visit to Lisbon, I went down with Spanish 'flu myself. As it was impossible for me to travel with the company, Kola stayed behind to look after me; and as Felix's passport had not come through he was to wait in Madrid and travel with us.

It was a miserable little band that set off a week after the rest of the company on the journey from Madrid to Lisbon. There was nothing to eat on the train, which was crammed, and nothing to drink, except water, which we were afraid might be contaminated. Felisa and the baby both cried most of the way. Felix seemed quite crazy, mumbling and grumbling to himself: he slept on the floor of the corridor.

When, at long last, we arrived at a station in pitch darkness and were told it was Lisbon, we were surprised to be greeted with gunfire. We had heard nothing about trouble in Portugal, but a man who loomed out of the night and offered to take us to a *pension* explained that a revolution had just begun. He led us out of the station into the Avenida. As we turned a corner our tails were nearly singed by a volley of rifle fire from soldiers lying flat across the road we had just left. Felisa, who had been moaning all the way from the station, fell to the ground and dropped the baby. Felix bolted up the street. How we ever got to that *pension* I cannot remember.

I was given a pretty room with a balcony, but as the shooting in our neighbourhood got steadily worse, we were all obliged to sit in a stone basement corridor for the rest of the night. By this time I was very sick and feverish, and as Felisa was in such a bad state she had lost her milk, so my baby was having a rough time too. When daybreak came the firing died down and I was taken back to my bedroom. Half the balcony had been shot away, and not only the wall but the headboard of my bed bore the mark of bullets.

As Felisa still could not feed Natasha, Kola went out in the teeth of the revolution to find a dairy, waving a large white handkerchief over his head. He had to cross the big square, from one side of which the Navy, crouched behind some statues, were shooting at the Army on the other. Kola was questioned, but made it understood that *leche* was necessary for the *chico* and was allowed to proceed. He came back with a little milk, but it wasn't enough to help Felisa's, so we sent for a doctor. He gave her stout, which did the trick; and before long we were all on the mend.

As soon as we had located the rest of the company we moved to a very nice hotel on the square where all the firing took place. We were really quite grand, with a big, handsome front room for Kola and myself, and another adjoining for Felisa and Natasha. The only drawback was having to keep the blinds down, because if a soldier or a sailor saw you peeping out he took a pot shot at you. Otherwise they fired at each other.

I had always thought there was something strange about Felix, and now, as I got to know him better, working with him and living in the same hotel, I observed how nervous and moody he was. At the time I put this down to the shooting, which upset him, and to depression at the loss of the personal success he had enjoyed in the cabaret where he worked. I thought he missed the applause deeply, and I doubted if Diaghilev had been right in taking him away from his natural environment. If anything upset him or if his brain were overtaxed in any way, he would lose control and shout. One night at dinner in the hotel, with the dining-room full of people, he became annoyed with me because I laughed. He began to bang plates on the table; then he picked up a bottle of wine and was about to throw it at my head when Kola snatched it from him. He was deathly white and jabbering with fury. A few days later there was another outburst of revolution in our square, and Felix was so petrified that he barricaded himself into an inner room with all the furniture he could find. It was not till all was quiet again after a couple of days and he was exhausted from lack of food and drink that he could be persuaded to come out.

Because of the revolution our season in Lisbon started a fortnight late, and it was not a success. The Royal Theatre being
closed, we were obliged to dance in a huge building which was
more like a circus. This was never full; and when Diaghilev,
anxious as ever to show his company to advantage, managed to
have the Royal Theatre opened, it was so dirty that our costumes,
tights and shoes were almost ruined. Being December, it was
bitterly cold, and both theatres were unheated. I think those
performances at the Royal Theatre must have been the worst
we ever gave: luckily there were only two of them.

The year 1918 began with not one engagement in sight. For
the first time in its history the Diaghilev Ballet was stranded.
On top of this, the news of the Bolshevik revolution, which cut
off the majority of our company from their home, made life more
desperate than ever. Diaghilev announced that we were to have
a month's rehearsals on half pay, while he went off to Spain in
search of new bookings.

The rehearsals were rather a farce, because Massine had de-
parted with Diaghilev and we had nothing new to do. It must
have been rather embarrassing for Grigoriev to keep up the
pretence of polishing the old repertoire. However, our time was
not all wasted, as it gave some of us a good opportunity to study
Spanish dancing under Felix. Woizikovsky, Slavinsky and myself worked particularly hard.

We were in Lisbon just over three months and for the last
part of this time we had no money coming in at all: Diaghilev
had none to give us. Grigoriev was very kind and at the beginning, when he had a little money to spare, he lent us what he
could, never thinking we would be stuck in Lisbon for so long.
What money there was in the company circulated, but in the end
we were all living on credit. As we stopped paying our hotel
bill, my good room on the first floor was changed for a back
room on the second, and finally all four of us, Kola, Felisa, the
baby and myself, moved into one room at the top of the building.

Felisa was fretting for home and Natasha was not doing very
well. We weaned the baby as best as we could, pawned something, borrowed a little more and bought Felisa a third-class

(a)

b)

(c)

(d)

Family Album
  (a) With Mother, Father and
      Beatrice at Hastings
  (b) Theatricals with Beatrice
  (c) Aged sixteen
  (d) With Natasha at Monte
      Carlo

Nijinsky and Karsavina in *Le Spectre de la rose*

(a)

(b)

(c)

FIRST ROLES

   (a) The Bacchanale in *Narcisse*
   (b) Papillon in *Carnaval*
   (c) Apple woman in *Till Eulenspiegel*
   (d) Ta-Hor in *Cléopâtre*

(d)

(a)

(b)

(c)

SCRAPBOOK
(a) 1913. Nijinsky's wedding in Buenos Aires
(b) 1915. The Cecchettis at Lausanne
(c) 1916. Larionov, Diaghilev and Kremnev
    at San Sebastian
(d) 1919. With Idzikovsky, Massine, Lopokova
    and Cecchetti, collecting for the Red Cross
    at the London Coliseum

(d)

As the Miller's Wife in *Le Tricorne*

(a)

(b)

Les Femmes de bonne humeur

    (a) Lopokova as Mariuccia
    (b) Tchernicheva as Constanza
    (c) Idzikovsky as Battista
    (d) Woizikovsky as Niccolo

(c)

(d)

(a) Tchernicheva in *Pulcinella*
against Picasso's set
(b) Massine in *Le Tricorne*
(c) Woizikovsky in *Le Tricorne*

(a)

(b)

(c)

(a)

1920'S SCRAPBOOK
(a) 1920. Chez Pasquier, Monte Carlo, with Antonova, Woizikovsky, Idzikovsky, Evina, Kremnev and Camishov
(b) 1924. With Kochno in London
(c) 1925. On the Lido with Woizikovsky, Lifar and Diaghilev
(d) 1929. With Woizikovsky at Vichy

(b)

(c)

(d)

As the Chosen Virgin in *Le Sacre du printemps*

(a)

(b)

(a) Red Riding Hood in *The Sleeping Princess* with Mikolaichik
(b) Columbine in *Carnaval*
(c) The Doll in *Petroushka*
(d) Chloë in *Daphnis et Chloë* (in an old *Faune* costume)

(c)

(d)

(a)

b)

(c)

Les Biches
  (a) Woizikovsky
  (b) and (c) As the Hostess

With Woizikovsky, Nijinska and Dolin in *Le Train bleu*

Massine in *Les Fâcheux* (against Sert's décor for *Cimarosiana*)

With Slavinsky, Lifar, Woizikovsky
and Nemtchinova in *Les Matelots*

(a)

(a) Gevergeva, Maikerska, Chamié, Tchernicheva, Sokolova, Soumarokova, Doubrovska and Danilova in *Zéphire et Flore*
(b) With Lifar in *Barabau*
(c) In *Le Bal*

(b)

(c)

DIAGHILEV
Painting by Elizabeth Polunin

ticket from Lisbon to Barcelona. It must have been an appalling journey, but we eventually heard that she had arrived safely.

Technically our contracts had expired, but most of us were determined to be faithful to Diaghilev if it was humanly possible to survive. One small group of dancers, however, were lured into signing a contract with a theatrical agent and, although Grigoriev did his best to dissuade them, they left us and went to Spain. We heard that they only danced a few performances and had little success. They were soon glad to come back to us, breaking their agreements with the agent and with their tails between their legs. Diaghilev was very angry about this desertion because it made it much more difficult for him to negotiate the new tour; in fact he was only able to conclude a new contract for the company when the renegades had agreed to return.

Time hung heavily on our hands in Lisbon. We could not afford to go sightseeing. Poker parties were in full swing among the gambling section of the company; but the rest of us just wandered about. One day Vassili, Diaghilev's servant, said to me, 'Your shoes are looking the worse for wear.' I replied, 'I'm afraid there is nothing I can do about it.' He told me to meet him the next day at the wardrobe where the baskets were stored, and gave me the high-heeled purple shoes I had worn in *Las Meniñas*. These saw me through for the rest of our stay in Lisbon.

At last the great day arrived when Diaghilev sent word that he had signed a contract for a tour all over Spain. What a relief it was to know that we should soon be working again! But I was once more faced with the problem of what to do with Natasha. She was now seven months old and I could not possibly take her on tour with nobody to look after her. Having made the awful decision to leave her behind, I found a Portuguese woman who agreed to keep her for me. She was a gardener's wife called Sra Abrantis, and it was with a heavy heart that I saw her take Natasha away.

Diaghilev raised as much advance money as he could, but we still had not enough to pay the whole of our hotel bill. We gave the management what we had, and I think they were glad to accept it and get rid of us. We had been shown exceptional

kindness and patience, for I think the proprietors were genuinely
sorry for us in our predicament.

We left for Spain at the end of March, 1918. The tour opened
at Valladolid. It was to be a long and arduous one, lasting over
two months, but it took us not only to great cities such as Sara-
goza, Cordova, Seville, Valencia and Alicante, but also to a number
of small towns, some of which were on the tops of hills and
could only be approached in horse-drawn vehicles. Our programmes were arranged in such a way that the big ballets with
elaborate scenery should only be performed in the larger towns,
and that these sets should travel on and wait for us at the next
big town, while we carried comparatively simple sets with us to
the smaller places on the route.

Dancers on tour are usually too preoccupied with their own
little problems—and often too tired—to be very discriminating
sightseers or to remember all the historic places and beautiful
buildings they have been lucky enough to see. The things I
remember from that journey are mostly quite trivial, and yet in
the course of it I felt I was getting to know and love Spain. As
we travelled south into the heat, the open windows would let
in a smell of blossom from the orange groves which was almost
overpowering; and at Andalusian stations children used to sell
pretty sticks with oranges tied ingeniously around them, with
a bunch of leaves and blossoms on the top. We visited cathedrals
hidden in narrow streets, containing madonnas with pearls for
eyes, crowned and hung with precious stones; and we saw the
blind and crippled beggars sitting on the steps outside. Wherever
we went I seldom missed a bullfight, if I was free to attend. The
colour, the music and the pure dancing movements of the men
always enthralled me, though I never liked to see the way the
horses were used, and would hide behind a fan until the picadors'
part was over. We got to know several of the *toreros* and their
troupes through staying at the same hotels, so we were often
able to go behind the scenes before the *corrida* began and usually
made a point of seeing the men off to the bull-ring in their highly
coloured brakes, with their horses decorated with bells, pompons
and glittering harnesses. Some of the *toreros'* marvellous costumes

used to cost as much as 4,000 pesetas each, and if you had the luck to be staying in the same hotel as one of these crack bull-fighters, you could see him go off twice in two different coloured costumes—that is, if you had not got a ticket for the *corrida*.

I shall never forget a bullfight I saw when all three *toreros* had either been tossed or gored, and we were only at the fourth bull! This bull had been particularly ferocious and had been booed by the public. The *torero's* second-in-command begged the president to let him try and kill the bull himself. The creature was lashing about the arena on its own and charging the barrier, while this man shouted and stamped and knelt, with his face like a ghost; but the president would not consent. Finally, an order was given, the door of the *toril* was opened and six young heifers were let in. The bull sniffed at them, the *peones* prodded him with little sticks, and off he went with his girl-friends, leaving considerable damage behind him. The two remaining bulls lived to see another gala day, much to the disgust of the crowd.

Some of the rough and rickety stages we danced on must undoubtedly have been the worst in Europe. One evening, in the middle of the male variation of *Les Sylphides*, Gavrilov went through a rotten board. He fell to the ground and had to drag himself off the stage by his hands, having torn his Achilles tendon. His foot was put in plaster, and the poor boy walked on crutches for a long time afterwards. He could never really jump and land properly on that foot again.

Logroño is a delightful place, famous for its wine, but it will be remembered by survivors of the Diaghilev Ballet for another reason. Having all managed somehow to pack into the one small hotel, where we were given a warm welcome, we made our way round to the little theatre. Here we found Grigoriev and Kremnev were having a lively argument with the management, who had sold every seat by dint of announcing that we were to perform the 'scandalous *Scheherazade*' and were refusing to accept *Carnaval* in its place. Spaniards were fascinated by the idea of a ballet about wives' infidelity with Negroes in an orgy followed by violent retribution. How could we give *Scheherazade* without the scenery, dresses and props? No doubt the management thought that in the tradition of strolling players, we ought to be able to put on any show we were asked for at a moment's notice. The stage was tiny, but we couldn't leave without our money, so something had to be done. Luckily, the box containing the musical scores, being very precious, always travelled with us. We dived into the extra basket which contained a lot of miscellaneous odds and ends and decided to make the best of a bad job.

There can never have been a ballet performance like the one we gave of *Scheherazade* at Logroño. We used the décor of *Carnaval*, which was just blue curtains, with a frieze painted round them, and which had only one opening at the back. Grigoriev as the Shah wore Idzikovsky's Bluebird costume, and as there was about two feet difference in their height, I cannot imagine how he got into it—I suppose the answer is, he didn't quite. His long legs, which nobody had ever seen in tights before, surmounted by little puffed trunks and ending in short boots from *Prince Igor*, were alone enough to double you up with laughter. But on top of it all he had to wear Lopokova's Firebird hat, back to front, with three large, flame-coloured ostrich feathers. For her role of Zobeide, Tchernicheva wore the bodice of an old *Cléopâtre* costume, her head wound round with a turban made out of an old scarf, and a skirt from *Prince Igor*. Kremnev, as the Eunuch, wore a long zig-zag patterned Egyptian chemise from *Cléopâtre*, with no belt and no keys to open the doors— which didn't exist anyway. We three Odalisques wore Grecian dresses, and everyone else used whatever they could lay their hands on. There were no cushions for us to recline on, no swords to kill us, and no steps on which to die. The sight of each other started us giggling from the very beginning; but to watch Luba trying to do her dance with Gavrilov, was the funniest thing I have ever seen. Everybody had hysterics, but we danced as never before and during the orgy the audience applauded like mad. At the end, Grigoriev, who had been lent an enormous old sword, stamped about the stage shouting at us, '*Die you fools! Die anywhere!*' I forget whether I was struck down by the one and only sword, died by auto-suggestion, or got a friendly colleague to strangle me. When the curtain fell, the applause was thunderous. We had triumphed in Logroño!

Next morning when we arrived at the railway station, we found the platform so crowded that Grigoriev, thinking there would never be room for us all on a small local train, passed round word that we should get into the van with the luggage. When the little train came in, the baskets were thrown into it with some of the boys on top of them, the rest of us piled into the end coach, and out we puffed. To our amazement, the crowd was still there on the platform, waving and shouting *Adios*. Almost the entire male population of Logroño had come to see us off, and except for us the train was empty.

On this tour we saw the dancing of several Spanish provinces, and if Diaghilev discovered any outstanding artists he would invite them to perform for us privately. While we were in Seville, I remember a party to which we went late one afternoon, driving in open carriages to an attractive café surrounded by orange groves outside the city. In the gardens there were two or three pavilions built in the tree-tops. We climbed up a ladder and went from one of these into another, which was about twenty-five feet long by fifteen feet wide, with windows at each side. The setting sun streamed into this room, and sitting there as we entered was a party of Gypsies, one of whom was softly playing a guitar. They were of various ages, all magnificent to look at. The women wore vividly coloured shawls on their shoulders over frilled and spotted dresses, while in their hair were combs and carnations. Waiters brought wine, and after several glasses, the atmosphere became friendly; then Diaghilev asked the Gypsies to perform.

Each dancer seemed to be better than the last. Spurred on by singing to the guitar accompaniment, clapping their hands in their special rhythm and drumming with their heels, they became more excited as the evening went on. The last of them to perform was a youngish man who looked as though he had stepped out of a painting, so true a Spanish Gypsy he hardly seemed to belong to the twentieth century. When he began to dance, we saw at once that his work had real technique and was beautifully executed. Diaghilev became extremely interested and watched every movement he made. Felix was with us, and I saw he was getting jealous of this potential rival, in a frenzy of impatience to show he could do better. During the applause that followed this boy's performance, Felix sprang into the middle of the room and began to dance as we had never seen him dance before. He tapped his heels faster and faster in an amazing variety of rhythms, and cracked his fingers as though they were castanets. He danced on his knees, leapt in the air, fell crashing on the side of his thigh, turned over and jumped up with such speed that it was incredible that the human body could stand the strain without injury. The Gypsies were themselves amazed and called out encouragement to him. Felix went on and on until he must have been exhausted, but he would not stop. We shouted *basta! basta!* but it was not until the Gypsies closed in and surrounded him that he would give up. After that evening Diaghilev must have made up his mind that he would never find a Spanish dancer better than Felix.

Our studies with Felix continued. He had a quick temper and screamed at us when we could not do a step, for he had no idea of teaching. We practised our castanets, but not one of us ever mastered the art of playing them correctly. Massine wrote down in a book every step, movement and footbeat he learned from Felix. Happy to see Spain and to be eating well, probably for the first time in his life, Felix waited for the day when Diaghilev would reveal him to the world.

In Madrid Diaghilev found a lovely girl called Zelita Astolfi, who was also an excellent dancer, and whom he thought he would be able to team up with Felix. She came once or twice to our rehearsals, but her family could not be persuaded to let her leave Spain, so she never joined the Ballet.

The long tour came to an end in Barcelona. Diaghilev must have realised that he could not expect any more Spanish engagements for the time being, and as he had no offers from anywhere else he told us that when our contracts expired at the end of the month, we were at liberty to look for other work. We had saved nothing from the tour, since we had been on minimum salaries. As there was nothing happening I decided to go back to Lisbon and collect my baby. Diaghilev gave me just enough money for a third-class return ticket. He told me to stay one night at his hotel in Lisbon, where I was to give the head porter a hundred-franc bill to arrange for my return visa with Natasha.

I set off in a navy-blue taffeta dress, white hat and shoes, taking only what I needed for one night. The journey was not comfortable as there were ducks and chickens in our crowded carriage, and I had to sit up all night on a wooden seat. I arrived at the palatial Avenida Hotel looking a mess, and with no change of clothing; then I set out next morning to find the village where Sra Abrantis lived. Crossing the river in a ferry, I walked miles into the country, under a scorching sun. At last I arrived at the cottage, trembling with excitement and exhaustion. The cottage had an earthen floor with practically no furniture; and lying in a clothes basket with nothing on but a little chemise, was Natasha. Sra Abrantis could speak nothing but Portuguese, but I made her understand that I had come for the child, and she got together what little clothing there was.

The journey back to Spain was a nightmare. I had no money at all, and nothing to eat or drink for twenty-four hours. Besides this, Natasha's milk turned sour in the heat and she never stopped crying or being sick. When Kremnev met me at the frontier, I was not only filthy but covered with bites, and the child was in an even worse condition. We only had enough money to get as far as Madrid, and on arriving there we took a room in a *pension*.

Night after night I walked up and down that tiled bedroom floor, rocking Natasha and trying to keep her from crying, for fear we should disturb the household and be turned out. Then, to our joy, we discovered that Diaghilev was in Madrid. For some time he had been negotiating with Oswald Stoll for a series of appearances at the London Coliseum. The difficulties of transporting us across Europe, of getting visas for France and of moving our scenery and baggage in time of war were considerable. Diaghilev had come to Madrid to facilitate his telegraphic correspondence with Eric Wollheim, the agent who was acting for Stoll, and whose telegrams I used to translate for him.

Although we were in a serious plight, it was reassuring to

have Diaghilev in Madrid with us. We used to meet him at ten o'clock at night in the park where the cafés were, and I came to love him dearly as a person during that anxious time. He often used to carry the baby himself, and let her play with his monocle.

One day Natasha was so ill I thought her last hour had come. Diaghilev took me to his bedroom, opened a wardrobe trunk and brought out a little leather bag. He undid the string and emptied on the bed a heap of copper and silver coins from various countries. This, I suppose, was all the money he had left. He picked out all the silver coins and gave them to me, telling me to get a doctor. Kremnev rushed to a bank and exchanged these coins for a few pesetas. A doctor came and wrote out a prescription, which we had made up by the chemist. After one dose of the medicine, the child had convulsions. Kola ran back to the shop with the bottle, and the chemist admitted he had made an awful mistake and had reversed the prescribed quantity of two drugs. He gave us the address of a woman who would help us. Kola fetched her—a very poor, middle-aged woman—and she immediately began to feed the baby at her breast, but Natasha appeared to be dying. The woman told me to go to the chemist and buy a tiny bottle of syrup of rhubarb. We gave the baby a spoonful of this, and the simple remedy saved her life. She brought up a substance which had been hindering her digestion for months. Then she settled down to a good feed. From that time on the child grew stronger and never looked back.

Diaghilev was full of sympathy for me and my troubles, while his own state of mind veered between hope and desperation. The telegrams varied. One, referring to the moving of baggage and scenery, read: 'Try from your end. Impossible from ours'; but it was hard to arrange the necessary transport from Spain through France. Diaghilev continually received help and advice from the Royal Palace.

One night I was enjoying the first deep sleep I had had for several days, when I was woken up by the sound of my name being called repeatedly. 'Eelda! Eelda! Get up!' As it was the early hours of the morning Kola and I were absolutely stunned to see Diaghilev at the foot of the bed. I jumped up to grab my dressing-gown, but he thrust a cable at me and begged me to translate it, so that he could be sure he had understood it correctly. The message was badly worded, but I realised what the sender was trying to say. Permission had been granted to ship our scenery and baggage from France to England; and it only remained for Diaghilev to move his company and their effects from Spain to France. With King Alfonso's help this would not be difficult. We could hardly believe it. Diaghilev embraced me and all three of us wept. The Diaghilev Ballet was to survive.

I was always glad that I had seen the gentler side of Diaghilev's character and had known how kind he could be in the days of deepest despair.

Some money was soon raised and we travelled back to join the company in Barcelona. One or two of the dancers had gone off to South America, but the majority had held out. It was a few weeks more before the French government could be persuaded to grant us transit visas, and this they only did on the personal intervention of King Alfonso. We were on the move again. For the last time during those years of war we lined up at a frontier while Grigoriev produced his album—know as 'The Rogues' Gallery'—containing all our photographs and particulars, calling out our names in turn to summon us before the officers who would check our faces by the photographs and pass us from one country to the next.

In Paris we were greeted by Big Bertha. For the first time the reality of war was brought home to us. The streets seemed empty but for wounded soldiers in dirty blue uniforms, some of them with bandaged heads or hobbling on crutches, others lacking a limb. We arrived in the early morning and took a bus to the Opéra, near which we found rooms. The first thing we had to do was to apply for food coupons. I next set off in search of milk and was sent from one dairy to another until I found myself at Auteuil, but all I succeeded in buying that day was half a litre. That night we had our first experience of total blackout. To find one's way around the Opéra neighbourhood in pitch darkness was far from easy. Paris was a sad place, so we were not sorry when we got our travelling orders and set off for England.

10

POST-WAR TRIUMPHS IN LONDON

Back to England — Reunion with Diaghilev — Diaghilev
and the spangled curtain — Twice nightly at the Coliseum —
London reception of a changed Russian Ballet — Armistice
night — Popularity of *Contes russes* (*Children's Tales*) — Lopokova gains admirers and loses drawers — The Alhambra —
The derangement of Felix and his last performance for
Karsavina — *La Boutique fantasque* — An embarrassing
dinner — Exit Lopokova — *Le Tricorne* — Massine-moulded
dancers.

Natasha was now nearly a year old, and my parents had accepted
my Russian wedding. I was forgiven, and Father moved heaven
and earth to get a permit for Mother to meet me at Southampton
Docks. The family were now living at nearby Bournemouth,
where Father had an official post in a munitions factory, and a
pass to enter the forbidden area was eventually secured. When
we docked at Southampton Mother and Beatrice were on the
quay to greet me. Floating mines were known to be in the
Channel, so they wept with joy at our safe arrival.

It was a strange homecoming to arrive at the little house at
Bournemouth which I had never seen. For three years I had
spoken mostly Russian—I was also fluent in Spanish and French
—and try as I did to talk plain English, Russian words kept
flowing out. Beatrice now gave up her job as a private nurse, in
order to devote herself to rearing Natasha: without her generous
action it would have been hard for me to concentrate on my
dancing. Food was very scarce and people looked undernourished.
I shall never forget the chocolates—they were like gravel covered
with unsweetened cocoa.

126

As soon as we got to London and found rooms at a little hotel in Soho the food question became less serious. One could get a French cooked meal of sorts in the hotel restaurants with one's coupons; and in Berwick Street I found I could buy butter and sugar without coupons, as well as seven-pound jars of marmalade to send to the family. The only thing I could not get them was fuel, and as the winter came on I think they sometimes had to stay in bed all day to keep warm.

It was thrilling to be back in London and working again. We were delighted to be at a fine theatre like the Coliseum, even if only as a turn in a twice-daily music-hall bill. Diaghilev probably thought it was a great come-down for his ballet to appear in a music-hall programme, but I don't think anyone else had such feelings. Everybody was kind to us from Oswald Stoll and our agent, Eric Wollheim, downwards; and we soon made friends with Mr Crocker, the stage-manager, and the musical director, Alfred Dove.

Diaghilev had left Barcelona for London ahead of us, so I looked forward to seeing him again under happier circumstances. I felt so much closer to him after the anxious days in Madrid, and my heart thumped when I saw him standing on the stage of the Coliseum. But when I went up to him he said, quite casually, 'Glad to see you. You've arrived safely?' Taken aback, I mumbled 'It's good to be here, isn't it?' 'Yes,' he said, 'Very nice.' Then, as he moved away, he asked as an afterthought 'How is Natasha?' I realised that the episode of our closeness in Spain was to make no difference to our relationship in the future—in fact, it was never to be mentioned again. He was always happy to see Natasha on the rare occasions she was brought to London, but no one was ever to know that the great Diaghilev had ever lived through those anxious weeks in Madrid, or sat on a park bench holding a sick baby. I told no one until after he died.

It might have been thought that Diaghilev, after nearly starving in Spain and being reduced to a point where he doubted the possibility of the Ballet's survival, would approach the London management which had come to his rescue in a spirit of deference or at least co-operation. Not at all. He immediately took exception to the Coliseum drop-curtain. This was an elaborate and dazzling affair, as befitted a music-hall, sewn with hundreds of thousands of sequins which caught the light and flashed magnificently as it swung up and down. Diaghilev said that after this coloured blaze the romantic picture and soft lighting of *Les Sylphides* would be completely killed: as the curtain rose you would see the two effects at the same time, and this was an impossible beginning. Stoll was naturally proud of his curtain, which must have cost a fortune, and was reluctant to give it up; but Diaghilev was adamant and got his way. During the week-end, the curtain was lowered and a crowd of women cut off most of the sequins. There are still a few on that curtain, but nothing like the solid mass there was before Diaghilev's protest.

The revolving stage interested the Russians. I had seen it before, but it was still a strange feeling to be standing or sitting ready in your group at the side of the stage and then to be hurtled round to the front. In 1918 it cost a shilling every time the stage revolved. Dancing on it was difficult; it sloped down slightly towards the middle, and the apron sloped down towards the orchestra. The brass studs, as big as tea-plates, scattered all over the stage, were also dangerous. There was a gap about an inch and a half wide between the part that revolved and the part that stayed still. With all the machinery underneath, it was a very hard stage to dance on and had no spring in it whatsoever. To jump on it, as I had to do in the Mazurka of *Les Sylphides*, jarred the spine.

If we had to adapt ourselves to working in a music-hall— even if it was a music-hall on the grand scale, in which not only great clowns such as Grock shared the bill with us, but also some of our most famous actors in one-act plays or scenes from Shakespeare—Diaghilev was determined that the theatre itself should play its part in catering for the needs of the Russian Ballet. He had always been accustomed to a lighting system that made possible the most subtle effects which, being a master of this art, he could devise; he would never dream of dispensing with long lighting rehearsals. At the Coliseum he realised at once that he could not get his effects with the floods and spots used in a music-hall. These, of course, were directed from either side of the gallery by men whose instructions were simply to follow the performers wherever they moved. Diaghilev installed a row of powerful lights in the centre of the dress-circle and a few in the upper circle—which can still be seen there today.

Nobody could achieve a lighting effect with the artistry of Diaghilev. Whoever saw his production of *Petroushka* must remember the bitter cold light just before the snow fell, which was so realistic that it made one shiver. Nothing could be more beautiful than his lighting in *l'Oiseau de feu* at the moment when the Princesses appeared on that enormously high rostrum in the moonlight, and then came slowly down the steps, to surround the magic tree whose golden apples shone with an unearthly glow. This was breathtaking. Diaghilev would start his lighting rehearsals with a full staff of electricians and a few scene-shifters on the stage. Although every ballet had its lighting plot, each theatre was differently equipped, so in important towns he rehearsed each ballet afresh and refused to leave the theatre until the effects he desired had been attained. Sometimes he would sit calling out instructions all night long, and we would find him still there, tired and unshaven, when we arrived to rehearse at ten in the morning.

After four years' absence the Diaghilev Ballet danced again in London. Our opening performance at the first house on Monday, September 2, 1918, was *Cléopâtre*, in which I danced my solo role of Ta-Hor. As the old Bakst scenery had been burned in South America, Diaghilev had commissioned a new set from Robert Delaunay. Luba's costume for *Cléopâtre* had a round mirror in the middle of her stomach and as Massine, dying from the poisoned cup, struggled up clutching at her body all he saw was his own face in the glass before falling dead at her feet.

Remembering how, as a girl, I used to flourish the *Dancing Times* at the bus stop just down the road, hoping people would realise I was a dancer, I found it exciting now to read in the dear old magazine 'as Tabor in *Cleopatra* Mlle Lydia Sokolova gave a truly wonderful character study. Her anguish over the dead body of her fickle lover held the huge Coliseum audience spellbound.'

Cyril Beaumont in his *The Diaghilev Ballet in London*, however, thought I was good, but 'lacked the range and subtlety of Fedorova'. Charles Ricketts, the art historian and stage designer wrote a description of the new production in a letter, published some years later:* '*Cleopatra* was a tragic medley. The hideous setting was by the post-Impressionist round the corner, pink and purple columns, a pea-green Hathor cow, and yellow Pyramids with a green shadow with a red spot; curiously enough, like many efforts at intensive colour, the effect is not coloured. A few of the old dresses, grown grey and tired, stood out amongst new ones. . . . These were eked out with dresses from *Le Dieu bleu*, *Thamar*, even *Joseph*, worn by very British supers with expressions on their faces signifying, "If you think I like these clothes you are blooming well mistaken." Massine dances well, but he is uninspired; he has huge square legs and in face is rather like Ethel Pye. He is stark naked save for rather nice bathing-drawers, with a huge black spot on his belly. Two or three idiot girls in the gallery shrieked with laughter when he came on. . . . Will the masses turn Bolshevist or suffer in silence this intrusion of art in their National Shrine?'

At the second house on the opening day, we danced *Les Femmes de bonne humeur*. Olga Kokhlova had stayed behind in France to marry Picasso, and I was given her role of Felicita. I had always considered this Scarlatti work a masterpiece and I was very happy to dance in it—the first time a ballet by Massine was given in London.

One day at the Coliseum I had to do the quickest costume change of my life. It was the custom to run two ballets for half a week; the one danced at the second house on one day would be given at the first house the next. We were due to dance *Scheherazade*, which meant, for me, bare feet and a turban fixed on my head with masses of pins; and I came down in a leisurely way when I heard the overture call. Suddenly I realised they were playing the music of *Carnaval*. I flew back upstairs. I had all those pins to remove. Then I put on tights and ballet shoes, did my

* *Self portrait, Letters and Journals of Charles Ricketts,* ed. Cecil Lewis (Peter Davies, 1939).

hair with flowers in it, got into my underskirts and costumes, put on my gloves, raced downstairs, along a corridor, through the big swing doors and across that vast stage. I got there just after the first bars of my music for Papillon had begun, and the beginning of my dance was the continuation of my run across stage. The whole thing had not taken more than five minutes. That is what comes from not reading the call-board.

The London public gave us a warm welcome, and many of our old friends came to see us, undeterred by the fact that we were appearing in a music-hall. After all our travels and troubles, it was a relief to settle down to a regular routine in London. Our old rehearsal room in Chenies Street, being a drill hall, was now occupied by the Army, but we had found another in Shaftesbury Avenue, immediately opposite where the Saville Theatre now stands. This first-floor club room was neither clean nor big, and the dressing accommodation was inadequate, but it saw some wonderful dancing and at least two great ballets were worked out there. Diaghilev had reluctantly been obliged to take on one or two English girls to replace Shabelska and the others who had gone to South America. It was at this time that the English Vera Clark, who later became Savina, was engaged. We already had two Italian girls, so we were opening our doors internationally.

At last on November 11, 1918, came Armistice Day. We gave our two performances just the same, but after the second house Kola and I walked down into Trafalgar Square, where crowds were collecting. We got caught up in a *farandole*, hand in hand with a lot of strangers, and I ended up on the bonnet of a bus in the Strand. Everyone seems to have been in Trafalgar Square that night: Sir Osbert Sitwell in his memoirs describes watching the crowds there with Diaghilev and Massine.

A few days later, the Diaghilev Ballet gave its thousandth performance. Diaghilev himself would not celebrate with the company: all he would let us do was to kiss him.

Of all the ballets we danced at the Coliseum at that time, I think the most popular was *Contes russes*, which in England was called *Children's Tales*: it was full of fantasy, excitement and humour, the music was so delightful and Larionov's designs were so vivid in colour. This work had been built up gradually. The first episode, *Kikimora*, had been given as a short ballet on its own, in San Sebastian in 1916, a few days after *Las Meninas*. The other two scenes, *Bova Korolevich and the Swan Princess* and *Baba Yaga*, were added and the three were given together for the first time as *Contes russes* in Paris during the season of 1917. For London, Massine arranged two amusing numbers to link the three episodes. One of these was a solo dance for Woizikovsky, and the other a number called *The Dragon's Funeral*.

The work held the very essence of Russian folklore. I loved dancing the ferocious and hideous witch, Kikimora, with her blue-striped face, who made her cat rock her in her cradle and then in a fury chopped off its head with an axe. Tchernicheva looked beautiful as the Swan Princess and Massine was the gallant Prince Bova who arrived on horseback to slay her captor, the Many-Headed Dragon, with a wooden stick. Idzikovsky, who was Kikimora's cat, wept bitterly into a large, red handkerchief at the Dragon's funeral. Kremnev, dressed as an old woman, played Baba Yaga, the demon who lay in wait in the depths of the forest and ate little girls. He had a wooden stump attached to the sole of one shoe, to make one leg longer than the other, and as he raced around the stage he would rise up on this hideous deformed foot and do four pirouettes on it. In this last scene there was a little house that ran about on legs. People used to adore that fairy-story ballet and go away the happier for having seen it.

The first performance in London of *Children's Tales* was on December 23, 1918, and, as I was going back to Bournemouth for Christmas and had to catch the last train at Waterloo, I took off the blue and black make-up of Kikimora in the taxi. Kola and I travelled on a mail train and arrived in Bournemouth at half-past three in the morning. We had to leave again at seven in the morning on Boxing Day to be in time for the matinée, but at least I had spent Christmas with the family for the first time for many years. I found that Natasha could walk.

Lydia Lopokova came into her own during that season at the Coliseum and attracted a devoted London public which grew with the years and never deserted her. She was so gay and feckless, never taking any trouble about herself and always coming to bits on the stage. One evening when she was dancing the Mazurka in *Les Sylphides*, she arrived at the part where she had to perform a *relevé* in *arabesque* several times over. Her raised leg fell lower and lower; then, to everyone's surprise, she stopped, tucked her hand under her costume and stepped out of a pair of tarlatan drawers. She threw them into the wings, picked up her music where she had left off and carried on as if nothing had happened.

Each dancer attracted his or her faithful followers, and these enthusiasts used to vie with each other in their devotion. It was at this time that the 'ballet fan' came into being. The same little crowd used to come to the gallery night after night, and as familiarity bred contempt they would begin to create disturbances. These ardent people from Chelsea developed very distinct preferences: they became intolerant, and if their particular favourite was not performing they would shout and stamp and draw attention to themselves in a tiresome way. Occasionally they made such a row that they had to be removed forcibly from the theatre. Autograph hunters at the stage door were often so numerous that we had to ask a policeman to move them on.

At the end of March, 1919, we finished our engagement at the Coliseum, having been part of the bill there for nearly seven months. We had had a lovely break after our wartime tribulations, and were very sad to leave and to say good-bye to the kind theatre staff, especially dear Mr Hyde, the stage door-keeper. Not that we were going very far away, for it had been arranged that we should open at the Alhambra, Stoll's other theatre, a month later. In the meantime we went North for a fortnight to show Manchester what ballet was like. The Lancashire audiences were somewhat slow to understand what it was all about, but once they got the idea they were very appreciative.

The Alhambra—whose Moorish decorations amazed the Russians—stood where the Odeon Cinema now stands in Leicester Square; and we took a furnished flat in Burleigh Mansions, opposite the back of the theatre, in the Charing Cross Road. At the Alhambra we were to have a real season, dancing three ballets a night, and not sharing the bill with anyone. Our opening night was a great success and we were happier than ever to be in London. Meanwhile, Massine's ballet about dolls with Rossini's music, and his Spanish ballet, were in active preparation. They were to be called, respectively, *La Boutique fantasque* and *Le Tricorne*.

Some time back it had been decided that Felix Fernandez was incapable of learning a sustained role such as that of the Miller, the leading role in *Le Tricorne*. Massine's proficiency at Spanish dancing was now so great he decided to take the part himself. As a sop to Felix, who had thought the Spanish ballet would be the vehicle which would carry him to fame, it was agreed that he should dance the Tarantella with me in *La Boutique fantasque*. The old Italian Tarantella was performed with castanets, so this lively number would have given Felix the chance to display more than one of his talents. However, Felix was accustomed to dancing his own improvisations and he found it almost impossible to fit himself into the set length of a dance in a ballet. Massine spent many rehearsals trying to teach him this Tarantella, but poor Felix would become nervous and hysterical. Massine gave him a metronome to help him to learn to dance in time. The climax came when Diaghilev arrived one day to watch a rehearsal. Felix had bought himself a cup of tea and an enormous sandwich. These he could not be persuaded to put down for more than a few seconds at a time, and he would keep breaking off the rehearsal to carry them to another part of the room. Diaghilev realised then that he could not entrust an important part to so unreliable an artist, so Leon Woizikovsky, who had been rehearsing the part of the Shop Assistant, was told to rehearse the Tarantella instead. As neither he nor I were much good with the castanets, Zoia Roszovska was given the refrain to sing in the orchestra pit while we danced. In the meanwhile an attempt was made to fit Felix into the *corps de ballet*, but he was so unreliable that he could only be given the simplest things to do. What he enjoyed best was being a pedlar with a tray of ribbons in *Petroushka*, for then he could play about and improvise to his heart's content.

Poor, simple, Andulasian Felix must have brooded over losing the great role which was to have been his and which was to have opened the door to his golden future. To be given a small part in the finale of the ballet was an additional humiliation. He must have wondered how he, who could hold an audience spellbound in a café at midnight, lacked some quality which would enable him to fit into this ballet company. The metronome, like a cruel god of Time and Order, whose laws he could not understand, became an obsession with him: he was even seen walking down Shaftesbury Avenue and making his footsteps coincide with its ticking.

As I was intended for the role of the Miller's Wife, Massine spent hours with me on the stage of the Alhambra in the afternoon, practising Spanish dancing and working out scenes and numbers we were to do together. We did amazing things with our heads, hands and arms, and tried out every combination of heel-beats which Massine had taken down from Felix or which he invented. In this way I became a really proficient Spanish dancer. Diaghilev would sit patiently watching us: I think he enjoyed seeing us master the subtle steps.

Felix, too, used to watch us at rehearsal, and he must have thought as he sat there how sadly he had been cheated: for he had taught Massine and the rest of us all we knew about Spanish dancing, and yet he was neither to dance the chief part in the ballet nor have any credit for his share in its creation. It must have been too much for him to see Leonide, who was not even a Spaniard, dancing what was to all intents and purposes his own *farruca*.

I do not think anyone realised how far Felix had gone on the way to a mental breakdown. Diaghilev cannot have grasped the situation. The Russian Ballet was never wanting in eccentrics, and he probably thought, as most people did, that Felix's odd behaviour was just a pose to keep himself in the limelight.

Shortly after our season at the Alhambra opened, Tamara Karsavina escaped from Russia and joined us. Everyone who knew her was overjoyed to welcome her back to the company where she was much loved and respected. It was not for a fortnight after her arrival, though, that she danced with us at the

Alhambra, for she was out of practice after her long journey and in need of rehearsal. Diaghilev decided that she should take over the role of the Miller's Wife in *Le Tricorne*; but I think he must have had difficulty in persuading her to dance a Spanish ballet, as she was quite untrained in this special type of movement and would clearly find it hard to perform the many numbers which follow one upon the other in the first act, without a lot of work and study.

In her book, *Theatre Street*, Mme Karsavina describes what must have been Felix's last performance. To inspire her for her role in the Spanish ballet, Diaghilev asked her to supper at the Savoy, and afterwards took her down to the deserted ballroom, where Felix danced. 'I followed him', she wrote, 'with open-mouthed admiration, breathless at his outward reserve when I could feel the impetuous, half-savage instinct within him. He needed no begging and gave us dance after dance. In between, he sang the guttural songs of his country, accompanying himself on the guitar. I was completely carried away, forgetful that I was sitting in an ornate hotel ballroom, till I noticed a whispering group of waiters. It was late, very late. The performance must cease or they would be compelled to put the lights out. They went over to Felix too, but he took not the slightest notice. He was far away. . . . A warning flicker and the lights went out. Felix continued like one possessed. The rhythm of his steps— now staccato, now languorous, now almost a whisper, and then again seeming to fill the large room with thunder—made this unseen performance all the more dramatic. We listened to the dancing, enthralled.*'

Perhaps the example of this great Spanish dancer fired Karsavina with enthusiasm: at any rate, she agreed to dance the Miller's Wife in *Le Tricorne*, and I had the pleasure of helping Massine to teach her the role.

It cannot have been more than two or three days after Felix had danced at the Savoy—and it may have been the very next morning—that his behaviour at rehearsal became stranger than ever. We were working in the club-room in Shaftesbury Avenue,

* *Theatre Street*, by Tamara Karsavina (Heinemann, 1930).

where the men had to dress behind a sort of bar or cloakroom counter. Felix began to pop his head up from behind the counter, wearing different hats and making faces. This was quite funny at first, and we all laughed, but he would not stop. Grigoriev tried to control him without success, and as Felix kept on and on, appearing and disappearing in a variety of hats, one could feel a wave of concern go round the room. At lunch time he went off, with his metronome ticking. Leon Woizikovsky followed him to the Hotel Dieppe in Old Compton Street, where he was staying, and found him lunching in his room—he was not allowed to have meals in the restaurant, as he behaved strangely and upset people. Felix was eating to the rhythm of the ticking metronome, stopping now and again to adjust it to a different speed. Leon could get no sense out of him and went away.

That night, when Felix should have been on the stage he was discovered in the men's dressing-room, his face spotted with a weird mixture of greasepaints, grimacing at himself in the mirror. Nothing could be done about this while the performance was in progress, and by the time the ballet was over he was nowhere to be found. He did not return to his hotel, and his disappearance was reported. Later that night he was found doing a demented dance on the altar steps of a South London church. He was certified insane, and was admitted to an asylum at Epsom. Felix's reason was the price fate demanded for the creation of a masterpiece.

With Felix gone, Massine and I had to work hard to teach Karsavina not only the dances of the Miller's Wife, but the whole Spanish style of dancing. I was then grateful for all the training I had had under Felix and Massine.

Before the first performance of *Le Tricorne* came that of *La Boutique fantasque*. This was probably the gayest and most exhilarating ballet ever invented. When it was first produced it must have been hard for people to decide what made it so delightful. Was it the variety of dances, the tunes of Rossini, the balance that was struck between the dances and the miming of the funny non-dancing characters, the bubbling personality of Lydia Lopokova—or a combination of all these elements? One thing the public could not realise, as I did, was that Massine had seized the opportunity to type-cast every dancer with absolute precision. The interpreters of even the smallest part could flatter themselves that Massine had taken as much trouble to show them off to advantage as if they had been the stars of the ballet: and every part was marvellously interpreted. To watch Maestro Cecchetti as the fussy old Shopkeeper, so ingratiating to his customers, was an education in mime; Grigoriev was ideal as the great bear of a Russian Merchant, with Mme Cecchetti as his fat little wife; even Bourman and Evina in the small parts of the naughty children of the American couple were able to create living and laughable portraits.

The Tarantella which Leon Woizikovsky danced with me was a wonderful and strenuous dance with a lot of Spanish footbeats in it. It had to be good, as we were the first dolls whom Gavrilov, as the clownish Shop Assistant, wheeled on to the stage. As the Snob, Idzikovsky was intended to be the caricature of an Englishman. His tiny, neat little figure with a grey top hat and the clockwork elegance with which he tripped across the stage and came to a halt, jerking himself off-centre in the exertion of giving a rakish twirl to his moustache, were unforgettable. He bought a slice of melon, ate it and was run over by a tiny barrow manœuvred by Kostetzky so neatly you could have sworn the same piece of mechanism was animating them both. Vera Clark and Kola Kremnev were the two French Poodles, dressed in all-over tights, one brown, one white, with little tufts of wool and painted muzzles. One day when this dance was being rehearsed, and the two poodles were sniffing each other up and down in the clever way Massine had arranged, Kola suddenly let out two very good 'woof-woofs'. We all burst out laughing and applauded; and to everyone's surprise Diaghilev allowed the audible bark to stay. This was the first time a ballet dancer had ever been allowed to give tongue on the stage, and there was much discussion afterwards as to whether it was morally and aesthetically justified.

As the Can-can Dancer, Lydia Lopokova wore a very simple blue dress with white frilly petticoats and a wreath of daisies in her hair. I once helped her do her hair before the Can-can and found that, regardless of the frantic exertions of this *pas de deux*, she had relied on exactly three hairpins to fix her hair and the wreath together. Massine had invented an extraordinary character for himself as her partner, which bore no relation to anything on heaven or earth. It may have started off as one of those capering, high-kicking fanatics one sees in old prints taking part in the revels of the Second Empire; but with a curious loose black velvet suit, black ringlets and chalk-white dehumanised face, it ended up half way to Charlie Chaplin. Anyway, he was immensely effective, though it was hard to imagine how the pretty doll in blue could have loved such an ugly fellow: they certainly made a freakish pair. With all the high-stepping, the kicking, leaping and spinning, this Can-can never failed to stop the show. Lydia had to do the splits at the end, and she complained 'It nearly cut me in two pieces.'

The gay setting by André Derain was his first work for the stage, and incidentally, the cause of a quarrel between Diaghilev and Bakst, who had expected to design the ballet.

The first night of *La Boutique fantasque* must have been one of the most rapturous in theatre history. The applause was deafening and continuous, and the stage was piled with flowers.

At this time Lopokova and Tchernicheva used to be showered with baskets of flowers by a pair of Russian officers who professed to admire them greatly. One night these officers gave a supper party in a private room at the Savoy consisting of Lydia and Barocchi, Luba and Grigoriev, Kola and myself. When we arrived we found there was a third officer, as well as our hosts. We were given plenty to eat and drink, including vodka, but it was an embarrassing and sticky party. As the meal progressed, Kola became drunk and aggressive. He told our hosts that he could see through their little game, even to understanding that the third officer had been asked to take care of me. He insulted Luba and Lydia, and accused their husbands of being go-betweens. Then just as it seemed everyone would have to come to blows, he passed out. One of the officers helped me to get him out by a back entrance and take him home to our flat.

I cannot think this appalling scene had anything to do with

Lydia's running away, but disappear she did a few days later. Diaghilev was in Paris, so she left a short note for Grigoriev, saying she wasn't well enough to dance with us any more. The newspaper-boys' placards announced, 'Famous Ballerina Vanishes'. Because of this Vera Nemtchinova got her great chance. She soon afterwards stepped into Lydia's role in the Can-can and danced it very well.

As the stage and backstage at the Alhambra were not as big as they might be, the problem of changing the scenery between our ballets became acute. Some of our works, such as *Petroushka*, *Scheherezade* and *Les Femmes de bonne humeur* had quite complicated sets to be built up, as well as masses of props, so that while one ballet was in progress, various flats and constructions had to be piled against the walls in preparation for the next. Because all this scene-shifting took time—not to mention the occasional need for dancers to paint their bodies all over for an oriental ballet —the intervals tended to be longer than was usual in London theatres. Diaghilev therefore decided to make an innovation: he engaged another conductor and made the orchestra play a short piece of music, perhaps lasting ten minutes, during the longest interval. This proved to be an admirable idea, as it enabled a number of fine new scores to be heard, which were sometimes too short for inclusion in an orchestral concert, and introduced the public to unfamiliar works by composers such as Glinka, Balakirev, Ravel, Satie, Arnold Bax and Lord Berners.

Massine had certain physical defects, which prevented him from becoming a classical dancer, but this did not alter the fact that he was an outstanding artist and performer. He had very tight hips and could never do a high *battement*. If I saw him practising at the back of the stage and was feeling mischievous, I would walk past deliberately and say, 'Higher, Leonide Feodorovitch, higher!' He had a slight defect in the shape of his legs, and after *La Légende de Joseph*, Diaghilev would never let him expose them again. Just below the knee, his legs receded and bent outwards. Once when I was watching him in *Les Sylphides* I though how straight and nice his legs were looking with little sign of the bow, so I asked Vassili to explain this. He told me that Massine had a fine strip of ermine sewn inside his white silk tights: this certainly did the trick. Massine's inventive brain had hit on another ingenious idea. When he wore long trousers on the stage, he had elastic sewn inside them from the waist right down under the foot, and this kept them from falling in and revealing that his legs were not quite straight. The black silk trousers he wore in *Le Tricorne* with his white shirt and short purple jacket were fixed in this way.

When we had sailed from Barcelona to South America in 1917, leaving the 'lucky few' behind, Diaghilev had seen in a Madrid theatre a short work which he was to transform into *Le Tricorne*. This was a mimed play by the writer Martinez Sierra with music by Manuel de Falla, based on a nineteenth-century novel *El Sombrero de Tres Picos* by Alarcón. Diaghilev liked this piece so much that he arranged for de Falla to fill it out with new numbers and rescore it for a larger orchestra. Rehearsing separate dances with a piano often gives a dancer very little idea of the true beauty of the score, and I remember how thrilled I was when we heard de Falla's joyful music played by the full orchestra. De Falla was a sweet person but he looked like a timid little official. It was wonderful to think that a quiet little man I knew with an umbrella and a black-and-white straw boater could have given birth to this explosion of melody and rhythm. I found the music of *Le Tricorne* so exhilarating that I preferred dancing it even to watching it.

Le Tricorne is about a Miller and his wife, who apart from being very flirtatious with their neighbours, are in love with each other. They live in a sun-baked, hilly, pink-and-white landscape—designed by Picasso—where the stars shine by day as well as night and the little river is crossed by two bridges, a small one for foot traffic and a big one for Madrid-bound coaches. The action takes place in the eighteenth century and the village must be somewhere about the middle of Spain, because its inhabitants not only dance the *Jota*, which comes from Aragon, but the *Farruca* and the *Fandango*, which are usually associated with districts further south. The local governor, a doddering old lecher, is attracted by the Miller's Wife and has the Miller arrested; when he returns by night to make love to the lady, she leads him on and then pushes him into the river. While he seeks refuge in the Miller's house his host returns, having escaped from prison, and throws him out to the delight of the laughing villagers, who celebrate his discomfiture by dancing and throwing his effigy in the air. This simple story manages to incorporate one or two spectacular dances for the Miller, no less than five for the Miller's Wife and a rousing finale in which two dozen villagers go mad with joy in Picasso's colourful striped and spotted costumes.

The woman's part was a long and exhausting one, which took a lot of rehearsing, but when I handed it over to Karsavina I was given only a small entrance with another girl in the finale, so that I could relax for most of the ballet and watch the succession of wonderful and varied dances. Leon Woizikovsky understudied Massine, and while the choreographer was watching and working out the rest of the ballet, Leon used to dance the Miller with me.

At the opening of the ballet, Leon mimed the role of the grotesque old Governor. Picasso gave him a fantastic make-up, with dabs of the same blue which was used in the costumes of his bodyguard of policemen. During rehearsals I greatly enjoyed stamping away on top of the little bridge and pushing the Governor over the side, to see him fall on a mattress and change his coat for one with stripes of black American cloth on it, so that when he reappeared it looked as if he were dripping wet. A day or two before the first night, Diaghilev, with his keen eye for effect, decided that he did not like the finale, which was performed in small groups, so Massine rearranged it.

The new finale had far more mass excitement; and the climax, during which the Governor's effigy was tossed on a blanket to the abandoned laughter of the villagers was a great moment of ballet. We had one full-dress rehearsal and the ballet was danced without a hitch. *Le Tricorne* was an immediate success: de Falla and Picasso had made their stage début in England with a bang.

Mother was staying with us for the first night, and as she did not like going out late in the evening I bought some chops, meaning to cook them for supper. We had no kitchen, only a gas ring, and just before the performance Mother said, 'What are

you going to cook the supper on? You have no kitchen utensils.'
I had an idea, and asked Camishov, the property man, whether
I could borrow the large, brand-new frying pan that was carried
on in the comic procession at the end of the ballet. When we came
out after the show and found our way through the crowds at
the stage door, Kola and I were carrying masses of flowers and
I can visualise Mother now trying to hold her own, brandishing
a big shiny frying pan at arm's length above her head for fear of
its being lost in the scrum.

All choreographers must agree that there are certain dancers
who excel in the particular type of movement they invent. Just
as Karsavina and Tchernicheva were essentially Fokine dancers,
so I am sure that Lopokova, Idzikovsky, Woizikovsky and myself were most suitable and adaptable to Massine's individual
kind of ballet. I have taught the role of the Miller's Wife to Mme
Karsavina, to Tchernicheva, Devillier and Dalbaicin, but I could
not teach any of them to do *all* the movements as Massine taught
them to me. I had practised Spanish dancing with Massine under
Felix, and we had learned so many of its intricate movements
together that he knew, working with me, he could safely put into
his dances all the subtleties and complexities he wanted. I res-
ponded to his type of movement because the whole system of it
seemed to be part of me. I was anyway so essentially a character
dancer that other people could not be expected to perform all
my contortions. This applied also to Lydia in *Les Femmes de bonne
humeur* and in the can-can from *Boutique*: nobody was ever able to
give quite the same accent and flavour to the steps which Massine
had invented for her. Leon Woizikovsky understood and danced
some of Massine's own roles almost as well as their creator; and
what Stas Idzikovsky did in the Scarlatti and Rossini ballets could
never be repeated by anyone else. That is why these perfect
ballets, although they are still done, are in a way *lost*, and when
Massine ceased inventing his extraordinary movements for Lydia,
Stas, Leon and myself we were lost too, and never did anything
so great again.

11

SECOND LOVE IN PARIS

Glamour and mystery of the Paris Opéra — *Le Chant du rossignol* — A kiss in the corridor — Falling in love again — Rome, Milan and Monte Carlo — Back to Paris in the spring —The perfections of *Pulcinella* — *Le Astuzie Femminile* — Unexpected success of my dance with Woizikovsky — A lesson from Diaghilev.

The Paris Opéra is the most exciting theatre I know, and nobody who has ever danced there can forget the experience of standing on that famous stage or finding their way about the immense building. I had danced there only once before during the 1914 season, when we created *La Légende de Joseph* and *Coq d'Or*, but that seemed a lifetime ago: by now in 1919, I was a real Russian dancer and a soloist as well as being a wife and mother.

The stage at the Opéra is magnificent, wide and deep, and the opening of the proscenium is unusually high. The theatre is so well-planned that the audience seems to be very near to you, but the orchestra-pit is so deep that it was difficult in those days before the conductor was raised, to see him. The *Foyer de la Danse* where classes were held in the old days and where dancers received their admirers—and, indeed still do—is immediately at the back of the stage. This room, with its huge mirrors, its paintings and its gilded pillars and cornices, was such a palatial place to work in that I never entered it without feeling I was at Versailles.

Backstage, the Paris Opéra has a mystery and glamour all of its own. The word 'backstage' is hardly adequate to describe the endless halls, corridors, dressing-rooms and offices, which are

144

planned on a scale unknown in England. In what other theatre
does the dancer arriving for work have to pass through great iron
gates and cross a cobbled courtyard before even reaching the
stage door? One walks between the lodges of the two *concierges*,
the one emitting a delicious smell of *escalope de veau*, the other
ragout de mouton; and the grumpy old *concierges* are the first people
one has to get to know. From each of these lodges, on either side
of the courtyard, there rises a wide and formidable staircase,
leading to a corridor of enormous length. There are two identical corridors on each side of the theatre, one above the other,
and it is often difficult to remember which floor one is on. All the
way down the inner walls of these corridors are the doors
leading to the dressing-rooms. Opening one of these you pass
down a narrow passage, at the end of which another door leads
into your comfortable, carpeted room. Once you are shut into your
dressing-room at the Opéra you feel so cosy and remote, quite
out of touch with whatever is going on miles away on the stage.
The only hint that you may be wanted comes from an enormous
electric bell which peals in the dark corridor outside and brings
you back to earth with a jump—this is fatal if you are painting
on an eyebrow.

To reach the rehearsal room from the stage door took about
seven minutes: one had to go the whole length of the theatre
climbing all the way, as it was near the front of the building. It
was a large square light room with a good dancing floor. Having
passed through long dark passages and eerie staircases it was
always a relief to arrive there. None of us ever undertook this
journey alone. There was a certain swing door in one of the narrow corridors where we were sure a ghost hovered, so we struck
matches or even lit candles when we went through it.

We arrived in Paris in time to open on Christmas Eve. Kola
and I stayed in a delightful hotel in the rue Cambon, a few doors
from Chanel's dressmaking establishment. It was a small, elegant
place, full of red plush, with lights on the little dining-room
tables and—joy of joys!—an electric clock on the wall facing my
bed. It was my first taste of real luxury and I liked it.

At the beginning of January, 1920, our season was interrupted by the orchestra of the Opéra going on strike, so that we had three weeks of free evenings to wander about Paris and enjoy ourselves before performances resumed. I had never before seen Paris at that time of year with the *boulevards* crowded with brightly-lit stalls selling sweets, toys, games and cheap jewellery. Meanwhile rehearsals continued; another new work was in preparation.

Stravinsky's opera, *Le Rossignol*, had not been a popular success when we gave it before the war: and now the composer and Diaghilev decided to reduce it and give a shorter version which would be entirely danced, with all the singing left out. Henri Matisse was called upon to do the designs for this—his first work for the theatre—and Massine began to work on composing the dances.

The new version was called *Le Chant du rossignol*, and its story, based on Hans Andersen, was naturally the same; but with the compression of the music the action was simplified, and the first scene with the fisherman was omitted. Grigoriev mimed the role of the Emperor of China, Karsavina was the Nightingale and Idzikovsky was the Mechanical Nightingale, rigged up in a great barrel-shaped body with a terrifying beak and wings.

I had the role of Death, and Matisse designed an extraordinary costume for me. The décor, very simple and yet giving the impression of a fastidious Chinese splendour, was all conceived in black and white—but mostly white—with a little turquoise blue. Most of the costumes, too, were white, with designs sketched on them in little dashes and squiggles of black. As Death I was the only note of brilliant colour. I wore scarlet all-over tights, with a very uncomfortable brass waistcoat, suggesting the ribs of a skeleton. On my head was a black wig and a very painful head-dress of brass supporting a china ball on which a skull was painted. Round my neck hung a necklace of *papier-mâché* skulls.

There was some question as to what make-up I should have, or whether I would be better in a mask. On the afternoon of the dress rehearsal I sat at a table in the wings while Massine tried out several designs on my face from pictures of Chinese theatrical make-ups. He decided in at the end that my face and neck should be red all over—the same colour as my costume. He drew white gashes down my cheeks from the temples to the corners of my mouth, then gave me a small black slit of a mouth, with slanting black eyes and eyebrows. He drew this gruesome design on paper for me, then coloured it; and I always carried it in my make-up box for reference.

Massine, as ever, had been very thorough: whatever he did he worked at with the utmost seriousness, and he had crammed in some homework on Chinese art. A choreographer must search far and wide for artistic material which will suggest movements or groupings to him, and I suppose he can never know what picture or sculpture may be the one to give him an idea. There were some very fine and highly ingenious groupings of men in *Le Chant du rossignol*. They built themselves up into flat friezes, rather in the way that acrobats do, but their bodies were packed tight and knitted close together, some men on one leg, some upside down resting on a bent arm, some in a kind of hand-stand. These groups suggested to me the grotesque combinations of figures on carved ivory boxes, and I wondered if it was from these that Massine had taken his idea.

The last scene was impressive. The Emperor—played by Grigoriev—was dying on his great carved and painted bed. He lay on an inclined plane covered in black material with his toes to the audience. Everything else was black-and-white except for me as Death in flame colour and gleaming brass. I was standing in a sinister way against one of the pillars supporting the bed canopy, to indicate that the Emperor's end was near. The antics of the Mechanical Nightingale failed to cure the Emperor's sickness; then the real Nightingale came in to lure Death away from the Emperor's bedside. In the original story, the bird was supposed to sing so sweetly about the beauties of cemeteries in the moonlight, with their white roses and scented lime trees, that Death, overcome with nostalgia for her native haunts flies out of the window. Karsavina, who represented the song of the nightingale rather than the bird itself, was dressed in such a way that she suggested all the beauty of the summer night outside: she was a white rose. As she moved lightly and sweetly about the stage, I came slowly down the steps from the bed to dance with her, making threatening gestures. At the end of our *pas de deux* I lifted my necklace of skulls over her head, gave it a sinister twist as though I were strangling her, and then glided sideways with her, in *pas de bourrée* off the stage. That was the end of me, but the spectacular part was to follow. The Nightingale returned to sing the Emperor back to health, while the court stood round expecting him to die. Suddenly the Emperor came back to life, and a mechanical device tipped his bed so that he stood upright. At this moment Grigoriev released the fastenings which held a mass of black material rolled up across his chest: this cascaded down the front of the platform on which the body stood, covering the whole of the central part of the stage, and revealed itself as an immense ceremonial garment like a train—only attached to the front of the body—embroidered with a huge golden dragon. The train was detached from the Emperor's shoulders and carried off. Grigoriev was lifted stiffly down and all the courtiers bent double in adoration, forming two lines converging at the foot of the bed. Then, with his hands supported on either side, he walked superbly along on top of them, using their bent backs as stepping stones, and disappeared into the wings.

Karsavina only appeared for one or two performances in Paris, then returned to London to rehearse for Barrie's play *The Truth about the Russian Dancers*. From this time onward I was given a number of her roles; and the fact that, though a character dancer, my classical technique was good enough for me to dance Columbine in *Carnaval* made it possible for Fokine's ballet to survive in the repertoire.

At the Opéra I had the joy of dancing for the first time in public that wonderful role which Massine had built up on me, and which we had prepared for Mme Karsavina—the Miller's Wife in *Le Tricorne*.

Towards the end of the London season I had been dancing with Leon Woizikovsky one evening in the *tarantella* of *La Boutique fantasque*, when he handled me rather roughly and tore off a thin, gold-chain bracelet on my wrist, sending it flying into the orchestra. I was so angry that I complained to Diaghilev and insisted that I could never dance with Woizikovsky again. Diaghilev calmed me down and everything went on as before. It was rather surprising, though, one evening in a long corridor at the Paris Opéra, to find Leon coming up quietly behind me, putting his arm round my waist and giving me a whacking great kiss.

Leon was as unhappy with his wife Antonova as I was with Kola—except that he was not the type to be very unhappy for long about anything. From then on I began to fall in love with Leon, and he with me, but there seemed to be nothing we could do about it and it was only an added complication in my life. As there were hardly any occasions when we could meet in private, we began to write each other letters. Although we were anxious to avoid drawing attention to our predicament, we grew self-conscious when dancing together—a state of affairs which cannot be concealed. Kola had been making jealous scenes for years, but now he had some basis for his accusations and he gave me no peace.

From Paris we went to Rome, and rehearsals began for Stravinsky's new work, *Pulcinella*, under the indefatigable Massine. Besides this, Diaghilev discovered the score of Cimarosa's opera-ballet *Les Astuzie Femminili* in an Italian library and decided to prepare it as an additional novelty for the Paris season. I was in every ballet in the repertoire except *Pulcinella*, as Diaghilev always insisted that soloists should work in the *corps de ballet*, so I was kept hard at it.

A sad event during our stay in Rome was the death of our wardrobe mistress, Margherita, the wife of Diaghilev's Italian valet, Beppo. Diaghilev was very fond of her and wept unrestrainedly at her funeral, which we all attended.

After a short and not very successful season at Milan, we returned to Monte Carlo for the first time since the war, and were very glad to be back there. The sun and sea air soon restored our energies, and rehearsals went on apace.

I remember how smart the company all looked, about seventy-five of them, waiting on the Monte Carlo station platform for the train to take us back to Paris; the girls in pretty hats with veils, with the latest dresses and smart shoes. We took delicious food with us on these journeys: chicken with Russian veal cutlets, salad and fruit.

So we arrived back in Paris for our short spring season of 1919. During the spring season of 1914 I had been in love with Kola, now I only thought of Leon. Paris was beautiful and the Diaghilev Ballet was ready with its new creations.

It was not etiquette to go to the rehearsal of any ballet in which you were not taking part, so I knew little about *Pulcinella* till I saw it on the stage in Paris. I had heard the women thought their dances charming and that the boys had a lot of fun, but even so I was hardly prepared for the masterpiece which had been produced in the three months since we were last at the Opéra. When Diaghilev had found the manuscripts of some eighteenth-century music believed to be by Pergolesi, he had decided that they should form the basis of a composition by Stravinsky for a ballet by Massine on a *Commedia dell' Arte* subject. Stravinsky readily lent himself to weaving a sophisticated orchestral web round the old tunes, and Massine found a typical plot, with the usual simple complications, in a book of comedies about the adventures of Pulcinella, dated 1700. The resulting work of art, with Picasso's decorations, was a marvellous evocation of place and period—high jinks by moonlight—Naples in the late seventeenth century—the *Commedia dell' Arte* at home, with Vesuvius sleeping across the bay.

The story of *Pulcinella*, which was unimportant, concerned two ladies who spurned their admirers because they were both seized with an infatuation for Pulcinella; the jealousy of Pimpinella, the peasant girl, over Pulcinella's supposed infidelities with these two ladies; the intractability of the girls' foolish old guardians; Pulcinella's feigned death; his impersonation by his double; his resurrection; the surprise of all concerned at the miraculous recovery; finally the successful pairing off of the various agile participants.

The score was delicious. Kochno described it well: 'Ironic embellishments of the trombone and bassoon transformed the melodies of Pergolesi. There were perhaps not twelve bars of music which were truly Stravinsky and yet everything bore his mark. When the emotion justified it, the small orchestra—lacking in romantic clarinets—would accompany a song or a distant chorus. There was a solo for the double bass; the flute joined in a funny trio with horn and bassoon or sang out on its own against a background of plucked violins . . . towards the end the dancers' steps were sometimes scanned in silence, dance alternating with music. . . .'

Picasso's set was so simple that it suggested the improvised screens of a troupe of strolling players, and yet it was as charged with atmosphere as the most thoughtfully composed easel painting: an irregular quadrilateral of white was the moonstruck wall of a house, a triangle of grey conveyed the shadow and mystery of a narrow street, a few marks on the back cloth—moon, boat and volcano—placed the action geographically and expressed Naples. This décor showed triumphantly what cubism could be and could do. One innovation was the omission of foot-lights. The chalk-white floor-cloth provided an arena for the action, and it was no doubt thought that all the lighting should come from above to suggest moonlight. This, incidentally, made *Pulcinella* a very difficult ballet to dance, as I found when I took part in it later; the absence of footlights revealed the faces of the audience and the dancers realised, to their distress, that they were under observation.

Luba Tchernicheva looked lovely sitting in her window in a tulle dress of jade green, a white hat trimmed with ostrich feathers perched over her long curls. Slavinsky as her admirer was dressed in powder blue, also with a plumed hat. After he had danced a serenade to her, ending on one knee in a romatic pose, Luba, with a brisk, neat gesture, upturned a *pot de chambre* over his head. Vera Nemchinova then appeared at the opposite window: both she and her swain were in pink. After they had gone through a similar routine, Karsavina appeared from the middle house nearest the harbour. She wore a red tulle skirt, with a black velvet bodice over a white blouse, and a green cap on her head. As I followed Tamara Platonovna in this part, I know how difficult the variation was which she had to dance immediately on her first entrance. It was very slow, with sustained hops on one point, the other leg performing *ronds de jambe*; and there was a lot of balancing. The two Pulcinellas, Massine and Woizikovsky, were of course both dressed alike with flapping white garments, red socks, black shoes and pointed white hats. They both wore similar masks with bulging cheeks and big Punch noses, which covered three-quarters of their faces —Massine had found an old mask and had it copied—and they both danced so exactly alike that there was no way of telling them apart except by a small difference in height: Massine was a little taller. It was amusing to see the four little Pulcinellas in similar costumes mourning the supposed death of their prototype, and their frantic capers when the 'dead man' was restored to life by his double in the guise of a magician. It was a really happy ballet, and the exciting finale had lots of lifts, turns and laughter. The difficulty, however, of performing unsupported *pirouettes* starting from *arabesque*, right downstage on a white floor-cloth which was freshly painted for every performance, and without footlights, was extreme.

Our next Paris production was *Le Astuzie Femminili*, a comic opera-ballet by the Neapolitan composer, Cimarosa. He had been for some years in charge of the orchestra in St Petersburg, and this work, first performed in Naples in 1794 was partly inspired by memories of his stay in Russia. Its Russian-Italian nature made it particularly attractive to Diaghilev, and, besides, he liked showing the world forgotten works of art. He engaged Italian singers for it, and Massine arranged their movements. Everything led up to the final danced *divertissement*.

I have never liked pom-pons or tassels, and there were so many of these on the costumes by Sert that they may have turned me against the new work, which we always referred to as 'Cimarosa'. This opera-ballet did not come off, and the whole production seemed fussy. It must have cost far more than *Pulcinella*, which was so much more successful in every way, and although the final *divertissement* had some excellent dances in it, they did not make up a complete ballet.

There was a difficult *pas de deux* for the two chief classical dancers, Karsavina and Idzikovsky, though I preferred watching this when the English girl, Vera Savina, took over, because she and Idzikovsky made such a neat and brilliant little pair. There was also a *pas de trois* in the ballet—which was spoilt for me by the girls wearing lampshades on their heads—and an effective *pas de quatre*.

I had a character *pas de deux* with Leon Woizikovsky, a kind of *tarantella*, which we enjoyed dancing, though we did not think it anything special. Sert designed for us the most hideous costumes we had ever been called upon to wear. Mine was a pair of red satin pyjamas with a fringe of black tassels round the neck and ankles. Leon's was made of very dark velvet, with a horrible pouch ending in a tassel hanging down in front, and a feminine hat. We were very surprised, when we first danced this *Tarantella* at a full rehearsal, to receive a round of applause from the members of the company who were watching. When such a demonstration as this occurred in the Diaghilev Ballet, which was very rarely, it was a spontaneous expression of approval, and all the more sincere because applause at rehearsals was discouraged by the management. Leon and I therefore realised there must be something particularly fetching about our dance or about the way we did it. On the first night, when we danced off the stage at the end of this *pas de deux* the applause was thunderous. We couldn't believe our ears and we took so many calls that the situation became embarrassing through being so unexpected. This led to an incident which made a deep impression on me.

After the performance I was walking along one of the endless corridors backstage at the Opéra—not the one in which Leon had kissed me, but the one in which Massine had his dressing-room—when I saw Diaghilev approaching from the other end. It is always awkward to approach someone from a distance—does one wave and smile to them the whole way, or does one look at one's feet and let them take one by surprise? As Diaghilev and I met and were passing each other, I felt the nervous necessity of saying something, so I remarked brightly, 'That was good, wasn't it?' referring to our ovation. I had made an unforgivable mistake. Diaghilev merely said, 'It could have been better,' and walked on. I learned a lesson which I never forgot.

12

LE SACRE DU PRINTEMPS

Diaghilev as matchmaker — Drama in Maiden Lane — Despair — Diaghilev as father — Holiday at Bournemouth — Drama in Liverpool — Diaghilev as disciplinarian — Beginnings of Massine's *Sacre* — Fined for assault — Private rehearsals with Massine — Romantic upheavals — Final rehearsals of *Le Sacre* at the Champs-Elysées — Savina's broken date — The ordeal of the Chosen Virgin — An evening of Triumph and Disaster — Roman detectives — The confidences of Savina — Massine leaves the ballet.

I am sure that by this time Diaghilev suspected that Leon and I were in love. He took a paternal interest in the slightest goings-on in the company—although he pretended to be entirely aloof from our private affairs—and had a feminine bent for matchmaking. He saw how well suited Leon and I were as partners and how well adapted we were to express Massine's particular style of choreography; and I have no doubt that he would have welcomed any relationship between us which might help to bind us more closely to the Massine–Diaghilev team.

Leon and I never met except at class or rehearsals or on the stage, but we continued to write to each other—on the understanding, naturally, that our letters should be destroyed. Life with Kola was more than ever impossible. He watched me even while I was dancing, and I was so afraid of jealous scenes that I hardly dared raise my eyes to look at another man on the stage, so that I got to know all the men in the company by their feet. He accused the other dancers of flirting with me and made himself a thorough nuisance. The thought of Natasha had kept me from leaving him, but I now decided the time had come to take action. After Paris we had a season in London, at Covent Garden, and I made up my mind to part with Kola at the end of that season.

A dancer's life revolves round the rehearsal room. I have mentioned the Chenies Street drill hall where we worked before the war and where Maestro Cecchetti gave me the prize, and the club-room in the upper part of Shaftesbury Avenue where *La Boutique fantasque* and *Le Tricorne* were worked out and where Felix made faces over the counter: now we had a new rehearsal room, very handy for Covent Garden, the basement of Chandos House, Maiden Lane, where Kola and I used to practise in the early days of the war, and where we had first met Idzikovsky. This dark and dirty cellar, with its poky adjoining room into which the girls could barely cram themselves to change their clothes, was to be the scene of another unforgettable event in my life.

Arriving in Maiden Lane for our first rehearsal in London, I walked into a hornet's nest. Leon's wife, Antonova, had found all my letters to him. While I had been burning his, he had been keeping mine, and she had found them in one of his pockets while he was out at class. The scene she made in that dressing-room I shall never forget. In a violent temper and using terrible language, she showed my letters and read extracts from them to any of the girls who would look or listen. Then, in the rehearsal room, she confronted Leon with the letters. Before everyone he denied having written to me. I was not only embarrassed beyond words, but desperately hurt and disillusioned by Leon's cowardice—after all it was he who had made the first move. I was in a frightful situation, between Leon, Antonova and Kola, and I do not know how I held up my head at that rehearsal. What made it all the more bitter was that I knew Leon had been threatening to leave Antonova for months past.

I wanted to give up both Kola and Leon and to live by myself: but if I had left him Kola would have told the whole story to my parents, and that I could not face. I had a bottle of laudanum which a doctor in Monte Carlo had given me for stomach pains, and I decided to finish myself off by taking daily doses of this drug. I cannot imagine how I managed to continue dancing. I had raging headaches and my teeth began to crumble. My friend, Hilda Bewicke, took me to a dentist. I was beyond caring what happened to me. The dentist told Hilda that my teeth and gums showed that something was poisoning me; and that I should see a doctor. That evening I decided to swallow all the remaining laudanum, hoping it might be a final dose: but the bottle had gone from the drawer where it was hidden. I have never known to this day who found the bottle and removed it.

Diaghilev must have noticed that I looked ill and was always crying, and he must have heard something of the trouble. One day he sent for me to the Savoy. I was very frightened. When one was interviewed by Diaghilev at an hotel, one never went up to his bedroom or his sitting room, if he had one. The only times I ever remember being in his private room in any hotel were in San Sebastian, when the dwarf spat cherries, and in Madrid, when Diaghilev emptied the old bag of coins onto his bed. On this occasion, he received me in a little lobby between the entrance hall and the restaurant. He was very kind. He made me tell him what I could through my tears, and then he said, 'I want you to think of me as a father, and remember I will come to you at any time of day or night if you should need me.' Years later, he kept his word. Knowing that I had the great man's sympathy I was comforted and no longer felt alone. I went back to work feeling braver.

I remember very little about that Covent Garden season, which ended unfortunately. Diaghilev made the mistake of cancelling our final performance because the management had not fulfilled their obligations over money. Naturally our devoted public could not be expected to understand what financial complications were behind this decision: disappointment was caused and the reputation of the company was somewhat tarnished. There were, as usual on a last night in London, masses of flowers at the stage door, and this made it all the sadder that we had not given our performance. I took four bouquets round to the Charing Cross Hospital—a thing I was to do frequently in years to come.

156

Kola and I went off to spend our summer holiday with my parents and Natasha, who was now three, and I decided to have another try at making a success of our marriage. Mother and Father had taken a lovely house called The Limes at Southbourne, near Bournemouth. Kola and I went on bicycling expeditions to Christchurch and Wimborne, and amused ourselves trying to ride Mother's tricycle—quite a difficult thing to do if you are used to a bicycle.

When Mother and Beatrice went off on a visit I had to keep house. I knew absolutely nothing about cooking at that time; but having watched a bread pudding with fruit being made so often in the past, I thought I would have a shot. There was clearly something wrong with my effort for it was as dry as a bone, but it was only later that I realised I had left out the fat. Father and Kola were kind about it, but even the chickens wouldn't touch what was left over. A few days later I found at the bottom of my wardrobe the helping of pudding I had given Natasha, complete on its plate.

Leon and his wife had gone off to Scotland to stay with Florrie Grenfell and her husband at Lennoxlove, and it was there he first met Oswald Birley, the painter, who later became a very great friend of ours. I was still unhappy in my mind about Leon's behaviour, and I dreaded returning to start work again with the company.

The ballet reassembled in London in autumn, 1920. As there were no more interesting engagements, Diaghilev had reluctantly signed for an English provincial tour. It was not a success; audiences in Bournemouth, Leicester, Nottingham, Sheffield and Leeds did not seem to understand our ballets, and the agent in Birmingham ran away with our takings. Finally we arrived for a fortnight in Liverpool, and here things looked up a bit.

In *Prince Igor* I was one of the veiled captive women with a bare midriff, and Leon was my partner. One evening when Leon lifted me and held a pose while I lay over his shoulder, supported by one arm, he began gently stroking my body. I was so livid with anger, having had no sign of an apology from him since his denial of me in Maiden Lane, that I could hardly restrain my feelings. As soon as the curtain came down, I walked straight over to him in the presence of the whole company and gave him a resounding smack on the face. This sent the sparks flying. Leon's wife had to be held back to stop her tearing my eyes out, and she shouted like a madwoman. She made such an uproar that I had to be escorted out of the front of the house for fear she might try to carry out some of her threats, and disfigure me with vitriol.

Next morning Diaghilev sent for Leon and me to go to his hotel. Neither of us spoke a word as we waited for him, seated side by side on a hard sofa in a passage. When he arrived, he sat down between us and appeared to be very angry. He made me tell him what had happened, and it sounded so futile that I was embarrassed. I think Diaghilev must have been secretly amused, as he revelled in other people's emotional upsets. Leon never opened his mouth, so I was reprimanded and told I would be fined. 'I don't mind,' I said, 'it was worth it.' The 'Old Man' told us that as we had got to work together in the same company, if we could not get on together without making disturbances we must not speak to each other any more; and this was agreed. Leon just sat there with his nose getting bigger and bigger, which it always did when he was annoyed.

We dancers knew little or nothing about the running of the company or about Diaghilev's financial arrangements, except insomuch as the trouble we had in getting a small rise in salary made it quite clear to us that money was always scarce with him. After all, we knew he was generous with artists and would pay us as well as he could. (At this time I received £20 a week.) During our summer holiday he had had great difficulty in finding engagements—our provincial tour was evidence of this—and there had even been a question of whether we could carry on at all. Throughout its history the Diaghilev Ballet was so regularly under the threat of bankruptcy that this could almost be called a chronic state; yet, as one lavish work of art succeeded another each recurring crisis was forgotten in the triumph of creation. Diaghilev had contrived to arrange a season at the Théâtre des

Champs-Elysées in December, but for the moment he could not afford any new productions; it was therefore decided to revive *Le Sacre du printemps*. Nijinsky's choreography had been forgotten, so Massine undertook to reset Stravinsky's great work.

I was happy to hear the music of *Sacre* again, and the beginnings of Massine's choreography were full of promise. I remember, one day at Liverpool, sitting on the floor in a row of girls performing some mechanical stitching movement and enjoying myself. Two days later I was called to rehearse alone with Massine. He tried out some movements with me which seemed to present no difficulty. I had in my bag a little notebook of Hilda Bewicke's in which she had drawn for me the pattern of the dress she was making, as I wanted to copy it. Massine made me write down in this the number of times the first step was to be danced; then he tried the next, and I wrote that down. After reflecting on the difficulties of the music, he said, 'I think we had better work this out with a metronome.' We tried several more movements, which I did not record at the time, but those first two steps remain in the small black notebook which I have always kept as a souvenir of the beginnings of the dance of the Chosen Virgin, perhaps the most extraordinary dance ever invented. Next morning, Massine said to me, 'Diaghilev is allowing us to go back to London to get in a good week's work alone on the *Sacre* dance.' I realised I had been chosen for the great solo role. I was so thrilled I wanted to throw my arms round his neck and kiss him.

When Grigoriev gave me my salary before I left for London, I found that Diaghilev had imposed on me the largest fine ever paid by a member of the Diaghilev Ballet; and Grigoriev wrote in his ledger, 'Sokolova: £5 for Assault.'

So Massine and I returned to London to work in that underground room in Maiden Lane. The only other dancer who came with us was the English girl, Vera Savina. She had made a lot of progress during the last year and was becoming a joy to watch. She had a lovely, long jump, with delicate hand and arm movements. Vera was evidently destined to be our ballerina, but I was none the less surprised to find her leaving with us for London.

When I rested or went into the dressing-room to memorise some of the movements Massine had given me, he would rehearse Vera in the Mazurka from *Les Sylphides*. She danced it beautifully and with a wonderful quality of lightness which I always admired and tried to achieve.

Day by day Massine and I worked on the dance of the Chosen Virgin, which was so difficult for him to plan and for me to memorise, because Stravinsky's music made its own rules and abided by none of them for long. First it was necessary to get used to the rhythm of each section, and the metronome was set at the tempo marked on the score. Without any music I would dance over and over again those first steps, then when I was imbued with the beat the music would be played by Rae Robertson, the pianist who had been specially engaged. Although I found the first steps fitted the melody pretty well, the second seemed to have nothing in common with it, but by ignoring the sound and keeping straight on, I eventually met the music on a given beat followed by a tacit bar. I began to understand how the dance must be worked.

Each step of the dance had a different set of counts, including several 'ands' for half-beats between them, which further complicated matters: but all this I learned easily. The difficult part was the execution of the actual steps and remembering how many times to repeat each one. For example, there were some enormous sideways jumps, which had to be performed very slowly, and every second one had an extra movement in it. It was not easy, while executing these exhausting *jetés*, to keep count of them and stop at the ninth. The only way I could register the number of times I had done any step in *Le Sacre* was by repeating the method I had used in *Narcisse*, which was to press down a finger each time I began a new step.

Once a step was worked out rhythmically we would plot it, then go back to the beginning and add a little more to the dance. These repetitions got me into training for the ordeal of performing this exceptionally long and exhausting dance on the stage.

The dance grew at terrific speed, and by the time the company arrived back in London three-quarters of it was done. It was all written down in the little penny notebook. That notebook holds the sole record of my dance in *Le Sacre du printemps*. The only other person in the world to memorise it was Leon Woizikovsky, who had a phenomenal photographic mind.

I was too preoccupied in learning the dance of the Chosen Virgin to see that something else had been going on in the basement room in Maiden Lane—something which would affect all our lives, as well as the fortunes of the Diaghilev Ballet: Massine had fallen in love with Vera Savina.

When Leonide Feodorovitch took Nijinsky's place with Diaghilev, he rapidly became far more important in every way than Nijinsky had ever been both to Diaghilev personally and to the creative life of the Ballet. From being the eager and receptive pupil Diaghilev needed emotionally, Massine soon became the indispensable interpreter of his artistic ideas. Although we knew he was dedicated to life with Diaghilev, Massine was desperately attractive to all the women and I think we were all a little in love with him. However, we had been warned by the episode in Washington.

Vera Savina, being English and not speaking two words of Russian, was as innocent as a new-born lamb, and she was the only person in the company who had no idea of Massine's situation. But Massine had fallen in love with her. Without realising any of the implications, she must have been flattered.

As for me, after being ill-treated by Kola Kremnev and let down by Leon Woizikovsky, I was in a state where anything was liable to happen. I was so thrilled by the role I was creating in *Le Sacre*—apart from the knowledge that I was ideally suited to the sort of ballets which were being invented by Massine—that if, at this particular moment, he had given *me* so much as a sign, I think I would have gone off with him like a shot!

It was a relief when the final section of my solo was arranged in Paris, because I had been impatient to know whether I would be able to keep up my strength throughout the whole seven minutes of the dance. In fact the movements I had to do just before my final jumps round the stage were the most exhausting

part of the entire solo. At last I knew the worst and I thought
I should just be able to get through.

The music of *Sacre* was, of course, familiar, but Massine's new
version of the ballet was very different from Nijinsky's, in
which I had danced at that same theatre, the Champs-Elysées, in
1913. This was a typical Massine production, clear-cut and
methodical, with each group counting like mad against the others,
but each holding its own. In Massine's choreography nothing was
ever left to chance, and if anybody was in doubt about what he
had to do or why he had to do it, he had only to ask and everything was explained. I think it was lucky for Massine that he had
never seen the Nijinsky production, which had been staged a
year before he joined the company: he might have felt obliged
to imitate something which had been conceived in a style quite
alien to him. The Nijinsky ballet had a sadness about it, with its
groups of ancient men with enormous beards, trembling and
shuffling; but although there were touching moments, I doubt
whether the ballet could have survived for long, even if circumstances had been different and Nijinsky had remained as choreographer to the company. It was a vague work, far less complicated and accurate than Massine's.

Without doubt the most terrifying experience of my life in the
theatre was the first orchestra rehearsal of *Le Sacre*. Igor Stravinsky, wearing an expression which would have frightened a
hundred Chosen Virgins, pranced up and down the centre aisle
of the Champs-Elysées, while Ansermet practised difficult passages of music with the orchestra. The cruel thing for me was
that I had to wait about for the whole of the first act, with all
the repetitions and corrections which were necessary. I became
so scared that I nearly ran away. When the second scene began
and my turn came to take the stage with the *corps de ballet*, I was
so stunned that I couldn't hear the music, but the girls pulled me
through the *ensemble* dances. When the other dancers retreated
to the back of the stage and left me alone I thought I was going
to faint. I stared at Ansermet: then I saw him make a sign of
encouragement before he gave me the upbeat to begin. I danced;
and I met the orchestra precisely at the two places where I

should, and we finished together. After that I knew I never had anything to fear from the orchestra when Ansermet was conducting. He understood the dance, and could tell exactly how I was progressing as it mounted to its final climax.

It was after this orchestra rehearsal that I happened to come down alone to the stage after most of the company had gone home. It was about six in the evening, and the place was dark. Vera Savina was standing in the far corner of the stage, when Mme Sert suddenly came through a door nearby. Misia Sert was a clever, attractive woman of the world, besides being Diaghilev's devoted friend, and there were no secrets between them. Crossing the stage, I overheard Vera say 'Mme Sert, have you seen Mr Massine?' 'No, Verotchka. Did you want him for anything in particular?' 'I have an appointment with him.' At this, of course, Mme Sert pricked up her ears—and so did I. 'Oh? Where is your appointment?' 'At the Arch *de* Triumph, but it's such a big place I don't know exactly where to meet him.' 'Then,' said Mme Sert, 'I should stand right in the middle of the arch if I were you.' I was staggered by this, but said nothing. I imagined Misia hurrying off to tell Diaghilev about the appointment, and Vera standing in the centre of the Etoile, waiting in vain.

When the time came to try on the old costumes for *Le Sacre*, which were to be used again, I was given one of the red ones from the first act. I found I could not get through my dance in this thick flannel dress and stuffy wig. A new tunic was therefore made in white silk, so that I should have the least possible weight on my body. A hideous photograph was taken of me by the press, wearing the red wig from *Narcisse*; but in the end it was decided that this was too heavy, so I wore my own hair. To prevent it falling across my face and obscuring my vision when I performed the big, hammering steps round the stage, flinging my body from side to side, the top part of my hair by my neck was stitched together by criss-cross tacking stitches with double thread.

The dress rehearsal passed off successfully a few days later. At the end of it I was going back to my dressing room when I heard Massine calling to me. His room was next to mine, and the door was open. As I walked in, Leonide Feodorovitch congratulated me for the first time in my life. He said, 'We could not have achieved this work without each other.' I was surprised and touched. I told him I was grateful for all he had done for me. He put his hands on my shoulders and kissed me quite naturally on each cheek. This was done with such sincerity, and I was so overwhelmed to hear these words from the handsome Massine, who never praised anybody, that I returned his embrace with emotion. As he moved away he suddenly froze. Looking round, I saw Diaghilev standing in the doorway. Without a word, he walked past me. I mumbled something and slipped out, leaving an icy atmosphere behind.

The next day, December 15, was our first performance, and although I was dancing my difficult role in *Le Sacre*, I was not excused from appearing in another ballet in the programme. That night we gave *Pulcinella*, *Le Sacre du printemps* and *Le Tricorne*. Tamara Karsavina was setting up house in London with her family, and besides taking over her roles in *Carnaval* and *Petroushka*, I had also inherited her role of Pimpinella in *Pulcinella* which I had to dance that evening.

Diaghilev and Massine had a little *griffon* dog called Micky which they kept in Paris and which they would leave behind in kennels whenever we went away. They treated it very badly, making it drunk and roaring with laughter to see it reel around on the table. When the dog was left alone in Massine's dressing room I used sometimes to find it eating its way through a great pot of grease used for removing make-up. No wonder the poor creature developed eczema. Diaghilev and Massine knew I was fond of the dog, because I often used to go and talk to it. When I went in to wish Massine good luck before the ballet the dog was sitting in its basket on the table complete with brushes, rug and four bottles of medicine. I wondered why.

Remembering the uproar at the first performance of *Le Sacre* in 1913, everyone wondered how the revival would be received; but a generation which had heard German guns was no longer to be shocked by the explosions of Stravinsky's music. The beautiful theatre was crammed. As I practised my strenuous jumps behind the stage during the first scene, I could not remember for the life of me what my music was like. As the curtain came down on Scene One to reassuring applause there was a lot of shush-ing, and quiet was restored for the intermission music.

There was a hush as the curtain rose on the second scene, and nothing now separated me from the public and my ordeal. I knew that Diaghilev, Massine and Stravinsky must be in suspense as to whether I should get through the dance without flagging or forgetting, and whether I should keep to all my different rhythms. One miscalculation and the whole effect of the scene might be ruined. I prayed for strength to get through to the end.

The second scene opened with all the men seated cross-legged round three sides of the stage. I was in one of three lines of girls who stood holding hands in profile to the audience. The outside two began by sinking with bent knees, then rose up again as the centre group went down, which gave an undulating effect. The three lines moved slowly round into a block, then executed a quiet, but forceful swaying movement. When they linked hands and filed away I was in the centre of the stage. From this moment I had to stand absolutely still for twelve minutes, waiting for my dance to begin. My left arm was held across my body, my clenched hand in the air above my head, my right hand was at my waist and my feet were turned inward. To keep still for so long in this position, with my back twisted, was almost unbearable.

At a given moment the crowd came to life. The music at this point is made up of overlapping sections, each of which was danced by a group of men or women or, at times, both. For every group there were different jumps, gestures and counts: the whole crowd counted audibly to themselves. They surged at me and receded in a frightening way. I tried to think of my coming dance, but in vain. As the victim of fate I was a heroic, as well as a pathetic, figure, and I knew I had to stare fixedly ahead of me as I awaited my end. I had learnt that the only way to prevent myself from blinking was to stare at a red exit light at the back of the auditorium.

At last the whole company converged on me. Two men held

their hands across my body and the others linked onto them on either side. Then, still counting, the whole line of men and women swayed from side to side, gradually opening out like a concertina and closing in again. This seemed to me to go on for ever. Only when the line began to wheel round could I at last lower my cramped hand and change my position. Having performed one whole revolution of the stage with me as an axis, the company were back in their line parallel with the footlights. The two men on either side of me then broke hands, and everybody slowly side-stepped upstage to twenty slow counts, as the music went down to a whisper.

I came in with a crashing step on the first beat of my music. I was the maiden chosen by the tribe as a spring sacrifice to their god. Possessed by an animal frenzy, I would dance myself to death so that the tribe might prosper and the crops not fail. As I danced, the forty others remained motionless at the back, their hands arched over their brows to shade their eyes, watching me. The watchers beyond the footlights seemed to be echoing with their opera-glasses this ancient gesture.

The steps Massine had invented for my sacrificial dance bore so little relation to any kind of dancing that had ever been done before and were so violently contrasted one with the other, and followed each other so swiftly with such sudden changes of rhythm, that I think the impression I gave was of a creature galvanised by an electric current. The dance was tragic: it evoked pity and terror.

Whatever it did to the audience, it nearly killed me. Rowers, after all, only have to keep rowing, and runners only have to keep going. I not only had to do my fearful movements, but I had to keep thinking, acting and counting all at once. Luckily the body has its own form of memory which carries on after physical exhaustion has stopped the brain from functioning consciously. The hardest thing was to remember how often I had executed one of the convulsive steps. At certain moments I was able to keep count on my fingers, but when this was impossible, Leon, who led the *corps de ballet*, was allowed to call out the counts. At last I came to my final spinning jumps round the stage. These consisted of *grands jetés en tournant*, in themselves difficult steps to do, but between each, on landing, I had to bend down sideways and place one hand on the stage while I raised the other in the air and beat my breast twice. Coming to a sudden halt in the middle, I pulled myself up on my toes, waiting for the curtain to begin to fall. I dropped to the ground and lay backwards, raising my body in a taut arch, like a victim meeting the knife, resting on my shoulders, elbows and toes. Just before the curtain touched the stage the last chord of music sounded, and I collapsed.

The curtain rose, I was told, several times on the final tableau; but I was not conscious of it. Then Woizikovsky and another lifted me to my feet and stood close to me on either side while we took our curtain calls in case I fell again. Gradually I came to my senses and my heart started to beat more normally. The applause was deafening. I was very tired but very happy to have succeeded, and Stravinsky had kissed my hand before the audience. I was twenty-four years old. When I got back to my dressing room the *griffon* dog Micky was sitting there waiting for me. Diaghilev and Massine had given him to me as a present.

It was in a more cheerful mood than I had been in for a long time that I went off to the supper party at Diaghilev's hotel, the Continental, where he stayed in those days. We had a big private dining-room. All Diaghilev's particular friends were there, Misia Sert, Chanel, and everyone connected with the organisation of the Paris season, but only the principal dancers of the company. Diaghilev sat at one end of the long table and Stravinsky at the other. We were all very merry.

Diaghilev must have known at this time that Massine was interested in someone, but I think he may have been uncertain whether it was Savina or me. As Mme Sert had undoubtedly passed on the information about the rendezvous under the *Arc de Triomphe* I suppose that his suspicions now rested on Vera. She was seated half-way down the table, and as the evening went on the Diaghilev group began to rag her unmercifully. As she spoke no Russian she was an easy butt. She wore a short pink dress with shoulder-straps, which looked very English among all those sophisticated gowns by Lanvin and Chanel. There was a lot of laughter and they kept saying, 'Have a little more champagne, Verotchka.'

If it had not been for the wretched complications of our private lives, it could have been an enjoyable party and a real celebration after the hard work of *Le Sacre*: but this was not to be. I had my problem with Kremnev—on these occasions there was always the likelihood of his drinking too much and making a jealous scene. Diaghilev must have been anxious about Massine; and Massine must have been longing for some sort of life of his own with Vera. I should have liked to sit quietly listening to Stravinsky, who could be very amusing, and who had, besides, many complimentary things to say about my performance. However, our conversation was interrupted by Massine who jumped to his feet and climbed onto the piano.

'Quiet, everybody!' he shouted. 'I have an announcement to make.' There were a few encouraging cheers, then everyone was silent. We all realised that he was tight, for he was much too quiet and well-behaved in the normal course of events to make any demonstration.

'The time has come,' he said. 'I have made up my mind that I am going to run away.'

Everyone shouted, 'Come on! Tell us who with? Who is it to be?'

'There's no secret about it,' cried Massine. 'I am going to run away with Sokolova.'

The guests all cheered and laughed, taking this for a great joke—pretending to think it funnier than they did—since they were all embarrassed. Diaghilev and Kola can have found it no more amusing than I did. Massine jumped off the piano, came round the table to where I sat petrified, and kissed my hand. Kola was in a flaming rage and got me away from the party as soon as possible. I could not imagine what had possessed Leonide Feodorovitch. Was it just a bit of nonsense on the spur of the moment? Was he trying to annoy Diaghilev, in a spirit of frustration? Or was he trying to put him off the scent? I am sure Massine would never have been so foolish as to do what he did if he had realised what I should have to go through that night from Kola.

I had so much work to do and had come to a point in my career when hard work had earned me a number of wonderful roles. With Mme Karsavina gone, I was taking over her parts in *Carnaval*, and *Le Tricorne*, besides *Petroushka* and *Pulcinella*. I danced in *Les Sylphides* and *Papillons*; had a solo in *Prince Igor*; danced the Bacchanale in *Narcisse*, Kikimora in *Contes Russes* and the tarantellas in *La Boutique fantasque* and *Le Astuzie Femminili*. I was in every ballet, either in principal or small parts. No wonder I had no time to spare for complications in my private life.

It was so hard to know what to do. I would have given everything I had to be able to go and tell Diaghilev that there was nothing in what Massine said and that he need have no fear that I would let him down. It was awful to think that he might be suspecting me of planning to run off with Leonide. After all, he had seen us kissing two days before. I was in an awkward position and there seemed to be nothing I could do without making it worse.

We had our second Christmas running in Paris, then set off for Rome, where we opened at the Teatro Costanzi on New Year's Day, 1921. Kola and I stayed at a nice quiet hotel near the priests' college on the Piazza Santa Maria sopra Minerva. The food was good there and the bedroom was comfortable. I got to know the hotel well because most afternoons, when I was stitching tights and shoes, I was locked into my bedroom by Kola; but I was too busy to care.

Rome was full of Russian aristocrats who had escaped from the revolution: they had formed a Russian library where they used to meet, and which became a club for them. Prince Youssoupoff organised a charity gala at which the company performed, and this was attended by innumerable people with famous Russian names, many of them related to the Imperial family. I made friends with a Princess Galitzine, who was the most beautiful woman I have ever seen. She had long dark hair and black eyes like Karsavina. Her husband had been so shocked by the revolution that he had developed a bad stutter. They were desperately poor and lived in two tiny rooms at the top of a boarding house: I used to visit them there and help bath the baby. The Prince got a job as a chauffeur, and the Princess, who was a fine musician, earned a little money by playing the piano for the British Ambassador's daughter, who used to dance at tea parties in the Embassy for charity, and who was horrid to her.

The dining-room at our hotel was usually rather empty, but shortly after our arrival I noticed there were two men who had their meals at the same time as we did, and who sat at the next table to ours. They left their old-fashioned motor-bikes outside the hotel, and when I saw them parked near our rehearsal room I began to wonder what was going on. It became clear that they were keeping an eye on me, and I learned later that they had been hired by Diaghilev to do so. However, as Kola and I never spoke anything but Russian, I do not think they could have learned anything much from eavesdropping on our mealtime conversations.

One morning, after class and just before the rehearsal began, Vera Savina said to me, 'Will you wait till they've all gone? I want to speak to you.' When the others had left the changing room, Vera said, 'Mr Massine wants me to go out with him.' Somewhat taken aback, I remarked, 'I suppose that's all right if he wants to show you some of the sights of Rome.' Vera said, 'But he says he's fallen in love with me.' I could not stop myself saying, 'But, Vera, that's an awful calamity.' 'Why is it a calamity', she asked, 'if he wants to marry me?' I was appalled that they were seriously considering marriage. I told her that she had not lived through the Nijinsky tragedy as we had, and that if she married Massine I was afraid they would both have to leave the company. Vera said, 'I don't see why'; and at that moment Grigoriev called us. I felt quite ill at having to share this secret, and before joining the rehearsal I had to go outside for some air.

After this, events moved very fast. Massine must have given away to Diaghilev the fact that it was Vera, not myself, with whom he was in love. When he announced his intention of going off in a *carrozza* to look at some villa or monument down the Appian Way, Diaghilev had the two detectives switched over to him, and I saw them no more. Leonide and Vera met and drove out together, but they never realised at the time that they were followed to the café outside the gates and that their conversations were reported to Diaghilev.

The next day as Massine walked in to start rehearsal, Grigoriev took him aside and quietly said something to him. Leonide Feodorovitch went deathly pale, turned and walked out of the room. As I had not breathed a word of what Vera had told me, the company thought something must have happened to Diaghilev—especially as the rehearsal was cancelled.

That evening at the theatre I went to see Vera to find out what was going on, but her dressing-room was empty. I asked the wardrobe mistress where she was and was told she had been put upstairs. I traced her to a room at the top, which she was sharing with three other girls. She had been banished to the *corps de ballet*. 'Isn't it awful?' Vera said. 'Diaghilev knows and I don't know what to do.' I told her she must stand by Massine whatever happened and not to say anything to anybody.

Massine had been dismissed. Savina left the company, and they were married almost immediately. We had lost our choreographer and our potential ballerina. Diaghilev was not seen for days, and Vassili told me later that he nearly died.

13

WITHOUT MASSINE

Reshuffle of roles — 'Love among the Ruins' — Eaves-
dropping at Lyon — Break with Kremnev in Madrid —
Diaghilev's problem — Arrival of Kochno — Catherine
Devillier — Maria Dalbaicin — A new choreographer chosen
— Dancers' accidents — A train robbery — *Chout* and *Cuadro
Flamenco* — at the Gaieté Lyrique — Dancing *Le Sacre* with
flu — Inconveniences of the Princes Theatre — Summer
holiday in Brittany.

The departure of Massine and Savina necessitated a shuffle of
roles, which gave more work to everybody. When Grigoriev
told me I was to dance Vera's part in *Les Sylphides* I nearly wept.
I said I could not possibly take on any more important parts,
particularly one so unsuited to me as the principal role in *Les
Sylphides*.

All the extra rehearsals that were needed brought home to us
what a terrible loss Massine was going to be to the company,
both as dancer and choreographer. As far as Leon and I were
concerned it was a personal tragedy. We had learned so much
from him, and it could almost be said that he had created us, as a
painter creates figures on his canvas.

Leon Woizikovsky took over most of Massine's character
roles, with the result that he and I were gradually thrown more
and more together—on the stage, at least. I found myself rehearsing with him the love scene of *Cléopâtre*, and it was quite
impossible to teach him the role of Amoun without conversing
at all, so the silence which had been imposed upon us at Liverpool
was soon broken. I felt in a way that Diaghilev had always intended us for each other. We made a date to meet secretly 'in

the ruins' and it was while we walked together among the fallen columns and cypresses of the Roman Forum that we decided to put an end to our unhappy marriages and arrange things so that we could settle down together.

I had something to look forward to, but in the meantime life was not easy. I was always conscious of the other dancers' whispered comments whenever Leon and I were rehearsing the same ballet, for we could not hide the fact that we were in love.

At last our sad stay in Rome came to an end—we were never to dance there again—and we moved on to Lyon. It was here that, by chance, I was able to fill the gaps in what I already knew of the story of Savina and Massine, and of the latter's parting with Diaghilev. One night I got a chicken bone stuck in my throat at supper, and as nothing would dislodge it a doctor was sent for, and I went up to my room to await him, leaving the door ajar. Our rooms at the Grand Hotel all opened onto a balcony which looked down on a central hall, and as I waited for the doctor I could clearly hear Diaghilev, who was sitting below with his close friend the singer Zoia Roszovska, telling her the whole story. I could not avoid overhearing. He told her how Leonide had been restless throughout the past year, and how this had resulted in increasing disagreements between them. He described the events in Rome which had led to Massine's dismissal, and I was delighted and relieved to hear that I was exonerated from all blame for having flirted with Massine or betrayed Diaghilev's trust. He ended up by saying, 'There is nobody indispensable in this world. I shall find someone else.' Poor Sergei Pavlovitch! He trained other talented dancers and choreographers, but nobody ever again took the place of Massine in his life, either as a pupil, an artist or a friend.

It was in Madrid, where we went after ten days in Lyon, that I finally parted company with Kola. At lunch one day in our hotel he was more than usually aggressive, and as we left the restaurant he smacked my face, sending me reeling against the wall. I ran out of the hotel and managed to get a girl friend, who was living nearby, to telephone Leon. He met me in the park and we drove about all the afternoon in a carriage, discussing what was best to do. I was afraid to go back to the hotel, so I went to the one where Diaghilev was staying and asked for him. When he came down I told him that Kola was in a really dangerous mood and that I thought he might make some sort of scandal at the theatre, if not on the stage during a performance. Diaghilev sent me home, assuring me that he would have Kola watched. It was late when I got back, and Kola had already begun his dinner. When he asked me where I had been and I told him I had seen Leon and Diaghilev he punched my face in full view of everybody in the restaurant, so violently that it knocked me over. The waiters carried me upstairs and the proprietor's wife bathed my face which was bleeding. Kola ran off to the theatre to give warning that I should not be able to dance. Soon after this Camishov, the property man, arrived and helped me to find a room in another hotel. So when I had collected a few things for the night I was able to go with him to the theatre and dance in the last ballet. Diaghilev sent for Kola, but I never knew what he said to him. Next day, when Kola was at class, I packed my wardrobe trunk and left him once and for all.

Diaghilev's greatest problem at this time was to replace Massine. Great discussions must have taken place between him and his artistic advisers as to which member of the company could possibly be moulded into a choreographer. Between the time when I had listened in to his conversation in the hotel with Zoia Roszovska and his arrival for our opening night in Madrid, Diaghilev had been in Paris. When he rejoined us he brought with him Stravinsky, Walter Nouvel, an old friend from Russia, who was to undertake the administration of the company, and a new young Russian friend called Boris Kochno—as well as some new ideas. His two immediate projects were first to go with Stravinsky in search of a *cuadro flamenco*—a team of Spanish singers, dancers and musicians—whose music could be rearranged by Stravinsky and who could be presented in a setting by Picasso; and, secondly, to entrust the tuition of the young dancer Slavinsky to the painter Larionov, with a view to making a ballet on a recently completed score by Prokofiev, the Soviet Russian composer, who was his latest discovery.

Boris Kochno, whose interests were divided between literature and painting, was destined to play a great part in the artistic history of the ballet, but for the moment he was merely being tried out for the position of secretary to Diaghilev. Diaghilev took him and Stravinsky to Seville during Easter Week in search of a suitable troupe of Gypsies, and Kochno has described how, in this first of the many journeys they made together, Diaghilev drove him straight from the station to the little-frequented art gallery in Seville, 'which was like a deserted country house with broken windows and swallows darting over our heads between the dusty canvases of Murillo and Zurbaran'. As a result of this excursion Diaghilev found his *cuadro flamenco*, and Stravinsky thought their music so perfect of its kind that he would not alter a note. Here they also met the famous English showman, C. B. Cochran, who was to present the Diaghilev Ballet later in the year, and who was himself in search of an exceptionally beautiful Spanish girl dancer with whom to astonish the London public.

I had been dancing the Miller's Wife in *Le Tricorne* for over a year, ever since Karsavina had left the company, and had recently been ordered to teach it to Catherine Devillier. Diaghilev was always eager to welcome dancers from Russia, and Katia, who came from Moscow, had joined us in Paris. She was a charming woman and a 'good scout'. She was as dark as a Gypsy, tall, plump and very feminine. I was very fond of her, and I think she liked me. She had never studied Spanish dancing, except the stylised kind which has a place in the old classical ballets, so *Le Tricorne* nearly killed her. She puffed and panted, and by the time she got half way through she had fallen back into a much more Russian style of dancing and was in a state of collapse. Poor girl! She had too much weight to carry round. No doubt if she had stayed with us longer she would have lost it, but ballet of our type was too much hard work for her, and she soon left us. However, she danced in *Le Tricorne* with Leon in Madrid, and the King of Spain liked her performance.

As the Miller, Leon gave a happier performance than Massine, although he was less Spanish, not having been through the same course of study under Felix. In some parts of the ballet most of us agreed he was better than Massine, but he could not do the subtle body movements necessary in the comic passage when the Miller draws a caricature of the Governor on the wall of the house. I preferred doing this ballet with Woizikovsky, because Massine, even when he was dancing as my partner, always seemed to be dancing a solo. He would not—or maybe could not—share a dance with you, and always remained detached.

Soon after we arrived in Monte Carlo from Spain, I was asked to teach *Tricorne* to yet another girl. This time my pupil was a real Spaniard, one of the *cuadro flamenco*, a beautiful creature called Maria Dalbaicin, but always known as Pepita. One might have thought she would have understood the dance at once and given a fine rendering, but most Spaniards are instinctive performers, quite incapable of counting or doing the same thing twice running in the same way, so that in complex ballets needing great precision such as those of Massine, she was just as much of a problem as Felix had been. I would willingly have passed onto someone else the work of teaching Pepita. She giggled most of the time and simply could not string the numerous dances together. I wasted hours and hours of sunshine teaching that flippant young woman the role of the Miller's Wife. It was a good thing Massine had so imprinted on me every step and gesture of that ballet that I could never change a single movement of head or hand and foot, for by the time three very different dancers had interpreted the role, it would not have been surprising if some of its details and special character had been lost. Without Leon as her partner I doubt if she would have got through.

Larionov began working with Thaddeus Slavinsky on the composition of *Chout*. Slavinsky was a Pole, a nice-looking young man of medium height, with a good, slim figure, but bad teeth. He danced easily and effortlessly, and if it had not been for his character he might have made a great success. He was unreliable, boastful and without a strict regard for the truth. Some of us had been shocked over the indiscreet way he described his love affairs, and since we thought of him as irresponsible and with no particular intelligence, it came as a surprise to us that Diaghilev should have thought him capable of producing a ballet.

Before doing so, Diaghilev had sounded a young dancer called Tcherkas, as well as Leon, to discover whether they had ambitions as choreographers. But Tcherkas admitted he had not the physical strength for the hours of study, the late nights and the social obligations which would have been entailed by an apprenticeship with Diaghilev and his artistic committee; while Leon loved his freedom too dearly—also he knew nothing about music. Nor, for that matter, did Thaddeus Slavinsky, and he took the whole thing as a huge joke. He would sometimes arrive quite tight for an evening's performance; and one evening I had a hard time dragging him through the tarantella in *La Boutique fantasque*. As we were pushed off the stage on our trolley I made him kneel in my place and stood over him, literally holding him up, as he was so winded from the dance that he would certainly have fallen off. Slavinsky had no more idea of inventing a ballet than flying over the moon, and what ballet there was must certainly have been the work of Larionov.

During this stay at Monte Carlo I was regularly dancing Tamara Karsavina's enchanting part in *Pulcinella*. I loved this ballet and was very happy when I was called on to take part in it. We were a merry little crowd, Luba, Vera Nemtchinova, myself and the men. The finale was one of the brightest of any ballet. We laughed, chatted, were lifted and raced round the stage, held hands and swung backwards and forwards, lifting first one leg, then the other. When the curtain came down we were usually in a gay mood, having thoroughly enjoyed ourselves.

But *Pulcinella* brought us one bit of bad luck. We were rehearsing during a violent thunderstorm, when Leon jumped, caught his foot in the wide trousers of his *Pulcinella* costume and fell to the ground. His ankle was badly twisted, and Grigoriev, thinking it would help, got hold of his foot and forced it back. Something snapped and Leon was carried away to be examined. He was told that he could dance no more that season, and for years later suffered from swelling of that ankle after a heavy stretch of dancing.

Leon was certainly battle-scarred. He had an appalling bruise all the way down his left thigh where he used to fall with a crash at the end of the *farrucca* in *Le Tricorne*, and his knees would get so badly bruised that he had to wear knee pads. It is strange how easy it is for a dancer to tear muscles doing something he has done hundreds of times before with impunity. Leon, making quite a simple movement in the second scene of *Petroushka* tore his thigh muscles very badly; and I myself, sitting down at a rehearsal of *Scheherazade*, once tore muscles in three places at the same time. These injuries are very painful and can take up to ten days to heal. Another frequent ailment which ballet dancers get from dancing on points is fluid at the back of the ankle—linseed poultices are the best thing for this; while inflamed toes, another common complaint, are treated with compresses soaked in a solution of zinc.

On my way down to rehearsal I would pass Leon sitting on the balcony of his hotel with his leg in plaster. I was living alone now and liking it. Although Kola continued to pester me to return to him I had no intention of doing so. I began to take part in the social life of Monte Carlo. I met the Dolly sisters, who sent me flowers; and at Comtesse Gautier-Vignal's luncheon parties we used to speak in six languages.

For the journey back to Paris I shared a four-berth *couchette* with Hilda Bewicke, her mother who had been visiting her, and Zoia Roszovska. Before going to bed we stood in the corridor for some time talking, and I admired a lovely jewelled necklace which Zoia was wearing. She said it was a family treasure and that she always wore it when she travelled because she thought it was safer round her neck. We went to bed and continued talking till about one o'clock, then knew nothing more till we were woken at dawn by Zoia crying out, 'My necklace! It's gone!' We then discovered that our handbags, which were still under our pillows, had been emptied as well. We learned that the lights of the whole carriage had gone out at about two o'clock; and it was thought somebody had given our compartment a whiff of chloroform to make us all sleep deeply while the thief stole Zoia's necklace and every penny we had. Luckily we were with the rest of the company, who helped us out of our predicament.

Apart from creating the awful problem of finding a new choreographer, the departure of Massine was followed by another severe financial crisis. Diaghilev must have been a giant in courage to rise above all these blows, personal, artistic, and pecuniary, which might have overwhelmed a lesser man. He had been unable to secure either the Opéra or the Théâtre des Champs-Elysées for his spring season and, swallowing his pride, had resigned himself to showing his glorious Russian Ballet at the Gaieté Lyrique, a not particularly distinguished theatre off the Boulevard Sebastopol. To Diaghilev the spring season in Paris was by far the most important in the year: if he could not dazzle and subject the capital of fashion with one or two novelties every spring, he would have considered himself a failure and closed down the company. While he valued his London public for their fidelity and because they could be counted on, given time, to appreciate the qualities in a new work, I think he felt that the audiences of other European capitals and lesser towns were lucky to see his Ballet at all. But the small public of *le tout Paris* was alarmingly fickle, unaccountable and derisive of failure, so that Diaghilev courted its approval with the eagerness and energy of a lover whose happiness depends on the whims of a capricious mistress. The opening programme at the Gaieté Lyrique contained both *Chout* and the *Cuadro Flamenco*, our two new presentations.

In presenting a ballet with a score by a brilliant, new composer in a setting which was nothing if not startling in colour and design, and by having the originality to include this team of fantastic Spaniards in his programme (not to mention the fact that they were dressed by Picasso), Diaghilev showed Massine and the world in general that he was keeping his end up.

The story of *Chout* was quite funny, and if it could have been worked out by somebody with a real feeling for telling a tale in theatrical terms, it might have had much greater success. As it was, only the fact that Larionov had good ideas and that Diaghilev kept an eagle eye on rehearsals and supervised every detail, prevented the wretched Slavinsky's first and last ballet for the company from being another *Till Eulenspiegel*. *Chout* was an old Russian folk tale, in which, for some reason, practically all the

characters, male and female, were buffoons. There must have
been as many buffoons in old Russia as Joneses in Wales. Slavinsky was *the* buffoon and I was his wife. In order to make some
money he demonstrates the supposedly magic properties of a
whip, with which, having killed me, he can bring me to life again.
Seven other simple-minded buffoons fall for this trick and buy
the whip. They all go home, kill their wives, then by cracking
the whip, try unsuccessfully to bring them to life again. To avoid
their vengeance, Slavinsky dresses up as a female cook, but
finding him attractive, they carry him off. A merchant, come to
choose a bride from among the daughters of the seven buffoons,
picks on the cook instead. Reduced to extremes in the bridal
chamber, Slavinsky pretends to be overcome by a natural want,
and is let down on a sheet out of the window. When the merchant
pulls the sheet up again, he finds a goat tied to the end of it and
concludes in dismay that his wife has taken another shape.
The buffoon appears in his own guise and demands the return
of his cook. As the merchant can only offer a goat in her place,
he is obliged to hand over a large sum of money. The ballet ends
with the buffoon and his friends having a party on his ill-gotten
gains.

One new idea in Larionov's décor, derived from cubism, was
to show different sides of a house simultaneously. His violent
colours were those of painted Russian toys, and in one scene
fragments of a house, clouds, lamp-posts and blossoming trees
seemed to be hurtling rhapsodically through the air in a way
which suggests some of the ecstatic pictures of Chagall.

I was not particularly happy in the part of the Buffoon's Wife,
although it was the leading female role, because I felt there was
no real dancing to get my teeth into; nor did I at that time appreciate Prokofiev's music. When I was not on the stage I used
to run away from its strident shrieks.

The setting used for *Cuadro Flamenco* was one of Picasso's early
projects for *Pulcinella*. He had done a number of designs for that
ballet before he could please Diaghilev; and he evidently forgave Diaghilev for being so difficult because he let him use this
old design—without payment, I believe—when the company

got into deep water after the departure of Massine. Moreover, he designed some stylised Spanish costumes for the Gypsy performers, who must have been surprised to find their traditional shawls and flounced dresses were not considered complete without the application of certain irregular and mysterious designs. *Pulcinella* had first been conceived as a performance on a stage within a stage, so that the Gypsies' platform was framed by the reddish proscenium arch of a nineteenth-century theatre, from the boxes of which they were admired by a painted audience of four. (To raise money on a subsequent occasion, Diaghilev cut out the two panels of canvas which depicted the boxes with their occupants, and which had been painted and signed by the artist himself, selling them for a large sum as genuine Picassos —which indeed they were—to a South American collector.)

Nothing quite like the *Cuadro* had been seen in Paris—at least since the early nineteenth century when Spanish dancing had been popular there. The singing of La Minareta, the beauty of Dalbaicin, the guitar playing of El Martel and El Sevillano, and the dancing of La Rubia de Herez, La Gabrielita, of Estampielo and El Moreno—not to mention the grotesque Mateo El Sin Pies, who, having no feet, danced on leather pads fixed to the stumps of his thighs—created a sensation.

During the season at the Gaieté Lyrique I underwent the awful experience of dancing *Le Sacre du printemps* with influenza. I had a high temperature, a sore throat, a splitting headache and a blocked-up nose so that I could hardly breathe. I could not have asked the management to take off the ballet—at least not while I had a breath left in my body; for to change a programme at the last moment produced incredible complications, and if the theatre was sold out, as it was on this occasion, disappointment would be caused to a great many people. All day I prayed for help—for strength, memory and breath to get through the ballet. While I waited during the first act my fear nearly overcame me, and I was soaking wet long before the curtain went up on the second act. As I held my pose in the centre of the stage I suddenly felt a great calm come over me and I became conscious of a strange phenomenon. I felt a light growing out of my head, and spreading as it grew higher and higher towards the flies. It was so bright that I thought the audience must see it. I took no notice of the counting masses round me, and when at long last the group moved back to twenty counts and my time came to begin, I went straight through my dance as if on air, made no mistakes and performed all my big jumps and turns without any discomfort or handicap. When I fell at the end, however, I could not move. The usual men picked me up and supported me until the curtain fell for the last time. I completely lost the power of speech, and it was only on the next day my voice began to return: but I gave thanks that night that my prayers had been answered.

Towards the end of our Paris season, Massine, who had formed his own company, persuaded several of Diaghilev's dancers to join him. These had somehow to be replaced before we opened in London.

In London as in Paris we danced in an unfamiliar theatre, and one in which, if he had the power to pick and choose, Diaghilev would probably have considered unsuitable for his elaborate productions. The Princes Theatre was built over a deep well, and when all was quiet one could hear the sound of the hydraulic pump below, which started off as soon as the water rose to a certain height. In those days the theatre was infested with rats, and the chief fireman told me you could even hear them play the harp. There were not enough dressing-rooms to go around, and what there were seemed too small for us. We were packed into these, and the supers had to dress across the road, much to the amusement of the crowds who saw Oriental janissaries and Russian peasants crossing Shaftesbury Avenue. The stage, too, was smaller than we were used to, and this worried me chiefly in *Le Sacre*, which we gave during June. There was no room in the orchestra for all the extra musicians which Stravinsky's score demanded, so that some were accommodated in the stage boxes, and two grand pianos had to stand on the stage. In *Le Sacre* it was hard enough to follow the music at the best of times, but with the sound coming from right and left I had to face further difficulties. These partly visible pianos distracted from the tragic illusion of the rite. After the first performance in London of

Massine's version of *Le Sacre du printemps*, Mrs Sickert sent me a trellis gate covered with white roses, which was so large that two ushers had to carry it onto the stage. As it would not go into my dressing-room, it stood for the rest of the performance on the stairs, and when I went to collect it at the end, there were exactly two roses left. Another evening I was given a colossal bouquet inscribed from five anonymous male admirers: I met one of these men over twenty years later.

Cuadro Flamenco was warmly received by London, although the footless Mateo aroused such sympathy that he was banned from appearing after a few performances; and Cyril Beaumont* has recorded the Londoners' surprise at the Gypsies' method of acknowledging applause by shaking their breasts.

Lydia Lopokova returned to us during the season to dance *L'Oiseau de feu* and other ballets; *Chout* was fairly well received; and our public proved as devoted as ever in spite of the recent fiasco of the cancelled performance at Covent Garden. Our prospects seemed to be looking up. C. B. Cochran, our impresario, however, had to appeal to his backers to make up a deficit. Ballet on the scale and of the quality of Diaghilev's could never really pay a profit.

There was a heat-wave that summer, and the dancers seemed to get thinner daily as the weeks went by. We all looked forward to our holiday. On the last night many of the bouquets and laurel wreaths were mislaid or lost. When at last Leon and I came out of the furnace and walked down Shaftesbury Avenue, we saw a laurel wreath hanging on the cross-bar at the top of a tall lamp-post in the middle of the road. Leon said, 'I wonder whose that is', and shinned up the post like a sailor up a mast. He tore off the card attached to the wreath, waved it and slid down to the ground: it was his own wreath.

At the end of this run we had the annual ordeal of visiting Diaghilev to renew our contracts, sitting with our faces in the light while Diaghilev confronted us in the shadow. It was a difficult half-hour, but both Leon and I came out with an increase of salary.

* *The Diaghilev Ballet in London* (Putnam, 1940).

Leon and I were in the process of getting free from our former marriages and looking forward to a time when we could be together. In the meanwhile we went for our holidays to St Malo and Paramé in Brittany. We bicycled everywhere, visited the oyster-beds at Concale and went with Florrie Grenfell and a party of friends to see Mont St Michel, where we watched the tide flow swiftly in over three miles of quicksand while we were having lunch.

14

THE SLEEPING PRINCESS

Diaghilev's reasons for mounting *The Sleeping Princess* — His
problems — Rehearsals begin — Enter Patrick Kay — An
elaborate souvenir programme — Links with the original
production — First impressions of the opening scene —
First-night accidents — Varying merits of the fairy-tale
numbers — My hated role — Four Auroras compared — The
fairy-tale has an unhappy ending.

Grigoriev writes in his memoirs of the Russian Ballet* that it
was the phenomenal success of the musical show *Chu Chin Chow*,
which decided Diaghilev to mount *The Sleeping Princess* in London.
He may, indeed, have been tempted, after all his vicissitudes, by
the idea of paying off his debts and even making money in the
course of a long run: but I think that he had always had a passion
for Tchaikovsky, suppressed during the recent years of innovation and experiment, and he longed to show the English
public the full glory of Tchaikovsky's ballet masterpiece, known
to them up till then only through a few waltzes. Perhaps, too, his
provocative spirit was amused by the idea of shocking his admirers of the *avant garde*, accustomed to the décor of cubist
painters, the angular choreography of Massine and the new
sonorities of Stravinsky, with the kind of melodious and spectacular work, lasting a whole evening, which had been the general
rule in the Imperial Russian theatres until the revolution in ballet
effected by Fokine, Benois and himself. Whatever the reason for
his decision to put on *The Sleeping Princess* (the fact that the
Alhambra Theatre was to be free in the winter must have had
something to do with it), there could be no doubt that he was

* *The Diaghilev Ballet 1909–1929*, by S. L. Grigoriev (Constable, 1953).

taking an enormous risk, and that he was going to have an appalling struggle to put it on in so short a time.

Looking back, one can see how Diaghilev's mind would have
worked, and one can imagine him ticking off on his fingers the
various problems he had to face, one by one. First of all there
was Tchaikovsky's huge score, parts of which were unsatis-
factory and parts inadequately orchestrated. Some of the weak
numbers must be cut and replaced by others from *Swan Lake*
or *Casse-noisette*; and Stravinsky must be interested in the music
and persuaded to re-orchestrate one or two dances: thus might
the nineteenth-century master appear to be given the blessing of a
hero of the *avant garde*. Secondly, Diaghilev had to find someone
who could remember even some of the innumerable dances
invented by Marius Petipa, thirty years back; and as it was not
in his nature to leave well alone, one or two new dances by a
young choreographer must be inserted. Thirdly, a suitable
designer must be found for the gigantic production: Benois, his
obvious choice, was in Russia, and Bakst had not spoken to him
since he had been passed over in favour of Derain as designer for
La Boutique fantasque. Fourthly, Diaghilev must engage a ballerina
—or perhaps more than one—with the technique, style and
authority to shine in the great classical role of Aurora: no one in
his company at the time was entirely suitable. Lastly, public
opinion must be swayed in favour of this five-act academic
ballet, which might prove more novel and sensational than anything he had ever put on, simply through being so old-fashioned.

While Leon and I were enjoying our holiday in Brittany,
Diaghilev had been working hard. When we arrived back in
London for rehearsals he had everything under control. Stravinsky had done some work on the score, Maestro Sergueev
from St Petersburg had been engaged to mount the production,
Bakst was designing a rich variety of costumes, three Russian
emigrée ballerinas—famous in Russia, though unknown in
Western Europe—had been engaged to dance Aurora, and a
press controversy about the merits of Tchaikovsky's music was
in full swing.

We needed plenty of room to rehearse *The Sleeping Princess*, so we were back in the drill hall in Chenies Street. It was here we met for the first time Nicolas Sergueev, who had been *régisseur* at the Mariinsky Theatre, and who looked like a funny little Russian civil servant. We began by rehearsing the *polonaise* which opens the last act *divertissement*. From that first rehearsal until the day he died, Diaghilev was never pleased with the way we danced the *polonaise*. How often were we to have special calls simply to rehearse this spirited dance for eight couples!

Having danced in so many difficult modern ballets, we found Petipa's choreography very simple, and therefore tended to get bored with it. But as the production grew, as dull bits were cut and new dances added, and as we gradually realised the scale and splendour of the whole work, we began to feel proud to be taking part in Diaghilev's revival of this great ballet.

I was not at all well during these early rehearsals; I became giddy and often found myself falling down at the slightest provocation. A specialist told me I had strained my heart, and after what I had been through with *Le Sacre*, this did not surprise me. With treatment and no early classes I was able to carry on: but I was badly in need of classes after the holiday, and my dancing suffered. I was never very good at *pirouettes* on point, and my best were done to the left, but in the *pas d'action* of the seven fairies with their pages, the *pirouettes* we had to do, each girl in succession, ending up in a supported *attitude*, were to the right.

The cast for *The Sleeping Princess* was so enormous that even with people doubling roles, our company was too small. A number of comparatively inexperienced English dancers and supers were therefore engaged, and among these was young Patrick Kay, called Patrikeeff on the programme, who later became Anton Dolin. Pat danced in the *corps de ballet* and was also one of the King's pages. Although this did not amount to much, it was impossible at rehearsals not to notice this boy who was always dancing in a corner somewhere and who showed keenness and ability. Young as he was, I feel sure that it was during this season he made up his mind to become a real member of the Diaghilev Ballet.

An old friend of mine from the days of Stedman's Academy,

Clarisse Wynne, who was now married with three sons, had a lovely house in Addison Road, Kensington, the top floor of which she had made into a flat; and it was here I lived during the rehearsals and run of *The Sleeping Princess*.

Looking through the handsome souvenir programme of *The Sleeping Princess*, one is struck by the absurd mis-spelling of the title as 'Spleeping Princess' on the cover, due no doubt to the fact that the cover and section of colour plates illustrating the designs of Bakst were printed in Paris. One realises what pains Diaghilev had taken to 'sell' the unfamiliar classic to critics and audiences. The first name on the title page after that of Perrault, whose fairy tale inspired the ballet, is that of Bakst. The statement that 'the entire production' is 'by M. Leon Bakst' seems to imply either that the spectacular aspect of the ballet was considered all important, or that Bakst was consulted about more than just the scenery and costumes. Tchaikovsky's name, however, which follows, is accorded the largest type, while Stravinsky, who orchestrated the prelude to the third scene and Aurora's variations in Scene Three, comes a close second. Next in size and order is the name of Marius Petipa; while those of Sergueev, La Nijinska, the scene painters and makers of the costumes, wigs and shoes follow in small capitals. Bronislava Nijinska, who rejoined the company, made her début as choreographer for the Diaghilev Ballet by producing the hunting scene, the variation for Aurora in the same scene and some of the fairy tales in the *divertissement*. The programme contains a note on the life and work of Bakst, a synopsis of the story, a reminiscence by Bakst of a youthful meeting with Tchaikovsky, followed by some very obscure theorising about modern art weirdly translated, an 'open letter' to Diaghilev from Stravinsky praising the music of Tchaikovsky, Perrault's Moral in verse which served as an epilogue to the original story, a free translation of this by Sir Arthur Quiller-Couch, and a cast list comprising the names of nearly all the most illustrious dancers of the period. Sprinkled between these and the eleven colour plates, the advertisements of dance frocks at eight and a half guineas by Harvey Nichols, and inexpensive tea gowns by Marshall & Snelgrove strike a period note; while others, illustrating a lady preparing a mustard bath (by J. & J. Colman Ltd., Norwich), and of an old dear playing patience beside a gas fire (by the Gas Light & Coke Company), remind me of the cold winter during which *The Sleeping Princess* was produced, and of the icy rehearsals on the stage of the unheated Alhambra Theatre.

The five scenes were given names: The Christening, The Spell, The Vision, The Awakening and The Wedding. Scene One immediately struck a note of pageantry. Into the marble palace of King Florestan and his Queen, came the seven fairies bearing gifts for the christening of the baby Princess Aurora. Choreographically the chief beauty of this scene was the great *pas d'action* of the seven fairies and their cavaliers: and the dramatic high spot was the apparition of the wicked fairy, Carabosse, in her coach drawn by rats, and her snubbing by the Lilac Fairy-Godmother. Scene Two contained the wonderful Rose *adage* for the now grown-up Aurora and her four suitors, which culminated in the Princess pricking her finger and falling asleep while the Lilac Fairy raised a thick forest of lilac to surround her castle. By Scene Three a hundred years should by rights have passed, but Diaghilev changed this period to 'many years afterwards, perhaps even twenty' to justify Bakst's use of Louis XIV costumes in the early scenes and of Louis XV costumes in the later ones. In this third scene the melancholy Prince Charming was seen hunting in the forest where he was visited by the Lilac Fairy, who showed him a vision of Aurora and then bore him off in a magic boat towards the enchanted castle. In Scene Four, which was short, Prince Charming awoke Aurora with a kiss. Their wedding was celebrated in the final scene by characters from other fairy tales who danced in their honour; the chief classical numbers being the *pas de deux* of the Blue Bird and his princess, and the *grand adage* of Aurora and her prince.

It was extraordinary to think that our teacher, Enrico Cecchetti had created the roles both of the witch Carabosse and of the airborne Blue Bird in the original 1890 production. Now, Diaghilev, who loved to forge links with the past, engaged the elderly Carlotta Brianza, who had been the first Aurora and was at this time teaching in Paris, to perform the mimed role of Carabosse. Cecchetti, who was soon to retire, gave one performance as Carabosse during our run to celebrate his jubilee on the stage.

I well remember the day we first saw the magnificent costumes for the opening scene on the stage. The main colour scheme for the courtiers was red, but the King and Queen were in white and gold with long blue trains. Vera Sudeikina, who played the Queen, was a very attractive woman and she made a breathtaking entrance wearing a huge head-dress of ostrich feathers. Her regal carriage and superb gestures were unforgettable. The dresses of the seven fairies were mostly white with small touches of colour. I was to wear one of these and my first thought was how on earth could we possibly keep them clean.

On the first night we found that there was so little room backstage at the Alhambra for such a large cast, that the wings could not contain the crowd of dancers to go on in the opening scene, and a number of us overflowed up a dirty, stone staircase. We waited in these drab surroundings as the orchestra struck up the first bars of the majestic score, a shivering procession, but clad in the richest costumes the company had ever worn. Then our cue came and we suddenly found ourselves on a stage blazing with lights, amid the splendours of the white and golden décor, part of an unbelievable pageant. To make an entrance into that scene by Bakst was really to be transported into fairyland. When the curtain went up one could hear the audience gasp. I would have given anything to have been in front on the first night and to have witnessed the effect as one gorgeous series of costumes succeeded another. Alas, the evening which began so well was marked by disaster. The Alhambra stage was small and we filled it to capacity. The changing of scenery had presented serious problems from the start, and Diaghilev had spent long hours rehearsing lighting and other special effects. When the moment came for the forest to grow the lights dimmed with an eerie effect and such a hush descended that we could hear each other breathe. The vast wooden structure supporting the painted forest came out of the trap door at the back in one

long piece and slowly began to rise. Then came a sound of cracking timber. The forest had risen half way when one side got
caught. The machinery continued to pull one end of the set up
in the air, while the other held fast, and the forest was broken
in half. The audience gave a groan of dismay, and so did
we. How Bakst and Diaghilev must have suffered! Finally, the
machinery was put into reverse and the broken wood and canvas came down again.

The Hunting, or Vision scene, with its blue, green and brown
costumes embroidered in gold was like a tapestry come to life,
a really wonderful evocation of the eighteenth century. This was
where Vladimirov made his first appearance, a dominant figure
in red. He was not good-looking, but he made an elegant Prince
Charming and bore himself with authority. The women dancers
were graded in the traditional Russian way: there were six litle
Marchionesses, five tall Duchesses and four Baronesses about
my height—five foot two. Luba Tchernicheva was the one and
only Countess and the combination of her beauty, her grace of
movement and the splendour of her dress was stunning: her
miming was in the grand style.

The production of the Awakening Scene was as lovely and
mysterious as the music which accompanied it; lit blue and pink,
the colours of dawn. Spessivtseva as Aurora lay stretched on her
monumental bier, like an effigy in an Italian cathedral.

I liked some of the fairy tales in the last scene much more than
others. In the opening *pas de quatre* of Pierrette, Columbine, Pierrot and Harlequin, Vera Nemtchinova was revealed for the first
time as an important classical dancer, and established herself
immediately as a *première danseuse*. She had always been an accurate performer but she developed an assured technique and
style through sheer hard work. The *pas de deux* of Puss in Boots
and the White Cat was danced by Schollar and a new English
boy called Errol Addison. He had the gift of doing as many
pirouettes as he pleased, but he had ability without finesse, and his
appearance together with a rather rough manner prevented him
from reaching the foremost rank. In the Bluebird *pas de deux*,
the astounding technique of Idzikovsky combined with the

delicious lightness and charm of Lopokova, made a dazzling and exhilarating impression. Long after the run of *The Sleeping Princess* these two continued to perform their dance in our programme.

The next number was that of Red Riding Hood and the Wolf, and it fell to my lot to dance this with Mikolaichik. It was one of the few dances in my whole career which I genuinely hated. I have since discovered that when I disliked a dance intensely it was because of the music, and certainly the tituppy, irritating little tune which accompanied the steps of Red Riding Hood, tiptoeing archly through the forest, is not Tchaikovsky at his best. Everything was done to make the episode more effective, and eight little trees were even carried on to form an avenue for my entrance, but it was sometimes as much as I could do to force myself to make that entrance on my points. I disliked the wig, the costume and the whole conception of the dance, and when I looked at the Wolf's mask, I could have run a mile—not through fear of his fangs, but in annoyance at ever having become involved in the stupid dance. In fact, half-way through the run I begged Diaghilev to let me off, but he refused with the excuse that there was nobody to take my place.

The scene of Bluebeard, Ariana and Sister Anne was not very interesting either, although Tchernicheva and Doubrovska had attractive costumes. Far more striking was the entry of Scheherazade, the Shah and his brother, to the music of *danse arabe* borrowed from *Casse Noisette*. Here the beauty of the Spanish girl, Maria Dalbaicin, really came into its own. She was carried in in an exquisite white sedan chair, and although she had little to do but sway her body and make exotic gestures with her hands, she created a sensation. From that moment excitement mounted and the applause increased. Kremnev as the Mandarin, with Hilda Bewicke and Sumarokova as the two Porcelain Princesses, gave a most delicate and witty performance which had a quality all of its own.

The dance of the Three Ivans, arranged by Nijinska and led by Woizikovsky, was the kind of tumbling number in which certain Russian and Polish dancers excel. Leon's high character jumps were thrilling, and the ending, when he took a run to land smartly on top of the other two men, was unexpected, so the whole dance went with a bang. Then followed the beautiful *pas de deux* of Aurora and Prince Charming, danced on the first night by Spessivtseva and Vladimirov, which seemed the quintessence of classical dancing. After this the centre of the stage remained empty for a moment, but with the King and Queen on their thrones, the pages, and the huge Negro guards with their pikes and feathered turbans, there must still have been a dozen or more people grouped on either side. Suddenly all the rest of the company, the dancers of the fairy tales, the male and female courtiers, and eventually the Prince and Princess, came shooting from the wings to wheel and wheel around the stage in a splendid Mazurka. When all forty dancers were spinning, and when there was no more room for another couple or for another flashing costume on the stage, the evening came to an end with the whole court sinking to the ground in a solemn *révérence*.

Olga Spessivtseva, our first Aurora, had the same dark hair, huge dark expressive eyes, delicate bone structure and bird-like lightness of movement as Pavlova, but she was taller, more beautiful and equipped with a better technique. Spessivtseva had very long arms and supple legs, with none of the over-developed muscles which deform so many good dancers. She performed such exquisitely gentle *ronds de jambe* as I have never seen since. The special quality of her dancing was flow: in this she differed entirely from Pavlova. If she had a fault it was lack of an innate musical sense, but all in all she was one of the most perfect of dancers.

Later in the season Aurora was danced by Vera Trefilova, a much older woman. She had retired from the Imperial Ballet with a very great reputation on her marriage, and since her husband died, had been working in Paris. Now, in her middle forties, she was persuaded by Diaghilev to return to the ballet in a role for which she had been famous. It was a wonderful opportunity for us to see Trefilova dance, as she seemed to embody all the highest traditions of the old Russian ballet. She was the daintiest little creature, though with very strong legs and feet; and she had a noble turn of the head such as I have never seen in any other dancer. Both she and Spessivtseva had such extra-ordinary qualities that it was hard to choose between them. Though Spessivtseva was the more beautiful of the two, I felt her movement would have been more ideally suited to a romantic masterpiece like *Giselle*. Trefilova, with her classical style and with the Olympian sureness of her stagecraft, was utterly suited to Petipa's choreography and I think she was my choice of the two Auroras.

Another Aurora was Lubov Egorova, who on the first night danced the Fairy of the Song-birds. I remember her in this, dressed in canary yellow with a long feather in her head-dress, running about the stage on her points faster than I could believe possible, fluttering her hands. Nobody did this variation nearly as well. When she danced Aurora she displayed an amazing assurance and was very strong. She was always unusually calm and controlled, showing neither exhaustion, fluster nor nerves. Egorova had not the glamour or suppleness of Spessivtseva nor the miniature charm of Trefilova, but I never had any fear that she might fail to bring off a step or give a satisfying performance. She had one strange characteristic: she was never at any time right on the very tip of her toes. We used to wonder how she could do such difficult steps just off the point. I was intrigued by this, and as I have always been fascinated by the different ways dancers 'fiddle' their ballet shoes, I took the chance of examining a pair of Egorova's shoes which she put down in the wings. Most of us had Italian shoes with rather square *papier-mâché* toecaps, but I think Egorova's were French. At any rate, I found she strengthened them with cork heel-lifts stuck in back to front with the thick end towards the toe, but with quite a gap left at the very end into which she would insert her toes. How her toes were not pinched I cannot imagine. I was impressed by the lightness of these shoes lined with cork, and tried to imitate her method of fixing the shoe, but without success.

Lydia Lopokova also danced Aurora, and although the technical problems of the role did not defeat her, she seemed to lack the necessary poetry. I felt that at any moment her nose would begin to quiver and she would burst out laughing or lose her drawers. She was delightful as the Lilac Fairy, a part which suited her style.

The theatre was filled to capacity for the first few weeks; but after this, in spite of the frequent changes of cast with which Diaghilev sought to interest his regular public, and although *The Sleeping Princess* was probably the most perfect and star-studded production of the century, receipts began to fall off. I have always been convinced that *The Sleeping Princess* was put on a few weeks too soon. If it could have been given at Christmas, instead of in November, and advertised as a 'Ballet Pantomime', it might have attracted a wider and less sophisticated public and enjoyed a longer run. It was suggested that Diaghilev might alternate some of the modern ballets in his repertoire with performances of the long classical ballet, but he was probably afraid that in the case of failure, Sir Oswald Stoll might seize the scenery and dresses of these works as well as those of *The Sleeping Princess*, and thus prevent his company from earning a livelihood elsewhere. Diaghilev had, of course, spent twice the sum Stoll had allowed him for the production: he and the English impresario were therefore not on the best of terms. Our run came to an end after one hundred-and-five performances. Stoll took possession of King Florestan's palace and gardens and the countless costumes of silk and velvet, heavy with golden embroidery; and we were given a month's leave with several weeks' salary still owing to us.

Nowadays the great work of Tchaikovsky and Petipa is given frequently at Covent Garden, as well as a number of other full-length ballets. Diaghilev's *Sleeping Princess* certainly began something in England: but since that February night when we closed at the Alhambra, so perfect a production on such a scale has never been seen, nor have so many incomparable artists of the dance appeared together on one stage.

15

DEPARTURE AND RETURN

The house at Hastings — Dunning Diaghilev — A change
of sides — In music-hall with Massine — Out of work —
Anello the shoemaker — Legal action — Return to Diaghilev
— Monte Carlo the new base — Changes in the company —
La Nijinska — *Les Noces* — Paris — The Fête at Versailles —
A holiday in the sun.

Father had been making quite an income from commissions on
the sale of property and, as Bournemouth was considered not to
be good for Mother's asthma and heart trouble, they moved in
1921 to Hastings, and bought a house in Pelham Crescent on the
sea front. The houses were five storeys high and some of them had
the old castle walls for their foundations. I was always afraid to
go into the forbidding cave-like cellars which ran under the road,
and one of the huge flagstones in the basement passage was loose,
which gave Mother the idea that it had been used by smugglers.
My father declared the house was haunted and that he used to
see a maid in cap and apron standing at the bottom of the staircase when he went up to bed. She would wish him, 'Good
night, sir', and he returned the greeting quite naturally.

Right in the centre of the Crescent there was a church which
fascinated Natasha. She was four at the time, and I used to watch
her from the window on Sunday morning wheeling her pram full
of dolls, which sometimes contained a kitten in a bonnet, to the
door of the church. She would wait until all the congregation
had gone in, then push her pram through the door, only to be
escorted out by a verger half a minute later. She never failed to
try this every Sunday, but she never mentioned to us her per-

196

sistent attempts to take the dolls to church. Years later it occurred
to me to go into the church to find out what could have intrigued
her, and I found a natural spring bubbling out of rocks just
inside the entrance.

Mother had found some boys throwing stones at a large sea
bird limping along the beach, covered in oil. She carried this
quite heavy creature home, and spent hours with Beatrice cleaning
the oil off its wings. It was called 'Jimmy the Squirt' because of
its messy habits. Fed on live fish, it became quite tame and waddled
in and out of the house whenever it was called. A fisherman told
us that Jimmy was a diver and it was rare for these birds to live
for long away from salt water. As Jimmy could not be house-
trained, after five months we allowed the fisherman to row him
out to sea and let him go.

There were thirteen rooms in the big Pelham Crescent house,
and Mother let the first floor to a religious sect, who turned what
should have been the drawing-room into a private place of
worship. This arrangement naturally helped the family budget.
I contributed towards Natasha's board and lodging, but when
The Sleeping Princess closed and Leon and I were out of work
with salaries owing to us, I could no longer provide any money
towards the running of the house. This was all the more serious
as Natasha was just beginning to go to school.

Leon and I decided to chase Diaghilev to Paris and try to get
some money from him. The day we arrived in Paris Leon telephoned his hotel. Diaghilev answered himself, which was very
unusual, but on Leon's asking for an interview he said 'Diaghilev
is not here,' and put the receiver down.

Next morning we went round to the hotel, rang up Diaghilev's
room and asked if we could talk to him. We were told to wait,
as he would soon be down. We sat for what seemed like ages in
the entrance-hall, then suddenly caught a glimpse of his back-
view disappearing out of the front door, which he had reached
from the lift by passing behind the chairs where we were sitting.
After a few days of this skirmishing, we managed to see him
and he finally gave us a little money. He was very undecided
about the future, and told us that he was handing over all his

responsibilities to his friend Nouvel, and that it was to him that we must look for further settlements. We knew quite well that Nouvel, like the rest of the *entourage*, was entirely dependent on Diaghilev, and we had no intention of considering him as our director.

Massine, meanwhile, had signed a contract for a London appearance, and was assembling a small company. I was reluctant to leave Diaghilev and sign up with Massine, but I had to make some money, and as it seemed possible that the Russian Ballet might never get going again, Leon persuaded me.

With Lydia Lopokova, Savina, Slavinsky, Woizikovsky, myself and a few others, Massine had a chance to do something really good, but the programme he arranged was a disaster. I believe there was an idea of turning the Royal Opera House into a dance hall, and the show we were in was scratched together with the intention of somehow preventing this. It was called *You'd Be Surprised.* We were at Covent Garden for a month, playing two performances a day to half-empty houses. The first part of the programme was taken by a film, shown on an enormous screen; the second part was us. Massine's ballet was so poor I can hardly remember anything about it. I know I was dressed in all-over brown tights with a black wig, had an African make-up and did a war dance. Leon and I were paid twenty-five pounds a week each, but we had never thought when we left Diaghilev that we should be letting ourselves in for a show of this kind. The 'Old Man' was rightly angry with us, but, after all, he had not been straightforward.

After Covent Garden the Massine troupe appeared in a *divertissement* on the bill of the Coliseum. This was almost as bad, and worse paid. There were various solos and *pas de deux*, and there was one frightful dance done by five girls, with Savina in the centre, to the waltz from *Faust*; this we danced in three-quarter-length ballet skirts with wands. I did a Chinese number entirely on points—quite an endurance test on that enormous stage. Massine, Vera, Leon and I had an arrangement that we would share certain expenses, but when Leon and I found that we were sharing rather more than we bargained for, and as we could hardly make both ends meet on the salaries we were getting, we split up the company at the end of the Coliseum engagement.

Massine had plenty of money of his own and went abroad. The rest of us were helped out by a Russian friend married to an Englishman, the clever and charming Vera Bowen. She arranged a little ballet for us to Mozart's *Eine Kleine Nachtmusik*, in which Lydia danced the chief part with Leon, and in which Slavinsky was very good. This went on at the Coliseum, and kept us going for six weeks.

We were living in a furnished room in a gloomy place called Richmond Buildings off Frith Street. It was clean and central, but we were often at a loss for a square meal. We did the round of the agents, and both Michael Mitchell and Eric Wollheim did their best to help us.

Leon's dancing boots were badly in need of repair, and he found an Italian named Anello living in a tiny house where the stage door of the Saville Theatre is today. Anello was working on a machine in the back room, mending shoes, while his baby son played on the floor amid the scraps of leather. He undertook to patch Leon's boots, and did them beautifully. After this I went to see him often, talked to him about ballet shoes and took a pair of my Niccolini ones to show him how they were made in Milan. He pulled some old shoes of mine to pieces, and seemed to understand their principle very well, but he said that being a poor man, there was no way he could possibly set about making them. Years later when we came to the Lyceum and the boots of the entire company were in bad condition, Leon suggested to Grigoriev that he should give some to Anello to mend. He was so successful with them that he was given the boots and shoes of all the ballets. Soon after this he started his first shoe shop in New Compton Street, a few doors from where the Anello shop is today. The Anello family were among the nicest people I knew; they were always grateful to Leon for giving them a start with the Diaghilev Ballet, and they often made me presents of my character dancing shoes. Diaghilev was quite fond of Anello; and the little boy is now the head of the biggest theatrical shoemakers in London.

o   199

We were so hard-pressed for money that we went to a lawyer to try to recover what Diaghilev owed us. The lawyer corresponded with another in Paris, and in due course an injunction was granted. Our measures seemed drastic, but once the affair was in the hands of French lawyers it was impossible to stop the proceedings. The Diaghilev Ballet had had short seasons in Monte Carlo and at the Paris Opéra, and in June they were to open at another Paris theatre, the Mogador. Before the curtain went up on the first night of the Mogador season, Diaghilev was presented with a legal document demanding payment of his debt. He must have been angry beyond words, but a sum of money was paid down, and an agreement was made that the rest would follow. We were very sorry about the whole thing, particularly as, by the time the lawyers had taken their fees, there was very little left for Leon and myself.

When Diaghilev had been in Spain the year before, rounding up the *cuadro flamenco*, and had met Charles Cochran in Seville, the English showman had been looking for an exceptional girl dancer to bring to London. The girl he found was named Trini and he announced her as 'The most beautiful girl in the world.' She was to take part in a new musical comedy at the London Pavilion called *Phi-Phi*, and Cochran engaged Leon Woizikovsky to partner her.

Evelyn Laye and Jay Laurier were the stars of *Phi-Phi*; another member of the cast was June, whom I had taught to dance when she was a girl. She was a natural dancer and could execute three or four *pirouettes* on her points without hesitation; I was delighted to find that she had grown into an attractive woman and a graceful dancer. The action of the play took place in ancient Rome, and there was a bathing scene for the comics. I arranged a swimming number for Leon in this, and he also danced a 'Greek' *pas de deux* with Trini, who was not a great success. Cochran paid Leon a very good salary for *Phi-Phi*, and we were at last able to take a furnished flat in Kensington. We further increased our income by giving lessons.

Towards the end of the run of *Phi-Phi*, which had lasted several months, Leon and I received letters from Monte Carlo asking us if we would like to return to the Diaghilev Ballet. I was over-joyed, as I was tired of not dancing and I had not really been happy since we left Diaghilev. We exchanged letters with Gri-goriev, arranging that the money owing to us should be paid, and clarifying our future position in the company.

Grigoriev came to London and we signed our new contracts. Both our salaries were raised. From April 1923 to August 1924, I was to receive 3,500 francs monthly in France. When I signed another contract the following year, I got 4,000 francs monthly or £100 in England; for the year after that, 4,500 francs or £134 12s. in England. Leon received about £200 monthly in England.

We returned with Grigoriev and Slavinsky to Monte Carlo, arriving on my twenty-seventh birthday, April 4, 1923. I was very happy to be back with the company, which meant even more to me than it did to Leon. I had been with it since before the war, so that it had become to me like a home and a whole way of life.

The only new works which Diaghilev had produced during my years of absence were a short opera, *Mavra*, with libretto by Boris Kochno and music by Stravinsky, and *Renard*, another vocal work by the same composer, which was interpreted by four dancers on the stage while the singers were banished to the orchestra-pit. He had also staged *Le Mariage d'Aurore*, which was more or less the *divertissement* from the last act of *The Sleeping Princess* done in the old scenery and dresses of *Le Pavillon d'Armide*. This display of classical dancing, with which Diaghilev had celebrated the centenary of Petipa's birth, proved immediately popular, and it remained in our repertoire until the end. By far the most important artistic event of the year, however, had been Bronislava Nijinska's emergence as a choreographer. Diaghilev had been very pleased with her work for *Renard*.

I was told that the company had been rescued from imminent extinction after *The Sleeping Princess* by the dressmaker Chanel, who had raised some backing. Shortly after this, something happened which was at last to provide Diaghilev with a measure of the security he needed for his troupe of wanderers. The Prince of Monaco had died and been succeeded by his son, Louis II.

The Heiress Apparent of Prince Louis was his daughter Charlotte, who was married to Prince Pierre de Polignac. Prince
Pierre was the nephew of Diaghilev's great friend, Princess
Edmond de Polignac, the American-born heiress of the Singer
sewing-machine fortune. She was well known as a patron of
musicians, and it was in her drawing-room that Stravinsky's
music for *Renard* had first been heard. Diaghilev had the brilliant
idea of installing his company permanently at Monte Carlo,
and his project met with success. From then until his death,
Diaghilev's Ballet spent six months of every year in the principality, thus having ample leisure to prepare new works, and, with
two months being reckoned for holidays, only four more to be
filled by outside contracts. We were to have a home at last; and
dancers who had been obliged to leave their possessions scattered
in hotels throughout Europe—many since 1913—were at last able
to settle down in flats or lodgings which were semi-permanent.

So in the security of our new-found base, a new era in the
history of the Diaghilev Ballet—the Nijinska era—had begun.
The company had taken on a new look, and was full of activity.
Walter Nouvel was running the administration in rather a feeble
way; and Boris Kochno was installed as principal idea-man and
Diaghilev's lieutenant—he seemed to have a finger in most pies.
Stravinsky was putting the finishing touches to his latest ballet.
Diaghilev's *entourage* had been joined by his cousin, Koribut-
Kobutovitch, a gentle, bearded, elderly man who did odd jobs
and became a dear friend to most of the company: he was so
very unlike Diaghilev that it was quite difficult to believe they
were related.

Some of the dancers had been dismissed or left the company.
(My friend Hilda Bewicke was married to a Persian prince.)
There were five new boys, who had been pupils of Nijinska in
Russia, Lapitsky, Unger, the two Hoyer brothers and Lifar, none
of whom were as yet very accomplished dancers. Serge Lifar
was a gay, dark boy with a real Russian snub nose, which he
later improved upon. We called him our Gypsy.

Bronislava Nijinska, known as Bronia, was very like her
brother Vaslav Nijinsky. She was blonde and wore her straight

hair screwed into a tight little roll. She had pale eyes and pouting lips, wore no make-up at all and had not shaved off her eyebrows as most of us had in those days. In appearance she was a most unfeminine woman, though there was nothing particularly masculine about her character. Thin but immensely strong, she had iron muscles in her arms and legs, and her highly developed calf muscles resembled Vaslav's; she had the same way of jumping and pausing in the air. Bronia was obstinate and once she had made up her mind nothing in the world would move her. She was brilliantly clever and inventive. No music seemed to present any difficulties for her, but her style of movement was even more pronounced and idiosyncratic than that of Massine, and she was not an easy person to work for in class or at rehearsal, because of her extreme mannerisms. If you excelled in interpreting her strange movements you got on very well, but a number of us, including myself, did not take to them easily. Her system of training seemed to depend more on improvisation than on traditional methods of technique, so that it struck one as lacking in foundation: but to watch her devise a sequence of steps and movements for one of her ballets was most interesting. I liked her, in spite of her moodiness and lack of humour. Nijinska had always been slightly deaf and she had a disconcerting habit of discussing the merits of one dancer with another during rehearsal, often within hearing of the person concerned.

We began working under Nijinska on the new production of *Les Noces*, one of the finest ballets Diaghilev ever presented. The music for this work—on which Stravinsky had been working since 1914—thrilled me, and to hear it played even today sends shivers down my spine. Strings and woodwind had been banished from the score, which was written for four pianos and percussion, and for four solo voices and chorus. The inspiration for the chiming, rhythmical music at the close of the ballet had come from church bells. Stravinsky's idea was to present a Russian peasant wedding with its primitive pathos and awkward solemnity; and Gontcharova has described how it was first intended to clothe these North Russian peasants from the Land of the Midnight Sun in the brilliant colours of folk art, such as she and

Larionov had used in *Coq d'or*, *Soleil de nuit* and *Chout*. Other commissions for the composer had prevented him from completing the ballet, and Diaghilev had not until now called upon him for the finished score; but Gontcharova had kept the theme continually in mind for seven years. She had made several versions of the designs since the composer had first told her of his idea before the war, without discussing it further with him. By the time it came to being produced *Les Noces* had been stripped of all local colour: it was elemental and austere.

There is a saying that 'Russians love their misery'. This was not a gay or happy wedding: on the contrary, there was much wailing and weeping, with a prevalent mood of tragedy. There were three tableaux: the Blessing of the Bride and Bridegroom, the Departure of the Bride for her Husband's Home and the Wedding Feast. *Les Noces* was difficult to dance. The women moved about mostly in *pas de bourrée*—that is to say on point, but rising and falling on and off the toes at high speed—forming into straight lines facing the audience, then packing themselves into strange congested groups. The men's formations were more semi-circular. The Bride had three-yard-long plaits attached to either side of her head, and there was a lovely but simple dance in which six girls braided these, moving backwards and forwards, never letting go. In the first two episodes mothers wept and fathers blessed, and these parents were almost more important than the bridal couple. At the end of the simple feast, when the time came for the Bride and Groom to start their married life together, they turned their backs to the audience and walked hand in hand through a doorway cut in the plain backcloth, beyond which could be seen a small bed piled high with pillows. Then a coloured curtain came down inside the doorway.

During our rehearsals Diaghilev went to Paris, where the ballet was to have its first performance, to see Gontcharova; and the story of how the designs for *Les Noces* were finally agreed upon, must be told by that devoted artist in her own words.

'Getting out of the car, Diaghilev told me that the music for *Les Noces* was finished . . . and that he was going to present the ballet that season. . . . He told me that four pianos would have to

be placed on the stage with the singers. This was rather sudden. . . .
I replied, "Very well." We stayed silent for a few moments in the
auditorium, then Diaghilev went up onto the dimly lit stage and
I followed him. We began to pace out measurements, and it
seemed to me that Diaghilev wanted to deceive himself about
them, wishing to find them greater than they were. A quiet talk
followed in the auditorium. I explained my new ideas for the set
and dresses: uniform costume for the women and another for
the men, both in brown and white. The décor was to consist of
three simple curtains. . . . All the explanations I gave Diaghilev
then were the result of years of work and thought. The lack of
precise instructions had been of great value, allowing me complete freedom . . . and I was ready to defend my ideas. So it was
rather to my astonishment that Diaghilev raised no objection.
He told me that the work was to be carried out as quickly as
possible. . . . This extraordinary man was able to foresee the
final result, the synthesis of all our efforts, and to create the ideal
atmosphere of bringing it about, without imposing his own views
in any way. The creation of other ballets was different . . . but
my own work for *Les Noces* had been completed without any
argument.'*

If it had not been for the difficulties presented by its production
—grand pianos, chorus and so on—I do not think *Les Noces*
would ever have left our repertoire. In Paris it was finally decided
to use two double grand pianos in the orchestra pit, but when
the ballet was given in London in 1926, three years later, they
were placed on the stage. This necessitated a deputy conductor
trying to guide the pianists, while he watched the orchestra
conductor through a hole in the set. The crashes of bells at the
end of the ballet made me think of all the churches in Moscow
ringing out their Easter chimes; and nothing has ever given
me more the feeling of what old Russia was like than listening to
Stravinsky's music for *Les Noces*.

During this season at Monte Carlo Diaghilev sometimes used
to bring friends or distinguished visitors to watch our rehearsals.
One day Princess Charlotte and Prince Pierre of Monaco came

* From an article in *Ballet*, Vol. 8, No. 3, translated by Richard Buckle.

to see us. She was small, dark and pretty; he was very tall with fair straight hair and immaculately dressed. They were given two high-backed red and gold arm-chairs, which were placed immediately in front of the door by which we reached our dressing-rooms and the lavatories. Although we appreciated the honour of having a visit from our princely patrons, we also found it most inconvenient not to be able to disappear or tidy up in between our classes and rehearsals.

When we arrived in Paris in July for the final rehearsals of *Les Noces*, I was suffering with internal trouble and my pains were so bad that I had constantly to lie down with ice-packs on my stomach, and I was taken out of the cast of the new ballet. We were back at the Gaieté Lyrique, where classes were held in a long, bleak room at the top of the building, with a bar down one side.

Les Noces was a great success with the public, and the Paris season went as well as ever.

Before we dispersed for the holidays, the Diaghilev Ballet gave what was perhaps its most remarkable performance. A fund had been established for the restoration of the Château de Versailles, and for this Diaghilev undertook to stage a gala performance in the Galerie des Glaces.

We spent three days at Versailles in brilliant sunshine, preparing for the spectacle. A stage was constructed at one end of the great hall, with a wide flight of stairs built up to form a background, down which we were to make our entrances. Needless to say there were hidden steps behind this setting, up which we had to climb to go over the top. It was an effective idea. Carpenters hammered away, great arc lights were installed near the ceiling, and I could never understand how no damage was done to the tall mirrors, the marble walls, gilded cornices or painted ceilings.

The women had for their dressing-room the bedroom of Louis XIV, and it was a strange experience to put on one's make-up, seated at a trestle table in this historic room, with the King's wig and death mask displayed on the wall in front of one.

People came from all over Europe, and even from America,

to see the gala. Tickets were 500 francs each, and supper was a great deal extra. The large audience was as splendid a sight as we were in our stage costumes, and we thoroughly enjoyed dancing that night.

The climax of the show was the entrance of a male singer, who sang *Le Roi Soleil* and whose costume was copied from the engraving of the King. He wore pale blue, with a shimmering gold sun embroidered on his front. His train was blue, covered with *fleurs-de-lys* and edged with imitation ermine: it spread out to the full width of the stage, and was carried up the steps at the back by little black pages. When this representation of the great King appeared in his rich costume with wig and feathers at the top of the staircase somewhere near the ceiling, and began slowly to walk down the steps to music, with his train, which seemed to grow wider and wider, unfolding behind him, one could sense a stir in the audience. We danced *Le Mariage d'Aurore*, with a few extra dances, and it was not easy to make our strutting entrance, which preceded the Polonaise, down that staircase.

After the show the guests went to supper in the Salle des Batailles; hundreds of people sat down at tables spread with fine linen and silver, to a meal which had been brought ready cooked from Paris and kept hot in the Palace kitchens. We dancers stayed behind to watch from the windows the floodlit fountains playing on the terraces. This was a rare and wonderful sight, but when fireworks began to rise up from among the shining cascades, flowering in the sky above the perspective of trees, water and stone, I knew it was something I could expect to see only once in a lifetime. Departing guests found the cobbled courtyard lit by flaring torches. Looking proud and immaculate, Diaghilev was in his element that evening.

For our holidays, Leon and I decided to go to a little fishing village called St Maxime, a few kilometres from St Raphael in the South of France. Nobody went south during the summer in those days, and we were told we were mad and that we should get sunstroke. From St Raphael we set off in a dirty local train which went round l'Estorel to Hyères and Toulon twice a day. Passing through forests, we arrived at St Maxime and were delighted to find that it was just the quiet, unspoiled place we had been hoping for. Down on the beach we found a small hotel to suit us—a long, narrow café-restaurant, at one end of which a wooden outside staircase led up to a balcony where six rooms looked out to the sea.

We had not had a holiday for two years, and this was to be our honeymoon. For eighteen francs a day we got a room and all our meals. There was nothing between us and the blue Mediterranean but a stretch of fine, silvery sand. The village had only one street, very few shops, and a typical little fisherman's church in which you could find someone praying at any hour of the day.

Every morning we would just put on our bathing things and run down the wooden steps onto the beach. We made friends with fishermen, and Leon would go out with them at night, lighting flares and catching fish in nets. Our friends sometimes took us in a little motor-boat to St Tropez; or we would bicycle to various villages inland. We discovered an old place with a castle on a hill, where they used to make the Dunhill pipes: here you could buy a thirty-five shilling pipe for the equivalent of five shillings. On Saturday nights the local people had a dance at the *café-concert*, and I was fascinated by the shuffling sound their feet made as they danced the one-step on the concrete terrace under the stars.

16

THE NIJINSKA PERIOD

Ninette de Valois and the ghost — Secrets of Monte Carlo —
Leon's mother — Dolin joins the company — *Les Tentations
de la bergère* — The charm of *Les Biches* — Leon's illness and
secret hoard — Vera Trefilova — *Les Fâcheux* — Diaghilev
detects dope — Dancing *Les Sylphides* and *Le Tricorne* in
Barcelona — Dressed by Chanel for *Le Train bleu* — Diaghilev
makes good a loss — Dolin for the high-jump — Lifar the
new favourite — Exit Nijinska — A New Year's Party of the
'twenties.

At the end of our holiday, which was the happiest I had ever
spent, Leon and I went along the coast to Monte Carlo to find
somewhere to live during the coming season. We took a large
flat in a villa called La Favorita for six months.

Before settling down for the winter, however, the company
rehearsed for a month in Paris, paid a brief visit to Switzerland,
dancing at the Fête des Narcisses at Montreux, then went on to
Antwerp. From Antwerp, Leon travelled to the Polish frontier
to fetch his mother, who was coming to stay with us, and I
returned to Monte Carlo with the company.

Ninette de Valois, a young Anglo-Irish girl, whom I had met at
Cecchetti classes in London, and whom I had pressed Diaghilev
to engage, now joined the company. Ninette was an excellent
dancer with a sure, incisive style and a quality all her own. She
was later to shine particularly in the 'finger variation' of *Le
Mariage d'Aurore* and as a nymph in *Narcisse*.

Ninette arrived as a stranger to Monte Carlo, and I put her
up for the first two nights at La Favorita until she could find
herself a lodging. We were both tired after our journey and went

209

to bed early, but we were not destined to have a good night's rest.

I had planned to give the best of our three bedrooms, which had its own bathroom, to my mother-in-law, but on that first night I slept in that room and gave Ninette mine. During the early part of the night I heard Ninette calling out frequently in her sleep, but I took no notice: it was only when she began shouting to somebody to, 'Go away and leave me alone', that I got up to investigate. She was certain she had seen someone in her room. Next day she found a place to live and moved out. I took possession of her room, and soon discovered it to be unpleasantly haunted. Leon arrived with his mother, a little round breathless woman, and we were soon joined by my sister Beatrice and Natasha, whom I was delighted to be able to send for from England. They had picked up, on their way through Paris, my new dog, an Alsatian called Dick. He and I were in complete agreement over the haunting. I used to find him outside the dining-room door with his hair standing on end, teeth bared, growling in terror; he hated going along that passage in the dark. As for me, I was continually woken up by the shakings of my bed and by loud bangs on the headboard. I was so strongly aware of a presence at the side of the bed, that night after night I would sleep in a chair. Sometimes when I was sitting in the bath, I would see the door handle turning on its own and then the light would go out. Even Natasha would call out at night, 'There's somebody in my room!' Natasha and I have often found such manifestations troublesome; one of the peculiarities we inherited from Father.

I later discovered that La Favorita had once been a low-class hotel and that a woman had been murdered there by her husband as she slept with her lover, and the lover had been stabbed in the corridor.

Monte Carlo was a very different place now from what it had been when I first went there in 1913, and it attracted a larger, less exclusive public.

Gamblers at the Casino frequently committed suicide. When they did so in the gardens outside the Casino, or on the lower road, a little black cross was painted on the ground where they fell. I remember one man shooting himself in the subterranean passage which led from the Casino to the Hôtel de Paris. If anybody shot himself at the tables, two commissionaires would immediately rush in and, supporting the suicide under each arm, walk him out of the nearest swing door as though he were ill. There was a door between the stage door of the Casino and that of our rehearsal room, which led to the seldom-used Salle Ganne. Sometimes a carriage would be waiting outside it, and a man would be brought out looking deathly white with his head bandaged, helped into the carriage and driven away. I realised that these unfortunate men were attempted suicides, but it was some time before I realised that they had come from a surgery inside the Casino itself. When Vera Savina, who returned to the company during the winter of 1924, cut her hand on her partner's jewelled tunic during a performance of the Bluebird *pas de deux*, I undertook to go with her to the hospital. I thought we should be taken some way out of town, but not at all: we were conducted just as we were in our costumes through some passages and up in a lift to the very top of the Casino. Passing through some glass doors, we found ourselves in the most luxurious and up-to-date operating theatre, which was held permanently in a state of readiness to patch up the unlucky and despairing gamblers.

Since the day before the war when Chaliapin had lost his whole season's salary at the tables, nobody appearing at the theatre was allowed an entrance ticket to the Casino, but this did not deter Leon who, like most Poles, was an inveterate gambler. He talked his way into the kitchen, and thence he soon penetrated to the Salons Privés. At *chemin de fer* he would stake sometimes more than our combined monthly salaries. There was no way of curbing Leon's passion for play, which was as much a part of his life as breathing. What with his gaming losses and my cook taking her usual percentage on the marketing, I found it increasingly difficult to run our household.

We were a comic lot at La Favorita. Leon and I spoke Russian to each other. His mother spoke to him in Polish, which I could understand but not speak. My sister and Natasha naturally knew neither Russian nor Polish. The cook, being Monegasque, spoke a mixture of Italian and French. Confusion reigned in the kitchen and our dinner table sounded like the League of Nations.

We were all amazed at the amount of food Leon's mother could put away, and between meals she used to eat cake and biscuits. She must have been a pretty woman once, in a Gypsy way, but now she was quite shapeless. She suffered from frequent migraines, which I had no doubt were due to overeating, and could often be found lying fully clothed on her bed, with slices of lemon on her forehead held in place by a large white hand-kerchief. When it became hot towards the end of her stay, she used to spend the evenings on the Fromage in front of the Casino, seated on a bench, wearing her carpet slippers.

In spite of the ghosts, the gambling, and Leon's mother, I enjoyed the winter of 1923–24 and the new experience of having my daughter with me for six whole months. Natasha was now six, and she attended her first fancy-dress dance in the Salle Ganne, wearing a traditional Russian dress and head-dress of pearls, with bunches of satin ribbons hanging down her back.

In Ninette we already had one Anglo-Irish dancer in the company: now we were to have another. Patrick Kay, who had danced under the name of Patrikeeff in *The Sleeping Princess*, was a pupil of Astafieva, and she had convinced Diaghilev that Pat's talents were exceptional. Diaghilev had evidently been impressed, and Pat joined the company as a potential soloist, without having had to work his way up through the *corps de ballet*. He was renamed Anton Dolin.

In his youthful enthusiasm, Pat never thought that Nijinska or the company might resent his position as a kind of outsider-soloist under the special patronage of Diaghilev. Many of the company had been working hard for years to get where they were, and it was difficult for them to watch this very green young man throwing his weight about. Whether it was because he was English or not, I know that at first I myself bore Pat a few hard feelings. One day I was practising behind the curtain in the rehearsal room, when he came up, grabbed the *barre* and said, 'Hello, Hilda. Can I join in?' I stopped my work and said, 'No, you can't. In ten days' time, when you have found your feet and calmed down a bit, come and ask me differently.' Poor Pat! He murmured, 'Sorry, I'm off.' Exactly ten days later he came up to me quietly and said, 'How right you were. I was behaving abominably and I realise it now. Why didn't you tell me?' I told him that he wouldn't have understood at the time, and that only experience could show him that it was not easy to walk into an established Russian company, and that he must exercise a good deal of tact if he wanted to make himself liked by the other dancers. He thanked me and we soon became good friends. Pat had an independent nature, and knowing Diaghilev's insistence on complete obedience both on and off stage, we thought it would be a miracle if they worked together in harmony for long. As it turned out, Diaghilev never broke Pat's spirit, although he tried.

Nijinska must have been doubtful of Dolin at the start, but he won her over. She gave him private lessons, and he worked hard, so that within a few months he turned into a real artist. Grigoriev was ordered to resurrect *Daphnis et Chloë*, with Pat and myself in the principal parts. It was some years since this ballet had been done, and as nobody could remember the *pas de deux* of the two lovers Nijinska arranged a new one. Grigoriev has written that he did not think me suited for the role, but Ninette de Valois put on record that one thing which stood out in her mind when she recalled that season, was the beauty of my performance in *Daphnis*. It was ten years since I had found myself whispering in English to my partner during a performance, and it somehow brought me down to earth. I was thrilled to be dancing the chief part in *Daphnis et Chloë*, however, because it was in this work that Fokine had given me my first little solo soon after I joined the company. Some of the costumes had been lost, so Juan Gris designed for Pat a simple white tunic with a black border, which showed up his fine figure and good looks. I wore one of the dresses from *L'Après-midi d'un faune*—the one with a red pattern; and I copied my style of hairdressing from a classical statue which stood in a niche half way up the steps leading from the Place de la Gare to the terrace and rehearsal rooms.

This was to be one of the richest and busiest seasons in the history of the Diaghilev Ballet, for not only were we enlarging our repertoire by reviving *Daphnis et Chloë*, *Narcisse* and *Le Lac des cygnes*, we were putting on three new ballets, *Les Tentaions de la bergère*, *Les Biches* and *Les Fâcheux*, besides giving the last act of *Les Astuzie Femminili*, without the singing, under the name of *Cimarosiana*. Diaghilev also produced three short operas by Gounod and Chabrier's *Colombe* in the course of this season, which ended on January 30, 1924.

After the season the dancers were to remain on in Monte Carlo, dancing as required in performances given by the resident opera company. Diaghilev's great aim at this time was to turn Monte Carlo into a centre of all the arts, and he planned a series of imaginative picture exhibitions, as well as other attractions. But although he succeeded that winter of 1923–24 in attracting crowds of clever or creative people to the principality, most of his great schemes were thwarted by the unimaginative Casino authorities and by M. Guinsbourg, the director of their opera company, who prevented him from mounting any operas of his own in the following year.

It may have been our glorious fête at Versailles which inspired Diaghilev to put on *Les Tentations de la bergère*. The ballet was arranged by Nijinska to a score by the seventeenth-century composer Montéclair, which Diaghilev had recently discovered. The music was pretty without being striking, and although the ballet was full of charm at rehearsal, as soon as it was dressed it seemed to lose half its gaiety. Nothing could have been more unlike his usual cubist paintings than the setting which Juan Gris designed. The stylised décor, representing the garden front of a Louis XIV *château*, with its subdued blues and greys, was in the best of taste, but it might have been the work of any professional stage designer for the last act of a revue. The costumes were heavy in texture and muddy in colour. I never felt the ballet came to life. Nijinska's talent was for inventing vigorous and forceful movements: she was not really at home in the stilted artificialities of that period, and the Montéclair music needed a lighter touch.

During the weeks when we were rehearsing and performing some of our old repertoire, before the new ballets were created, we were entertained by listening to Francis Poulenc playing snatches of *Les Biches* on the rehearsal-room piano. Poulenc was one of the French group of composers known as 'Les Six' who were the latest fashion—three of whom were to write ballets for Diaghilev which were first given in 1924. Poulenc was very young at the time, barely twenty, and his music was the happiest and gayest we had worked to for years.

There was no story to *Les Biches*—it was far too chic to have anything so obvious. In fact it was quite the most chic ballet ever invented. It was like one of those drawing-room comedies which are all about nothing at all, and yet if wittily planned, and acted with style and innuendo, can seem to be works of art. When the ballet was given in England, it was called *The House Party*, but it was certainly a very odd kind of house party. There was a large blue sofa, a number of girls and a rather more mature woman, the Hostess, with a lot of pearls and a foot-long cigarette holder. When three men arrived on the scene, wearing very little, they seemed primarily concerned with their physical exercises, and only when Nemtchinova tip-toed on, with her little blue-velvet bodice and white gloves, did one of the men begin to take interest. It was never quite clear whether or not she was meant to be a page-boy.

Marie Laurencin may not have been a great painter, but her designs for this particular ballet were perfect. The set was just white canvas, subtly lit, with only an enormous window sketchily suggested on the back-cloth, and the all-important blue sofa on the left to indicate that we were in a drawing-room. The simple costumes, which approximated to evening dresses of the period, were mostly pale pink, except for Nemtchinova's, and that of the Hostess, which was beige lace. On her head the Hostess wore two waving ostrich feathers. The men wore one-sided singlets and blue sashes over their sun-burnt torsos, with pale bluish-grey shorts and white socks.

Nijinska was completely in her element. She improvised and invented steps and dances at such speed that the girls found it impossible to follow her; demonstrations and explanations would develop into an uproar. Silence would then be called for, and the whole thing would begin again. The ballet seemed to take shape overnight.

Vera Nemtchinova was never seen in anything as striking, or so suited to her, as her solo and the *pas de deux* in *Les Biches*. She had very good feet, strong and arched and once she was on her points she could stay there for ever. Her legs were fine, too, with invisible knees, so that her elegant line, revealed by white tights and close-fitting jacket, was perfect. Vera's hands were not expressive, and it was clever of Marie Laurencin to give her long tight sleeves to the wrists and white kid gloves. Her dark hair was screwed back tight to her head. This neat little 'page-boy' entered on tip-toe from the wings, then, stood still, with her right hand laid against her right cheek and the other straight down against her leg: her appearance never failed to cause a stir. Nemtchinova took her *pirouettes* from her points and stopped them dead in an open position, as clean as a whistle. I am sure that the craze for *pirouettes* which has since swept the ballet, dated from her first appearance in *Les Biches* at Monte Carlo.

Next came Nijinska's solo as the Hostess, followed by her irresistible Rag Mazurka danced with two of the men, which gave an extraordinary picture of a spoilt, capricious woman carrying on a sophisticated flirtation. She flew round the stage, performing amazing contortions of her body, beating her feet, sliding backwards and forwards, screwing her face into an affected grimace, enticing the men and flinging herself in an abandoned attitude onto the sofa. She danced as the mood took her and was brilliant. I was to succeed her in this role, and although it was one of my most successful characterisations, the dance as I eventually worked it out differed in many ways from Nijinska's inimitable performance.

The Rag Mazurka was followed by what I always considered the weakest number in the ballet—a dance for Tchernicheva and myself. We were two inseparable 'friends' in grey with camellias in our hair—inseparable in the most tiresome way: for if there is anything I dislike it is trying to dance when I am physically linked to someone else. Moving slightly behind me, Luba had one arm right round my neck and bosom. We came down in this clinch, and remained in it throughout the dance. I thought this female *pas de deux* was wrongly conceived and badly constructed: Nijinska cannot have understood the type of women we were meant to be, and certainly few people ever have been less Lesbian than Tchernicheva and myself. The finale, however, went with a swing, and we all knew long before the curtain went down on the first night that *Les Biches* was a smash hit.

Les Tentations de la bergère was first given on January 3, 1924, and *Les Biches* three nights later. Leon had fallen ill on New Year's Eve, when he and I had given a lovely New Year's party at La Favorita (nobody guessing that this was all done on borrowed money, for Leon's investments in *chemin de fer* were not paying dividends, and Grigoriev was continually called upon for our salaries in advance). He complained of a sore throat, and next morning he could hardly swallow. He had a high temperature and became slightly delirious as the day wore on. Beatrice, who was a trained nurse, felt sure that it was something worse than influenza, and that if we called a doctor he would be taken to hospital, so we decided to try to treat him ourselves. We put him in a hot mustard bath for ten minutes, then sponged him with mustard and water every three hours, frequently swabbing his throat with iodine and glycerine. Eventually we got his temperature down, but I did not see how he could dance the principal part in the new ballet on January 3, in only two days' time. When the night came, however, we bandaged him in Thermogene wool and drove him down to the theatre in a carriage. He somehow got through the ballet; and three nights later danced in the opening performance of *Les Biches*.

While Leon was ill I had found myself with no money at all to buy medicine for him or food for the household, and I had once again been obliged to go to Grigoriev for an advance. Shortly after this I overheard Leon telling one of his friends that all the time we had been nursing him he had had 28,000 francs stitched into the lining of his waistcoat; and that he had lost it all the first time he went back to the Casino on his recovery!

Diaghilev engaged Vera Trefilova to dance in his two-act version of *Le Lac des cygnes*, which had not been performed since the early days of his company. Her technique was superb; she was entirely devoid of mannerisms and she brought a miraculous lightness to the role of Odette. As Odile, the sorceress in the second act, she did an amazing series of *fouettés*. It thrills me merely to remember the exquisite turn of her head and shoulders, and I was happy to have seen this great classical ballerina both in the *The Sleeping Princess* and *Swan Lake*, her two most famous roles. Trefilova was always in the theatre two hours before a performance began, practising quietly and preparing herself for the ordeal of dancing the revealing choreography of Petipa and Ivanov.

The third of our new ballets to be presented in January, 1924, was *Les Fâcheux*. The music was by Georges Auric, another of 'Les Six', and it was a dry, crackling score, which appeared strange and thin, but was interesting in texture. The subject was taken by Kochno from the Molière play, in which a young man on the way to meet his mistress is waylaid by a series of bores. Braque designed the setting, which was a town square, smudgily suggested in browns and greens. The costumes were Louis XIV and very difficult to dance in. Some of them were one colour in front and another behind, mostly in greens, greys, yellows and browns; they were unbecoming and with heavy flat hats tilted over the eyes, and heavy wigs, they gave an impression of weight.

Nijinska, dressed as a man, had an amusing variation, and Dolin as a Dandy caused some excitement by dancing on his points. Although this was an original idea for a man and Dolin found no difficulty in doing it, the first impression one got was the size of his feet. Pat's *pirouettes* on point were quite easy, but a man has very little flexibility in his ankle and instep and no effortless *relevé* from the flat of the foot to the point, so that one had the feeling that Pat was walking on stilts. The whole production appeared laboured, and grew boring half way through.

One of the most remarkable creations of Nijinska in this busy year was her ballet in the Moussorgsky opera *La Nuit sur le*

Mont Chauve, in which she covered the stage with a writhing, whirling mass of bodies and conjured up the most convincing Witches' Sabbath I have ever seen.

After Princess Charlotte had given birth to Prince Rainier, she decided to have some ballet lessons, and Tchernicheva was deputed by Diaghilev to teach her. I, too, had a distinguished pupil, a rich and handsome Frenchwoman with a lovely villa on the other side of Cap Martin. So twice a week Luba used to go to the Palace, and twice a week I would either receive my pupil at the Cinéma des Beaux-Arts where the opera performances were held, or go to her house along the coast. She was a talented dancer and I arranged a Greek dance for her which she later did bare-footed, in a gold lamé dress, for a charity gala in Paris.

One evening when I was giving her a lesson I complained of a splitting headache. My pupil said she had something which would take the headache away, and she gave me a little box of powder, telling me to take a pinch and sniff it up as if it were snuff. I followed her instructions, and she drove me back to the flat in her car. I suddenly felt an extraordinary tension round my face as if my jaw had been bound up, and I could neither eat nor speak. However, the headache disappeared and I went to a rehearsal. By the time it came to my turn to dance I was feeling on top of the world: I threw myself into the role as I never remembered doing before or since, and enjoyed myself immensely.

Diaghilev was watching, and when I had finished dancing, he called me over to sit beside him, saying, 'You seem very excited.' I replied, 'I'm not excited. I just feel very well, and I was enjoying dancing and having a lovely time.' He looked at me for a few seconds in silence and then said, 'Who gave it to you?' I asked him what on earth he meant, but he merely repeated his question. 'Are you going to tell me who gave it to you?' I said, 'I don't know what you mean.' 'Weren't you given some powder to smell?' he asked. 'Yes,' I told him, 'for my headache. And now I feel so much better.' Diaghilev got up and walked away. From that day onward I neither gave that lady another lesson, nor did I ever speak to her again. The 'Old Man' had diagnosed the effects of cocaine: his measures were prompt and drastic.

At the end of our season in Monte Carlo, Beatrice and Natasha went back to England, and we installed Leon's mother in an hotel. When we saw her off to Poland from Holland a month later she left with a large trunk heavy with loot, and that was the last time I ever set eyes on her.

After this we had to face the long and tedious journey to Barcelona. All-night train journeys always left me giddy and weak in the legs; and in the course of this one I was told that Nemtchinova had remained in Monte Carlo with mumps, and that I should have to dance the principal part in *Les Sylphides* on the night of my arrival. I never slept a wink. The lyrical dancing of *Les Sylphides* was quite outside my range, and as I had refused to tackle it when Vera Savina left the company, I had no idea how I should do it now. Pat Dolin, who was to be my partner, was also new to the ballet. The Teatro Liceo in Barcelona had the biggest rake of any theatre I knew: it was so steep that the dancers could hardly help themselves from crowding forward to the front of the stage, leaving a void behind them. My legs seemed like heavy cranes, and when Pat tried to lift me I felt like a sack of coal. That was the worst performance I ever gave, but Pat pulled me through.

All this was forgotten after the excitement of my appearance with Leon in *Le Tricorne*. Barcelona had never seen our Spanish ballet before, and we were very nervous. Even Zoia Roszovska, who had to sing to the accompaniment of our clapping hands before the curtain went up, was apprehensive of making a fool of herself in front of the critical public of the largest city in Spain. But no sooner was Picasso's décor revealed in all its warmth of lighting, with Leon alone on the stage making his first Spanish movements, than the audience settled down to watch us intently, and at the end of the first part they showed their enthusiasm by a tremendous burst of applause. By the end of the ballet they were worked up into a frenzy, and we took so many curtain calls that some of the dancers were dressed and on their way out of the theatre before Leon and I could leave the stage. We were very happy.

One day while we were in Barcelona Diaghilev called the whole company together on the stage. He was holding a piece of paper in his hand, which looked like a letter or telegram. 'I know you will all be very sorry to hear that poor Felix has died in the asylum near London', he said. Naturally everyone put on sympathetic faces and made the right noises. In fact, I did feel very badly about the poor boy who had done so much towards the creation of *Le Tricorne* and had lost his reason as a result. Fourteen years later when I was visiting Massine in a London dressing-room, he told me that he had just been visiting Felix. I was amazed. I went later to see him myself. In fact, he died in 1941. Why Diaghilev made this false announcement—whether he was misinformed or whether he was afraid that while we were performing *Tricorne* in Spain, Felix's family might make some claim on him—I have never known.

Then followed our first visit to Holland. Of this short tour I remember our astonishment at the crowds of people on bicycles, the fields of tulips, the novelty of cheese for breakfast and the paper coverings of lavatory seats in the theatre.

Paris was to see all the new ballets we had given in Monte Carlo, and one more. Feeling the need of a new work which would show Dolin off to advantage, Diaghilev had asked Jean Cocteau to devise a scenario; and Cocteau, fascinated by some acrobatic jumps and hand-stands he had seen Pat performing between rehearsals, invented *Le Train bleu*. It took the company some time to realise there would be no Blue Train in the ballet: it was all about the sports which people indulged in when the train deposited them on the beaches of the South of France. Nijinska was to be a tennis champion in a white dress and *bandeau* like Suzanne Lenglen, who leapt about the stage whacking at an imaginary ball. Leon Woizikovsky slouched about as a British golfer (looking most un-British) in a pullover and plus-fours, pretending to be at home with a pipe, when he had never even smoked a cigarette. I was a bathing-belle in a dashing pink hand-knitted costume. Leon discovered me in a bathing hut, with two metres of pink georgette round my shoulders. Relieving me of this garment, which was typical of the period, he took a good look at me, put his pipe in his pocket, and danced with me the famous *Train bleu* waltz. He had to throw me up spinning in the air, then catch me as I came down, and I cannot imagine how we never came to grief, because my woollen costume was impossible to grip. Dolin in the role of a sunburnt and reckless youth, *Le Beau Gosse*, performed some breath-taking acrobatic stunts and created a sensation.

Darius Milhaud, another of 'Les Six', had written the score for *Le Train bleu*, which was tuneful, unpretentious and danceable like a musical comedy with no singing: hence the designation of *Opérette dansée*. The dresses were by Chanel; the set, with its lopsided sea, bathing huts and two great fishes, was by the sculptor Henri Laurens; and a painting by Picasso of two running giantesses was enlarged to become a curtain.

Leon and I were staying at my favourite little hotel in the Rue Cambon, which was handy for the fittings at Chanel's establishment a few doors away. When I tried on my pink bathing dress, which we all thought very daring, the question of what I was to wear on my head arose. Three women stood round me binding my long hair with various pieces of material, until at last they decided on a dark suède. The neat little skull cap they made for me set a fashion. I could not decide on what shoes to wear, and eventually settled on a pair of the little rubber slippers which women wore for bathing in those days, and which were most uncomfortable to dance in. After the dress rehearsal of *Le Train bleu*, Mlle Chanel came to my dressing-room and said, 'I must think up some accessories for your costume'; and on the opening night I found on my dressing-table the first of the large pearl stud earrings which were soon to be seen everywhere. They were very smart but so heavy that they pulled at my ears and made it hard for me to hear the music. Mlle Chanel had invented a new kind of pearl, which was made of china and coated with wax. She used to wear a great many ropes of these; and I remember her at a party she gave for the ballet at her house next to the Elysée Palace, dressed in a skin-tight, champagne-coloured lace gown, knee-length in front and ending in a fish-tail train at the back: it was cut high over the chest, but showed her bare back below the waist, and with it she wore ropes and ropes of her heavy pearls. At that same party I had a similar dress of chocolate lace with just one row of pearls.

Our season was to be at the Théâtre des Champs-Elysées, but we rehearsed at the Mogador. One day I was watching a rehearsal of *Prince Igor* from the stalls, when I saw Leon catch his hand in the little gold chain which he always wore round his neck: it broke and fell through a crack in the stage. He knelt down to see if he could recover it. Diaghilev, who was sitting beside me with Kochno, turned to ask me what it was that Leon had lost and which seemed to distress him so. I told him that it was his gold confirmation cross which his mother had given him many years ago. At the next performance a small box was handed to Leon, containing a beautiful gold cross and a chain. Diaghilev very seldom gave presents, so that this became Leon's most precious possession.

The Paris season went well, and of all our new works *Les Biches* was the most popular. It was a cheerful and prosperous time for the company. Among our friends I enjoyed calling on Picasso and Olga, who now had a little red-haired son, in their new apartment in the Rue la Boétie.

After the holiday, which Leon and I spent visiting Bordeaux, Biarritz, Pau, Lourdes and St Jean de Luz, the ballet reassembled in September for a long tour of Germany, which took us to Bremen, Hamburg, Stuttgart, Hanover, Cologne and Berlin. It was enjoyable, not only because of the pictures and churches we saw, but because audiences were appreciative and critics understanding. Bronislava Nijinska was married in Germany.

On one of our train journeys we were waiting in a station, when the door opened and a very fat man entered our carriage full of girls. He signalled to two of them to make room, and lowered himself onto the seat. As he did this one of the girls, assuming he would not understand, remarked in Russian, 'Sits and bursts.' Quietly puffing at his cigar the fat man said, also in Russian, 'Sat and did not burst.'

Diaghilev had at last come to an arrangement with Oswald Stoll: he was to pay off his debt incurred over *The Sleeping Princess* by giving three seasons at the Coliseum. So, in November, 1924, we returned to London for the first time in two years.

The time had come for Anton Dolin, the Russian Ballet's English *premier danseur* to enjoy a triumph in his own country. *Le Train bleu* was an enormous success, an even greater one than it had been in Paris. Unfortunately the Coliseum stage is made of teak, and the jump with which Dolin made his downstage entrance seemed to lose its effect. Then somebody hit on the idea of installing a springboard in the wings: this enabled him to run and bounce high into the air before landing on the stage. The men in the company took a poor view of this contraption, and said, 'If he wants to jump off a springboard let the public see him do it.' Pat's knees and feet were always bleeding from some of his extraordinary jumps and falls. Leon's public, who were used to seeing him dance like mad, found it amusing that he should wander about in plus-fours, puffing at a pipe. *Le Train bleu* took London by storm, and the English all decided that they must go to the South of France without delay.

The press acclaimed Pat, and he was foolish enough to give an interview to a journalist. He was young and inexperienced, and had not yet learned that there were some things one must never do in the Diaghilev Ballet. He revealed that his real name was Patrick Healey Kay, and even mentioned that I was English too. When this appeared in print, Diaghilev was furious. He found me alone in my dressing-room and accused me of talking nonsense to get cheap publicity. I assured him that I had done nothing of the kind, but nevertheless he ignored me for weeks.

We had already noticed signs that Diaghilev was not interested exclusively in Dolin. In Paris, before we went to Germany, Leon and I had seen Diaghilev one evening on the boulevard with Kochno and the young Serge Lifar. Lifar had never struck us as being particularly intelligent, but Diaghilev must have noticed his enthusiasm. The 'Old Man' could do wonders, given the slightest flicker of response.

When Bronia found that Diaghilev was working secretly with her pupil Lifar, in the hopes of turning him into a choreographer, she became extremely indignant. She was a stubborn woman, inclined to sulk and reluctant to listen to reason, and when she was disturbed by anything she would go about mumbling her misery to anyone she came across. This try-out of Lifar as a choreographer seemed to her like a betrayal. Nothing would persuade her to remain longer in the company, and she left at the end of our London season. 'Nobody is indispensable', said Diaghilev, but Lifar was anything but ready, and who was to be his choreographer?

Diaghilev's decision to engage four dancers, recently escaped from Russia, who were dancing at the Empire Music Hall, was more momentous than he could have guessed at the time. They were Alexandra Danilova, Tamara Gevergeva, Nicolas Efimov and George Balanchivadze. We were also joined by a little English girl of fourteen called Alicia Marks, who was to come out with her mother and study with us in Monte Carlo. Vera Savina, too now separated from Massine, returned to us at this time.

Discipline with regard to social engagements was less strict than in the old days. I spent delightful evenings with the Morleys in Charles Street; and there were wonderful supper parties given by Florrie Grenfell at her house in Cavendish Square. Usually, however, when there was to be a party, Diaghilev accepted or declined for us, and decided who should attend. Half a dozen of us were taken by him to a crush on the last night of 1924. Cars fetched us, but it was late when we arrived and the large house was jammed with people. We managed to get upstairs and leave our coats, but we couldn't get down again for the crowd. Leon fought his way to the bar and returned with one neat whisky and we sipped this together as the New Year came in. There was a trumpeter standing beside us on the staircase who deafened us by playing *Auld Lang Syne* and *For He's a Jolly Good Fellow* to the shouts and applause of the guests. Then the hostess, whom we saw for the first time that night, came up and paid him a guinea, whereupon he downed his trumpet, snatched his hat and coat and went off. Our hostess disappeared into the crowd, and I did not catch another glimpse of her. This was typical of the 'twenties.

17

RETURN OF MASSINE

Accumulated roles and worries — Mother comes to Monte
Carlo — Cupping Alicia Markova — An abortive strike —
The Balanchine era begins — Massine returns — *Zéphire et
Flore* — Cruelty of Diaghilev — Cecchetti's classes — A new
'Nightingale' — Success of *Les Matelots* — Exit Dolin — Im-
promptu performance in Venice — Legat replaces Cecchetti
— Balanchine's *Barabau* — Moving in to *Les Jasmins*.

The Nijinska period was over.

In my twelve years with the Diaghilev Ballet I had worked
under Nijinsky, Fokine, Massine and Nijinska. All but the first
of these had bequeathed me wonderful roles; and in the next
year or two the variety of characters I was called on to interpret
in the course of our ordinary repertoire was remarkably wide.
I had never been and never could be a classical ballerina, but the
fun I had in taking such different parts, invented by choreographers of such varied genius, was more rewarding to my way
of thinking than all the laurels and fortunes of Pavlova. What
other *première danseuse de caractère* had ever had such roles in stock?
I still danced the Slave Girl from Fokine's *Cléopâtre*; I did the
Bacchanale in *Narcisse*, Chloë in *Daphnis et Chloë* and the Doll in
Petroushka. Massine had given me the Chosen Virgin in *Le
Sacre*; I danced the Miller's Wife in his *Le Tricorne*, Pimpinella in
Pulcinella and Felicita in *Les Femmes de bonne humeur*, besides the
Tarantellas in *La Boutique fantasque* and *Cimarosiana*. Nijinska had
invented for me the Bathing Girl in *Le Train bleu*, and now that
she was leaving I spent the last Sunday in London learning from
her the Hostess in *Les Biches*.

Although I was earning a good living and had made a success of my career, my private life was destined never to be free from worry. Not only did Leon's gambling keep me in a permanent state of uncertainty over money, but Father's peculiar way of life was continually creating problems at home. He would disappear for weeks on end, and had begun to involve himself in a series of shady undertakings. Mother had recently decided to sell the house at Hastings, and Beatrice moved into a furnished flat at Surbiton, which was convenient for Natasha's school, and as I was unable to help her very much, she took a job. Mother's health, meanwhile, had gone from bad to worse, so I decided to give her a change and take her off to stay with me in Monte Carlo, and she set off with me on the longest journey she had ever made in her life.

We found a small flat on the Boulevard des Moulins, one of four, built out on descending terraces behind a new cocktail bar. We later discovered that the only reason it had not been snapped up, was that a man had cut his throat in the one above and the blood had flowed down the steps to our front door. Monte Carlo seemed to be as full of tragedies and bloodshed as a cheap thriller, but at least this time we were not haunted— and we had a lovely view of the sea.

Little Alicia Marks, who had been renamed Markova, was a quiet, well-behaved girl, and I was fond of her. She had not been long in Monte Carlo, however, before she caught a cold which turned to pneumonia. She was a delicate creature at that time, and nobody thought her dancing career would be very long. Alicia and her mother and governess were living in a small *pension*, and as none of them spoke French I went along to see if I could help. The French doctor had prescribed the old-fashioned remedy of cupping, and as Mrs Marks, being English, had no idea how this should be done, I undertook to put on the cups. These were made of thick glass and were rather like containers for fairy-lights. The method was to wrap cotton wool round a thin stick, dip it in spirit and then rub the inside of the cup. A lighted taper was then inserted into the cup to ignite the fumes of the spirit, and before it had time to burn out, you clapped the cup on the patient's body. If there was no congestion it was supposed that the cup would not hold on by suction; if there *was* congestion the cup would stick fast, and the flesh would gradually turn blue like a bruise. Alicia had nearly a dozen of these on her thin little back. When she got better she used to sit in my dressing-room and watch me make up. Eventually she began to try this out herself; and we would sit side by side, rubbing 'fleshing'—as foundation was then called—into our skin, looking at ourselves in the mirror and chatting away. It was in this way that Alicia had her first lessons in make-up.

The cost of living had risen, and the company had decided to ask for a rise in salary. Schollar and Wilzak, who had always been rather Bolshy, organised a meeting and suggested that unless Diaghilev would agree to certain demands we should all refuse to dance that night. Diaghilev, whom Grigoriev fetched to speak to the company, was furious. He pointed out that we had individual contracts and that he had never yet refused to listen to personal complaints. We all felt very small. He said he would do what he could for us as soon as he could afford it, but in the meantime he declined to make any specific promises: anyone who failed to take part in the evening's performance would be dismissed. In the end the performance took place, though half an hour late, and the only dancers not to appear were Schollar and Wilzak. It was decided that a small deputation should address Diaghilev after the curtain had gone down and Leon, being the universal comrade, was chosen to lead it. Diaghilev sauntered towards the group with a face like thunder. Leon went up to him and tried to put the dancers' point of view in some detail. After listening to him in silence, Diaghilev said, 'Leon, where are your friends?' When Leon turned round there was not a soul in sight. Everyone had scuttled. 'That will teach you to speak for others,' said Diaghilev. 'If you have a grievance come and see me privately.' With this he turned and walked off the stage. Schollar and Wilzak were sacked, and Pat Dolin stepped straight into most of the latter's roles.

One of our newcomers, Danilova, who began to show promise, took over some of Schollar's parts. Another, Alice Nikitina emerged as a potential soloist. Vera Nemtchinova, who had proved herself in *Aurora's Wedding* and *Les Biches*, and who, though she lacked the gift of expressing emotion, was a fine classical dancer, appeared for the first time in *Le Lac des cygnes*. In this ballet Dolin was certainly an excellent partner. During the last two years our classes had been given by Nijinska, but now Maestro Cecchetti was induced to return from La Scala, Milan, where he had been teaching, to give private courses to our principal dancers.

It was during this season that Balanchivadze, who was now known as Balanchine, was given his first chance to do choreography for the opera-ballet, and his work was so satisfactory that Diaghilev ordered him to rearrange *Le Chant du rossignol*.

In the previous summer, Massine had formed a company with the backing of Comte Etienne de Beaumont and had stolen from us nine dancers, including Idzikovsky and Evina. Although one or two interesting ballets were created, this venture failed and Massine went to America. Diaghilev had not forgiven him for the Savina episode, and that he should have dared to start a company on his own and even to lure away artists from the Russian Ballet was an additional source of resentment. However, the time had not yet come when Diaghilev could depend entirely on Balanchine, and rumours began to fly around that a truce had been arranged and that Massine was coming back to us. Poor Vera Savina was very perturbed.

Sure enough Massine arrived, and from the first day he appeared embarrassed and uncomfortable with the company. When he said, 'How do you do?' he just pressed his lips together and curled up the corners of his mouth: that sufficed for a smile. At rehearsals he spoke to no one, except to give directions: he and Grigoriev exchanged civilities and that was all. By this time he had married again and Savina was ignored as if she did not exist. She was deeply hurt. Diaghilev and Massine were never seen together, and we gathered there was little love lost on either side. If in the old days it had been impossible to get a glimpse of Massine's inner thoughts and feelings, now he seemed to exist in complete isolation. It would have been interesting to know his

opinion of Dolin, Lifar and Balanchine. He was lonely, but refused to be friendly, and although some of our 'old gang' were
secretly glad to have him back it was clear that an earthquake
would be needed to make him show any emotion. Massine's
immediate task was to produce *Zéphire et Flore*, which was the
ballet that Diaghilev had hoped, in vain, to entrust to Lifar,
and which had been the cause of Nijinska's leaving the
company.

Zéphire et Flore, a mythological subject, was a work in the
style popular at the end of the eighteenth century. Diaghilev and
Boris Kochno had devised a scenario between them, and as
Diaghilev was avoiding Massine, it was Kochno who kept an
eye on rehearsals in his place. It seemed strange to have this
elegant young man seated in a chair to represent Diaghilev at
our rehearsals.

The music of *Zéphire et Flore* was by a young Russian called
Vladimir Dukelsky, who surprised us by being tall, gay and good-
looking—in fact a heart-throb. He loved jazz music, and would
play anything on the rehearsal-room piano that the girls asked
him for. Of all our composers he was the most friendly with
the dancers, and we all loved him. One evening he was strum-
ming away with a crowd of girls round him, when Diaghilev
came in unexpectedly. It was quite funny to see them all scatter, as
if they had been caught in some improper conspiracy.

I could never understand why Braque had to torture his
dancers by making them wear caps and head-dresses. The movement of the dancer's head and neck are so essential in lending
meaning to the body, that a hat, besides being an uncomfortable
weight, can detract enormously from the expressiveness of a
dance.

Much the best part of this not very effective ballet was the
appearance of three young people, Nikitina, Dolin and Lifar,
who were all slim, long-legged and attractive; but of these,
Lifar looked best because he wore least. All he had on was some
gold pants and sandals; his sleek, black head and his youthful
brown figure were irresistible. Dolin, on the other hand, wore
a jockey cap and a tunic made of overlapping satin petals, with

a cape and tasselled girdle. As Flore, Nikitina had little green leaves sprinkled on her bodice and her white tights; her tu-tu had no front and was more like a bunchy frill round each thigh. Nikitina's hat looked to me like any old flowered hat from a jumble sale.

There were nine Muses in the ballet: among them Danilova, Tchernicheva, Doubrovska and myself. We wore 'sack' dresses, with tiaras resembling Russian head-dresses and long dangling earrings. Massine gave us each an angular, and uncomfortable little solo and these were danced in rapid succession. Although my dance was all over in about a minute, I hated it almost as much as the Red Riding Hood number.

I still had internal trouble and was often in pain. We had to travel from Monte Carlo to Marseilles for one special performance at a time when I was feeling particularly ill; and this was the only occasion I can remember when Diaghilev was really unkind to me.

I was to dance in *Les Sylphides* and *Prince Igor*. Although Fokine's choreography for *Prince Igor* had been religiously preserved, Nijinska had inserted for herself, at Diaghilev's request, a spinning, turning, stamping solo with the idea of providing a more vigorous opening for the ballet, and when she left the company I took over this number. If there was any dance in the repertoire more calculated to make one giddy, I never knew it. The company went all the way to Marseilles in a bus, but I could not face the bumpy roads when I was feeling so ill, so I travelled alone by train. Hoping to be able to pull myself together and get into the way of dancing a little before the company came on stage, I dressed early and began to practise on my own, wearing my *Sylphides* costume: but I fainted dead away just before the ballet was due to begin. I was revived, and somehow got through my part in the first ballet. Then I begged Diaghilev to let me cut the Nijinska solo from the beginning of *Prince Igor*, and revert to the Fokine choreography. He flatly refused. As soon as the last ballet began, I realised that it would be a physical impossibility for me to execute all the turns and stamps, so I cut them out and inserted some of the traditional Fokine steps. The 'Old Man' was

on the stage in a flash. 'Who gave you permission to alter the
Nijinska choreography into a Fokine one? How dare you take
such a thing on yourself?' He raged at me and I was soon in floods
of tears. Diaghilev was certainly ruthless in the cause of art, and
he lacked the imagination to understand how somebody else
could be feeling ill when he was well himself.

This was the last season that the Russian Ballet had regular
classes with Maestro Cecchetti. At his first lesson we would be
placed in alphabetical order round three sides of the room, and at
every subsequent lesson every dancer moved up one place.
The old teacher had no patience with illness, and if one were
obliged to stay away from class he accused one of laziness. For
adage and *allegro* work, he moved the men into the centre, and
this gave us a chance to measure the progress various dancers
had made. Cecchetti was a wonderful professor, with an eagle
eye for the slightest fault, but he had one shortcoming. Although he himself could *pirouette* like a top, it would have been
impossible to do a *pirouette* on stage in the way he taught it in
class—his preparation from the open second position would have
taken much too long.

Massine was no good at *pirouettes* and never included them in
dances he invented for himself; Leon did a fine character *pirouette* which was more of a spin; and Vladimirov, who was tall,
had no trouble with turning successfully. But the one person
who had a perfect technique—although he was not with us during
this season—was Idzikovsky. For him to do a series of *entre-
chats-huit* at the end of a solo and finish on one knee, was child's
play. I loved working behind him in class, to watch him take four
pirouettes and stop clean with absolute accuracy: but when I
whispered, 'Lovely four, Stas', he would glare round at me and
say, 'Eight, you mean!'—and he really believed it. Dolin was
incapable of starting his *pirouettes* without a series of fussy hand
movements, rather like someone doing card tricks. The only way
to control this bad habit is to watch yourself carefully in a mirror
and start again as soon as you see the trick beginning to show.

Lifar was continually having private lessons with Cecchetti,
and it must have been obvious to Dolin by this time that the

young Russian's star was in the ascendant. It was a sure sign that a young man had been promoted to the position of official favourite, when he had his teeth fixed or appeared wearing plus-fours. On the day that Serge appeared in these fashionable garments, I turned to Pat and said, 'Your number's up, chum!' If Pat had shown signs of wanting to create ballets for the company, I am sure he could have held onto his position much longer; but perhaps he had no such ambitions.

Mme Matilda Kchessinskaya, who had been loved by the late Tsar and was now married to the Grand Duke Michael, was living in a villa on Cap d'Ail with her husband and a party of other Grand Dukes. They were much in evidence. She was small, pretty and vivacious, with sparkling eyes; and she loved gambling. Vladimirov and his wife, Doubrovska, were great friends with her and went to her poker parties. Kchessinskaya had danced in Diaghilev's second London season in 1911, and I was fascinated to see something of this famous woman. She lived in great style at this time, but the money and jewels she had got out of Russia did not last for ever; the villa was soon sold and Kchessinskaya settled down to giving lessons in Paris, like so many of the other Russian ballerinas.

Summer 1925 was spent between London and Paris. We were to dance again as part of the music-hall programme at the Coliseum throughout June and July, but with a break in the middle into which was squeezed an unusually short Paris season of one week.

Zéphire et Flore had been first shown in Monte Carlo, but it was a novelty in Paris. Our other new productions were Balanchine's version of *Le Chant du rossignol* and Massine's *Les Matelots*, both of which we had made ready before leaving Monte Carlo.

It was in *Le Chant du rossignol* that Alicia Markova had her first solo part as the Nightingale. A special costume with sequined trousers was designed for her. Her little neck was so thin that when, during the performance, the time came for me to twist the necklace of skulls round it, I suddenly felt an overwhelming desire to strangle her in earnest. However, I mastered the impulse.

233

In working out *Les Matelots* Massine really seemed to be back in his old form: it was one of the most successful of our light-hearted ballets. There were only five characters in the ballet, three sailors and their two girl friends. Vera Nemtchinova's role was that of a rather better-class girl than mine: she looked pretty in a short red satin dress with a spotted apron, and a neat scarf on her head. In keeping with my more oafish character, I was given an ugly and shapeless garment which consisted of a dark serge skirt with a grey top, a little white bolero jacket with criss-cross braid embroidery, and a fish-net snood with a tassel. Slavinsky, Woizikovsky and Lifar represented an American, a Spanish and a French sailor. There was very little plot: when the sailors had gone off to sea, they returned unexpectedly in false beards, and I was supposed to persuade Vera to be unfaithful to her boy-friend. She resisted, however, and the ballet ended happily. There were several sets by the young Spanish painter, Pedro Pruna, very simple, pretty and straightforward in a Picasso-ish way. One of the scenes had a cube to the right of the stage which revolved, each of its four painted sides indicating a change of locality.

With the exception of Lifar, we were all old hands at Massine's choreography and he knew exactly what he could expect from each of us. He gave Vera a charming, wistful little dance on points, in which she lamented the absence of her sailor friend. Thaddeus Slavinsky had some big free movements to execute. He did one extremely difficult step in the course of his variation. Starting on one side of the stage in an arabesque, he crossed to the other in a series of sixteen slow hops, and each time he jumped onto the supporting leg, he threw it up behind and touched the extended leg with his toe. Leon, being short, square and very dark, could have passed for a Spaniard any day. Massine remembered the flashing hand movements and foot tricks Leon had done in *Les Femmes de bonne humeur*, so he gave him an entrance with the same fast, fidgety gestures of the hand held close to the body, and a series of rapid, comic steps for the feet. This was one of the best numbers Leon ever danced, and it became famous.

Lifar looked about sixteen: he was slim, agile, flexible in movement and altogether delightful to watch. His variation was a waltz, with a number of slow turns in attitude or arabesque, which showed off the great advance of his technique. We all enjoyed dancing this ballet, not only because of the amusing steps Massine had given us, but because Auric's music was danceable and easy to understand. Nina Hamnett, the English painter, has described* how she whistled sea shanties to Auric which he included in the last scene.

Auric had written some interlude music to precede the final scene; and somebody had the idea of sending me on the stage during this lull in the action, to stand with my back to the audience, staring at the drop curtain. I just stood there with my feet apart and my hands clasped behind my back. This experience taught me that it is not necessary to look at an audience in order to control them. I had thought, for instance, that when I stood motionless in *Le Sacre* and felt the audience were with me, it was because they were able to watch the expression of my face and see my unblinking eyes: but I learned in *Les Matelots* that even with my back turned, I could command attention, simply by concentrating on the character of my role. If my thoughts wandered for a moment, people would begin to cough or whisper or shift about in their seats, so I had to hold onto them tightly with my mind. I received many compliments over this 'feat of personality'.

Les Matelots was a wild success in Paris, but we could never manage to put *Zéphire et Flore* across the footlights. I so much hated my little dance as a Muse that one day, in Belgium, I plucked up enough courage to speak to Diaghilev at a rehearsal. He was in a good mood, so when I asked, 'Please take it away from me, dear Sergei Pavlovitch. I dance it so badly', he said, 'I'll think about it and let you know tomorrow.' Next day he was sitting as usual on a hard, little chair in a corner of the foyer, watching us rehearse, his walking-stick between his legs and both white hands folded over the top of it. He beckoned me to him and said, 'Hilditchka, I have done what you asked and made arrangements for Dora Vadimova to dance in your place in

* *Laughing Torso*, by Nina Hamnett (Constable, 1932).

Zéphire.' I bent over and kissed his cheek, and said 'Thank you. You are a real dear.' Then as I was about to run off, delighted with my escape from the hated role, he caught me by the hand and said, 'But there is one condition.' I thought he was joking, but he went on, 'In exchange I am asking you to teach Tchernicheva your role in *Le Tricorne.* She has always wanted to do it.' I was taken aback and exclaimed, 'Oh, Sergei Pavlovitch, I have already taught three people to do the Miller's Wife—Mme Karsavina, Devillier and Dalbaicin. I *can't* do it again.' 'Well,' he said, 'that's the condition.' So I taught Luba the role, and it was a good thing I did, for when I became ill the ballet was thus able to remain in the repertoire. When she had learned the difficult sequence of dances we began to alternate in the part; and this, too, was a good thing, because it gave my costume a chance to dry off between performances.

With the promotion of Lifar, Dolin's position in the company was less assured, and it was with the greatest difficulty that he had been induced to fulfil his contract and remain with us until the end of July. The re-engagement of Idzikovsky had seemed a further challenge to Pat's superiority; and after the Paris season he left us.

Leon and I decided that before settling down for our holiday in the South of France, we would visit Venice. We knew that Diaghilev would be there, but we thought that if we kept away from the Lido, where he always stayed, we should be able to avoid him: we did not want to give the impression of trespassing on his favourite holiday resort. The very first morning, however, as we were coming out of our hotel to go sightseeing, we ran straight into the Diaghilev 'family'—that is to say, Nouvel, Lifar and the 'Old Man' himself. To our surprise he seemed delighted to find us there. We were bundled straight into a motor-boat and carried off to the Lido. We spent a happy day together; and when Leon and I explained that we were only staying four days because of the expense, Diaghilev said, 'Nonsense! Now that you are here we will arrange a party and you two and Lifar shall dance.' As we had been dancing for nine months without a break, it was the last thing we wanted to do, but

Diaghilev could never resist the opportunity of organising a party on a grand scale. Venice was crammed with smart people from all over the world, and no doubt he thought that this might be a chance to get a little publicity for his company.

The Cole Porters were living at the Palazzo Papadopoli on the Grand Canal, and Diaghilev took this over for the evening, complete with gorgeous gondolas and liveried gondoliers in gold, red and black. A stage was built against the garden wall backing onto the Grand Canal, and dressing rooms were contrived for us on either side. Diaghilev constructed three arches to form a background; he covered them with trailing vines and borrowed three priceless statues from a museum to stand under them. Floodlighting was arranged, and the auditorium was just a sloping lawn filled with borrowed garden chairs and strewn with coloured cushions.

The programme was a short *divertissement* made up of two male variations from *Les Matelots*, the Tarantella from *Cimarosiana*, and the dance of the Hostess with her two men from *Les Biches*. Costumes were easily found, but it proved impossible to find artificial pearls in Venice, and without these my get-up as the Hostess and performance of the Rag Mazurka would be incomplete. I needed at least six long strings, besides the one I played with, which had to be nearly four feet long. All that the shops offered was coral, and this was neither appropriate nor cheap; so an S.O.S. was sent out to a number of the ladies who had been invited to the party, asking for the loan of their 'Chanel pearls'. These beads were so heavy that when I had put on as many as I needed, I could hardly stand up. When I danced the Hostess, I used to have the necklaces tacked down on either side of my bodice in such a way that they would appear to be hanging freely, yet could not fly up and hit me in the teeth when I did my jumps and intricate footwork, tearing across the stage.

The night before our performance there was a tremendous thunderstorm. Gondolas were overturned, houses were struck by lightning and people were even drowned. To add to the confusion, all the electricity in Venice failed and steamers stopped running. Leon and Lifar had to make last-minute preparations for the show, and they were obliged to walk miles through unknown streets and alleys before they could find anyone to ferry them across from the Zattere to San Marco.

By the next evening the weather was perfect again. I never saw such a beautiful sight as the arrival of the guests in their decorated gondolas hung with coloured lanterns. The women were in pretty summer evening dresses, and the air was full of music and song. All went well until *Les Biches*, the final number, during which I gave an impetuous twirl to my longest string of beads. The thread broke and off they flew! I had a pang of anxiety to think of all the ladies in the audience who might be cursing me for destroying their precious property, but I kept on dancing. There was naturally no rake to the stage, so the pearls lay where they fell, and we had to get through the rest of that long number as best we could, sliding and tripping over them. In spite of this our performance was enthusiastically received; and the evening ended with a ball and fireworks over the Grand Canal. We were each of us sent £25 by Diaghilev the next morning.

At the end of the summer the company gave a few performances in Belgium, then returned for the last of our several seasons at the Coliseum, after which Diaghilev would have paid off his debt to Stoll. *Le Train bleu* was no longer given, because Dolin was irreplaceable. His part in *Zéphire et Flore* was taken by Tcherkas, while that of Nikitina, who had hurt her ankle, was filled by Alexandra Danilova. Tcherkas was shorter than Dolin, and Danilova in those days was on the plump side: so with the changes of cast this ballet lost what little charm it had ever had, and it was soon dropped from the repertoire. It was while we were at the Coliseum, giving one ballet per programme, that Maestro Cecchetti, who had finally left us and retired to Milan, was replaced as ballet master to the company by Nicolas Legat.

Legat, who had been a famous teacher in Russia—and under whom Kremnev had worked in the old days—was a charming and friendly person. His method was lighter, much less strict and accurate than Cecchetti's so that although our classes became gayer, we lost strength and precision. Legat used to give us quite long *enchaînements* of five or six steps to practise, but as he played the piano himself at class, he could not possibly make all the corrections necessary in such a large company. A dancer easily falls unconsciously into the way of taking advantage of a lenient professor; and unless one is continually corrected, one tends to leave out or slur over difficult passages.

Lydia Lopokova, who had been married in August to Maynard Keynes, the economist, came back to us again. Although she was the most elusive of his dancers, Diaghilev always welcomed her back, for nobody could really ever take her place. Her high spirits and her personality were unique. She could always be relied on to invent some funny word, or to express herself in a peculiarly vivid and personal English. On one occasion, when she was presented to Queen Mary during an interval, the Queen looked in amazement at the little, dripping, breathless figure, whom I can so well imagine smiling up appealingly at her; but as Lydia did nothing but dab at her face with a towel, Her Majesty said, 'Thank you for dancing for me; it must have been trying on such a hot afternoon.' Lydia bobbed and exclaimed, 'Pleasure pain, Ma'am'. On another occasion, at a party given by Florrie Grenfell, Lydia proposing the health of the hostess, decided on an impulse to make her toast include other members of the family. The fact that Florrie's mother, whom Lydia had never known, had been dead a number of years, did not prevent her crying out, 'And let us not forget dear Florrie's mother who compiled her!'

George Balanchine, unlike Massine, had a great sense of humour in private life, although his demeanour was rather serious and he seldom laughed. He was extremely musical and could entertain one for hours at the piano. It was also obvious that he was a born choreographer. Diaghilev now set him the task of composing a farcical ballet. Maurice Utrillo designed the setting for *Barabau*, the action of which took place in an Italian village at the beginning of the century, and Vittorio Rieti wrote the music. Leon Woizikovsky was in his element, with long black moustaches, eating imaginary spaghetti, swilling it down with Chianti straight from the flask, doing amazing tricks and dancing on top of an enormous barrel. Lifar was very dashing as the sergeant of a group of tipsy soldiers who pass through the village; and there was a chorus of mournful-looking citizens in black bowler hats and gloves who popped up from behind a fence, and sang a deadpan commentary on the action.

The principal female part of a clownish peasant woman was given to Chamié, but she did not quite bring it off, and nobody laughed when they should have done. It was not long before I took over her role. I realised I must do something to make it a success. The costume was a blouse and skirt, red stockings, black boots and an upturned straw hat. I got a switch of false hair and pinned it on top of my head, then planted the hat on top of that. Next I stuck a piece of wax on the end of my nose, raised my eyebrows and reddened my lower lip only. I was rewarded by a burst of spontaneous laughter as I came onto the stage—the first time that such a thing had happened to me, and it was a wonderful experience.

Our Coliseum appearances were a success, and several hundred people signed a petition asking for two ballets instead of one on the last night. Unfortunately, this would have interfered with the time schedule, and so they were disappointed.

From London we went to Berlin, where our performances were very badly attended, possibly because the Germans were reluctant to go to the theatre over Christmas. This raised fresh money problems for Diaghilev, but he managed to pay us, and we were back in Monte Carlo in the New Year.

Leon and I had bought, through a Russian estate agent, the lease of an apartment in a villa called Les Jasmins on the Monte de Tenao. This was our first real home—in fact it was the first I had in the course of my two marriages. Payments for the lease and contents of the flat were spread over a year. Les Jasmins was quite high up the hill, immediately opposite the Carmelite church, and one had to climb several flights of steps to reach it. There was a *salon*, attractively furnished with Empire furniture, an elegant dining room, a large kitchen with a mimosa tree outside the window, and a bedroom with a communicating bathroom. The drawing-room and bathroom had French windows leading onto a balcony which ran the whole length of the flat. We had a splendid view of the bay and the mountains, and our back windows looked towards Roquebrune and Cap Martin. It was a new and delightful experience to be collecting my own household equipment. I even had feather pillows, made by the blind, sent from England.

Leon was an admirable man in the house; he could do everything—except, perhaps, plumbing. He was a first-class cook, specialising in Polish dishes. He laid the carpets, made all the curtains and cushions, and upholstered most beautifully our set of Empire furniture. If only he had resisted gambling, we might have been so happy.

18

AN ENGLISH YEAR

Roméo et Juliette — Lambert and the lemonade — Winning
over Lord Rothermere — Surrealists at the Sarah-Bernhardt
— In the dome of His Majesty's — 'The Queen of English
Dancers' on ice — An operation in Chelsea — *The Triumph
of Neptune* at the Lyceum — A last-minute hornpipe — Airborne Britannia — Talk of diamonds — *L'Oiseau de feu* revived — Flowers for a reluctant Princess.

Even in Monte Carlo, where we were always glad to settle down
into a regular routine, life was never dull in the Russian Ballet.
Somebody was always behaving badly and getting fined; there
was always a new flirtation or drama; new dancers arrived, or
other dancers left. The fines we paid, according to a scale specified
in our contracts, were mostly for being late, and these all went
towards the purchase of a library which we carried round with
us on tour in wooden crates. The books were all Russian, except
for a few French novels, and a favourite author was Jack London,
translated into Russian.

The first excitement of this 1926 season was the sudden departure of Nemtchinova and Zverev. Being keen disciples of
Tolstoy, they had refused on principle to put their names to a
written contract with Diaghilev. Massine and his new wife
Eleanora Marra, who had been appearing successfully in revue
in London, were now planning a new show with C. B. Cochran,
and as they needed a pair of good classical dancers, they got
Cochran to offer Nemtchinova and Zverev a large salary. Both
dancers had been with Diaghilev over ten years, and he had
built Nemtchinova up to become our classical ballerina. How-

242

ever, she and Zverev left with hardly a good-bye. This was a real blow to Diaghilev. I never knew if their Tolstoian ideals prevented them from signing a contract with Cochran.

The year 1926 was destined to be a somewhat 'English year' in the history of the Russian Ballet, for we were to do two ballets by English composers, and a new English backer was to play a part in our lives. It was at one of our morning classes that we first set eyes on Lord Rothermere, the proprietor of the *Daily Mail*. He was a big man with a slow way of speaking. It was soon evident that he was prepared to take an interest in individual dancers as well as in the ballet.

Our new ballet, *Roméo et Juliette*, was by no means a literal adaptation of Shakespeare's play: it was about a troupe of ballet dancers who were rehearsing episodes from the play. The first scene was a class; then the *maître de ballet* tried to arrange a *pas de deux* for the two principal dancers, who kept interrupting their work to make love to each other; there followed some scenes from the play in terms of dancing; and finally Romeo wearing a leather coat and airman's headgear, eloped with Juliet in an aeroplane. The composer of the score was Constant Lambert. He was young, inexperienced, shy of the Russians and terrified of Diaghilev. His timidity, however, did not prevent him from having very definite ideas of his own. He had, apparently, wanted his friend Christopher Wood to design the scenery, while Diaghilev insisted on employing the two surrealists Ernst and Miro, so that relations between the composer and his employer were always rather strained.

One afternoon Constant had arrived to accompany a scene which Nijinska had arranged and which Diaghilev was coming to see at our two o'clock rehearsal. It was discovered that Thaddeus Slavinsky, who opened the scene alone, was not present. After a few minutes of waiting the atmosphere grew very tense, and Diaghilev began walking about, banging his stick and haranguing Grigoriev. As Slavinsky made no secret of his private affairs some of us knew very well where he might be enjoying his afternoon siesta. At last Diaghilev turned on Grigoriev, who always got a red spot on his cheek when he was disturbed, and shouted, 'If you think you know where he is, go and fetch him!' Poor Grigoriev rushed away, and shortly afterwards Slavinsky appeared, making excuses. By this time Diaghilev was in such a state that he screamed abuse at Slavinsky. They nearly came to blows and some of the male dancers had to pull Slavinsky away. Florrie Grenfell, who was present to watch the rehearsal, told me that Diaghilev apologised to her afterwards for this degrading scene. Constant Lambert, seated at the piano, could not understand Russian and had never seen a Russian or a Pole in a rage before. I suppose his anxiety over the music, his animosity towards Diaghilev and his fear of the mad foreigners amongst whom he found himself, all came to a head: he went deathly pale and was about to faint. Noticing this, I grabbed a bottle of fizzy lemonade which I had brought to rehearsal, and poured it into his mouth as he was on the point of slipping from his chair. This brought him round.

Faced with the loss of Nemtchinova, Diaghilev had succeeded in persuading Karsavina to make a come-back especially for this ballet. He liked to think that his new young favourite would dance with his first and most beloved ballerina. It was not so funny for Mme Karsavina, who was out of practice, to find herself landed with Lifar as a partner. The great dancer, used to the support of such artists as Fokine and Nijinsky, discovered that the inexperienced young man hardly knew how to lift her. She never complained. Her manners were as beautiful as her face. She would just raise her eyebrows and say, 'But Serge, if you will do it this way it will work.'

Diaghilev thought that the rehearsals of an 'English' ballet, inspired by Shakespeare and composed by Lambert, must surely interest Lord Rothermere; but the main point of this ballet, as we soon realised, was to be an expression of the latest art movement, Surrealism, and it is doubtful whether the newspaper magnate had much interest or sympathy with that. However, he came to our rehearsals.

I played the Nurse, and I had to come onto an empty stage carrying a scroll, which I then had to open and read. The whole company were at rehearsal one afternoon when, preparing to make my entrance, I realised that my scroll had got lost and had probably slipped down behind the benches where Diaghilev was sitting with Lord Rothermere and his *entourage*. When my music cue was given I was still rummaging for the scroll, and several voices called out, 'Sokolova, you're late! Why don't you start?' Turning to face the crowd, I said, 'I can't start. I haven't any paper.' There was a burst of laughter, and several dancers ran towards me waving newspapers or paper bags. Lord Rothermere asked Diaghilev for an English translation of the remark which had caused such amusement; and I blushed.

Roméo et Juliette was performed on a stage quite empty except for a few mysterious objects designed by Joan Miro. There were two drop curtains by Max Ernst painted with abstractions which I think were meant to represent Day and Night; and between two of the scenes the curtain was lowered to within a few feet of the floor, so that the audience could see the dancers' legs as they walked about to take up their positions for the next episode. This idea was thought to be very ingenious by the powers that be, but the public sometimes tittered, thinking that the machinery had gone wrong. Most of the dancers wore a kind of practice dress, and the only three who had period costumes were Karsavina, Lifar and myself. The costumiers decided to fit a basketwork frame round my middle to give me the pregnant line which was fashionable in the Renaissance, and made me look like the lady painted by Van Eyck in the National Gallery. I protested at this and succeeded in having the awkward appendage reduced in size.

By the time of the dress rehearsal Diaghilev and Constant were at loggerheads, and the composer decided to try to prevent the performance of his work. I never knew what caused the disagreement, but I did know that Constant went into the orchestra pit and removed important parts of the music. Poor soul, he did not realise that he could not win against Diaghilev. Those parts were back on their stands before the opening night.

Meanwhile we had been seeing quite a lot of Lord Rothermere. He had a villa on Cap Martin and a charming dancer called Rita Redhead, who had been with Pavlova, was staying there.

As I admired the glorious variety of tulips which grew in the villa's garden, Lord Rothermere took to sending masses of these round to my flat. He also used to send some of us large boxes of chocolates from a shop in Monte Carlo called La Marquise de Sévigné.

As I was not one of the Ballet's beauties or glamour girls, I never understood why Lord Rothermere paid such attention to me, but I think he genuinely admired my work, and perhaps our common nationality was a bond between us. Diaghilev now decided that he knew the English millionaire well enough to ask him to underwrite our next London season. He was anxious to instal himself at His Majesty's Theatre, an ideal one for the ballet, but probably more expensive than most. Having noticed that Lord Rothermere liked me, he sent for me and explained his plan. He had already approached Lord Rothermere about the backing, but nothing was settled, and he wanted me to clinch the deal for him at a supper party he was giving for the newspaper magnate and his principal dancers. I felt this to be a fearful responsibility as I was not by nature a gold-digger, and had no experience of extracting large sums of money from rich men. However, Diaghilev seemed convinced that only I could persuade Lord Rothermere to give his word to back us and he said, 'You must realise that on your ability to get this support depends the whole future of the Russian Ballet.'

The supper party took place at the Carlton Hotel, Monte Carlo, and I was seated between Diaghilev and Lord Rothermere. At what he judged the right moment, the 'Old Man' whispered, 'Now you must go and dance with him.' I was very nervous, and it was not until we had had two dances that I summoned the courage to approach the subject. Lord Rothermere did not make it easy for me. Eventually, after a little persuasion, he said, 'All right, I will do what you ask. But I want you to make it clear to Diaghilev that I am doing this for you personally.' I was dumbfounded. When we returned to our table I asked Lord Rothermere to excuse me if I spoke to Diaghilev in Russian, but when I did so I had not the audacity to repeat in front of the other dancers what he had really said, so I told Diaghilev that the backing had been granted and left it at that. Diaghilev beamed; and when Lord Rothermere asked me if I had repeated his exact words, I merely said, 'Yes, of course. Thank you very much.'

Other events during our 1926 season in Monte Carlo were the loss of our ballet master and the attempted suicide of one of our dancers. Nicolas Legat had a row with Diaghilev and returned to London. He was replaced by Tchernicheva, who remained *maîtresse de ballet* for the rest of the company's existence. The attempted suicide was a Polish dancer, Statkevitch by name, tall, plain and with a slight cast in one eye, who tried to kill himself for love of a pretty little dark girl in the *corps de ballet*. Vassili found him in the men's big dressing-room just as he was on the point of putting his head through a noose. Later in Paris he also shot himself, but as Leon pointed out, well above the heart where it was most unlikely to kill him. These demonstrations proved effective, as the girl subsequently married him. (The couple survived dreadful experiences in Poland during the war, and Statkevitch is now ballet master at one of the provincial theatres there.)

We opened in Paris on May 18, 1926, at the Théâtre Sarah-Bernhardt, a grand old theatre but gloomy and mysterious behind the scenes. The dressing-rooms had old-fashioned fireplaces and very tall windows. Mine, needless to say, was haunted. When I exclaimed to the dresser, on moving in, 'What a dreary dressing-room!' she replied, '*Oui, madame,* a lovely girl threw herself out of that window. And she sometimes returns here.' She went on to explain that the great Sarah had been so jealous of this young actress that she had made her life unbearable and the girl had killed herself.

Paris audiences are unlike those of any other country. You were never conscious of a friendly 'ballet public', and it was always a surprise to see that there was an audience in front of the house. On the other hand, as painting and music were far more part of people's lives in Paris than in London, they naturally took a keen interest when Diaghilev presented works by the latest painters and composers: in fact, I had the feeling that in Paris dancing

R 247

took a second place. The performance of *Roméo et Juliette* on our opening night was marked by a demonstration made by surrealists, who objected to Ernst and Miro working for the 'capitalist' Diaghilev. Leaflets and insults were showered from the gallery, the new ballet was interrupted and could only be resumed after the house lights had been turned on and a number of people were ejected by the police.

We showed two other novelties in Paris, the first of which had no importance. *La Pastorale* was all about the making of a film, and the only memory it leaves behind it is that of Doubrovska in the guise of a film star unlike any seen before or since, wearing a short, fringed skirt and a long velvet train, extending her elegant white legs, pointing her lovely arched feet, being followed about by a silly little camera on a tripod and interrupted by Lifar riding a bicycle.

The other new work, *Jack-in-the-Box*, was taken over by Diaghilev from Comte Etienne de Beaumont, who had set up a rival company with Massine two years before. It had music by Erik Satie, décor by Derain, choreography by Balanchine and good parts for Idzikovsky and a black-faced Danilova, but it was very short and had very few performances.

A great season in London now began at His Majesty's Theatre, which nothing but illness could have spoilt for me. We had not had a London season to ourselves since *The Sleeping Princess* closed at the Alhambra; the public were in ecstasies to see such a varied programme of old and new ballets after the snippets they had been doled out at the Coliseum; and we were all delighted to find ourselves performing in this historic theatre with its noble tradition. Sir Herbert Beerbohm Tree's rooms were all in a line on the first floor. I was given his make-up room, which was small but had its own bathroom with the largest bath I have ever seen.

Soon after our arrival Lord Rothermere appeared, and the principal dancers were all invited to go up with him into the dome, which contained Tree's private apartments. There was a large room, which the manager told us was now used for board meetings: it was comfortably furnished—that is to say, there was a kitchen, a big bed which slid into the wall and several suits of armour. I could not stop exclaiming at the unexpectedness of this secret flat, and Lord Rothermere said, 'Perhaps you'd like me to buy the theatre for you?' (Not that it was for sale.) Taken aback, I replied inanely, 'I'm sure Diaghilev would be so very pleased to have it.' He frowned and changed the subject. I never had any idea of the right way to talk to rich and powerful people. I always put my foot in it. But I think Lord Rothermere forgave me for not being able to feel romantically towards him.

That our wonderful season, with Karsavina in *Roméo et Juliette*, Trefilova in *Le Lac des cygnes*, Lopokova in *La Boutique fantasque*, Doubrovska in *Les Noces*, with Tchernicheva, Danilova, Woizikovsky, Idzikovsky, Lifar and myself was a success from a financial as well as an artistic point of view, must have made Lord Rothermere think that his first plunge into the theatre had been worth while. It certainly did us no harm to have the *Daily Mail* behind us. In one headline I was called 'The Queen of English Dancers'.

By this time, however, I was in a state of being quite afraid of publicity. The more my name got into the papers, the more demands Father began to make on me and the more money he was able to borrow. Sometimes, what with my illness, Leon's gambling and Father's scandalous behaviour, I would wonder whether my life was worth living—then 'cheerfulness would break in' once more.

Unhappily my internal pains were getting worse, and I spent half the time with ice-bags on my stomach. There was a charming woman in charge of the smooth running of His Majesty's Theatre. She did all she could to make us as comfortable as possible and but for her kindness I should have collapsed much earlier than I did. As soon as the curtain came down on any ballet in which I was dancing, this good soul got a waitress to run through the theatre fetching me a bag of crushed ice. Mrs Samuel Courtauld often came to see me in my dressing-room, bringing young Randolph Churchill and other friends, whom I used to entertain clutching an ice-bag to my middle. One day Mrs Courtauld followed me into my bathroom and I told her the trouble. She made an appointment for me with a gynaecologist friend of hers, to see how he could help me get through the remaining weeks of the season. This doctor told me that if an operation was not performed immediately I would be in danger: but I was reluctant to give up.

Five days before the end of the season I could dance no more, and I was taken into the Chelsea Hospital for Women, where I had an operation. It all happened so quickly and quietly and so soon before the last night, that I thought there would be no publicity. However, a few small paragraphs appeared in the papers after the operation was over, and I had stacks of letters of sympathy from all over the country. One of them, posted from the north, was addressed to 'Lydia Sokolova, London'. Lord Rothermere sent so many bouquets and so many boxes of roses so regularly that I used to pass them to the other wards, and they gave pleasure to most of the hospital. Leon told me over thirty years later that it was Lord Rothermere who paid for my operation. Thinking it over, it seems likely that there was something left over when the hospital bills were settled, for this would account for Leon's being able to afford a trip to Poland at this time, his first visit home for many years.

The ballet danced at Ostend and Le Touquet without me, then went on holiday. After three weeks in hospital and a few days with Mother, I went south to convalesce at the Golf Hotel at St Maxime. The little place was hardly changed, though there were a few more houses and the railway system had improved. I was glad to be about again and in the sun.

Diaghilev, not knowing how long I would be ill—or even if I should be able to dance again—engaged a Polish girl called Vera Petrova, to take over some of my roles. She was a reliable dancer with a good technique, and later substituted for Nemtchinova in *Les Biches*.

As soon as the holidays were over, rehearsals for our second English ballet began in Paris. I was better and found I could still dance. The starting point for *The Triumph of Neptune* was Diaghilev's admiration for the rather French music of Lord Berners, the wit and lightness of which appealed to him. He asked Sacheverell Sitwell to help him find an English subject and an

250

English designer for the ballet. Many ideas were discussed and many painters rejected—for Diaghilev could not discover one living artist in England whose talent he thought suited to ballet design. At length it was decided to arrange a kind of mock pantomime with a story partly inspired by the science fiction of Jules Verne: there was a villain, policemen, a fairy queen and a transformation scene, but the sailor hero, in company with a journalist, was shot to the moon. The twelve quite elaborate scenes were to be painted in the style of Pollock's 'twopence-coloured' toy theatres. This whole ballet was clearly going to be enormous fun, with plenty of opportunities for comic as well as classical dancing. It was the biggest production Diaghilev had undertaken since *The Sleeping Princess* and we all looked forward to it. As His Majesty's was not available, we were to appear for the first time at the Lyceum, exchanging the haunt of Beerbohm Tree for that of Henry Irving.

The Triumph of Neptune took time to prepare, and we continued to rehearse it after our London season had begun. In the Russian Ballet one was never told what roles were in store for one, the only warning being a notice on the call-board: but as time went on and I was never called, I began to wonder when I was going to hear something about a part. As it was an 'all-British' production and the whole company was involved, I could not believe that I alone should be left out. When I was called at last, Balanchine gave me one of those little classical fragments which I so much disliked, because I was not primarily a classical dancer and needed something with character to get my teeth into. I resolved to make no comment until I saw the finished ballet.

At the orchestra rehearsal, on stage without scenery, I saw how insignificant a part I was to play in our delightful pantomime ballet, and I asked Grigoriev if he could get me a minute alone with the 'Old Man'. Going into the stalls, I waited till Diaghilev beckoned me and asked me, 'What's the matter?' I was tearful and shaking with nerves and resentment, but determined to say my piece. I said, 'Sergei Pavlovitch, I am terribly disappointed you have left me out of this ballet except for one tiny dance. And I offer to pay a fine for missing every performance, because

I would sooner be left out altogether than have the press and the public talk about how little I am given to do in our English ballet.' He was not a bit angry. Perhaps for once he recognised that I was right, and that he had been careless to have over-looked me; for there were so many good parts in *The Triumph of Neptune*. He said, 'You must speak to Lord Berners.'

So I went up to Lord Berners, who was on the stage, looking, with a hint of mockery, like the quiet kind of dandy he was, and I repeated what I had said to Diaghilev. 'I can't understand it', he said. 'I had naturally imagined that you would be having a principal part in my ballet. It doesn't make sense, and I must do something about it.' Diaghilev, Kochno, Lord Berners, Ba-lanchine and Lifar all went off together, telling me to be on stage immediately after lunch. When they came back Lord Berners told me cheerfully that a perfect place for my appearance had been found. A gay hornpipe tune was played during one of the scene changes, and I was to dance this in front of the drop curtain. 'Go and get a dance fixed up', he said. George Balanchine had the quickest invention of any choreographer I ever knew. We went under the stage together and I showed him a few steps from the Scottish reel—one of which Ninette had taught me some time before. We hummed, sang and got the hornpipe organised in no time, without a pianist. Meanwhile the orchestra had continued rehearsing, as the ballet was to be run through again with the scenery. When my time came, George pushed me out on the stage on my correct beat, and I rattled through that dance without a mistake. To my amazement I had a round of tapping on the music-stands from the orchestra. The story must have spread among them, and they knew that an hour before there had been no dance at all.

The next question was how to dress me. Diaghilev, Kochno or Sitwell—or all three of them—went to Fox's, the old-estab-lished theatrical costumiers. Rummaging about in boxes, they found two extraordinary costumes which had never left the shop in living memory and dated from goodness knows how long before that. The one which fitted me was a queer tight-fitting tunic falling to my thighs, and done up with enormous Victorian hooks and eyes: it was entirely covered in pear-shaped coloured stones set in pewter, which caught the light and tinkled as I danced, sending thousands of flashing rays across the footlights. With this costume, the heaviest ever worn to dance a hornpipe, I sported a Glengarry, tartan gaiters, a little dagger, and red shoes. To crown my pleasure they called me 'Britannia'.

There were some flying fairies in the Frozen Forest scene, arranged by Mr Kirby, and when Balanchine wondered how to bring me into the finale somebody had the idea of hoisting me up in the air above a big statue of Neptune, which occupied the centre of the stage. I was to rise straight up behind Neptune and have a spotlight turned on me, so Mr Kirby got busy and fitted some harness under my arms. Before the curtain went up on this scene at the dress rehearsal I called across the footlights, 'What shall I do with my feet?' The answer came back, 'Cross them and rest them on Neptune's right hand.'

As a series of dances came to an end, I felt the wires grow taut between my shoulders. My first emotion as I rose in the air, was to laugh outright at the sight of little Idzikovsky as Cupid, dancing round the stage in a short, pink silk Grecian tunic, a gold tiara and large horn-rimmed spectacles. A second later I felt only pain as the wire wrenched at my body, and I realised what it must be like to be hanged. I could not possibly find Neptune's hand with my feet; and as I reached my destination I began to rotate. Everyone roared with laughter, and when it was seen that my tunic was open at the back to admit the reins all the company and spectators were in fits. There were cries of 'Put your foot on Neptune's hand! Stay still!' but I was beyond anything except pleading gestures to be let down. After this I was fitted with more straps between the legs to take some of the weight, and I had a ring on each middle finger with strings held by men in the wings, which kept me as firm as a rock.

Although it was slightly on the long side, and many scenes were cut after the first night, *The Triumph of Neptune* was a success from the start. It had plenty of incident as well as dancing. My hornpipe turned out to be one of the hits of the show. It was so quick and unexpected, and was danced moving across the stage.

It had a clean finish on one leg, and this was always followed by a burst of applause. When I ran back to take a call, I instinctively took up the position in which the dance had ended. This always brought more applause, and I would repeat the procedure, without the slightest idea that I was being funny. I was soon up on the carpet before Diaghilev. 'How dare you hold up the show? Do you think this is a music-hall?' I was forbidden ever to take the call like that again.

Other good dances were those of Balanchine as Snowball, a drunken negro; and another hornpipe in the final scene for Danilova and Lifar in which she wore a boater, and trousers under her ballet skirt. Both of these were brilliant and could have been encored at every performance.

I had a large solitaire ring made by a jeweller in Monte Carlo whose speciality was to copy expensive pieces, substituting white topaz for diamonds; I used to wear this when I danced the Hostess in *Les Biches*. One evening at the Lyceum I was standing in the wings, waiting to go on, when Diaghilev, Rothermere and his secretary came and stood by me. Catching sight of my ring, Lord Rothermere said, 'I can't understand an artist like you wearing an imitation.' I told him, 'It's a real stone—a white topaz.' He said, 'I think we should get you a diamond'; then, turning to his secretary, 'See that she has one tomorrow. Don't forget'. I was delighted, and feeling I must include Diaghilev in the conversation, I turned to him and said rather naïvely, 'I'm going to have a real diamond ring for *Les Biches*!' He gave me a forced smile and looked away; then murmuring to Lord Rothermere, 'Come, let us go and watch her dance', he led the two men through the pass door. Needless to say I did *not* get the diamond.

During rehearsals in Paris Diaghilev had told us that he intended reviving *L'Oiseau de feu*. This was a considerable undertaking as the ballet had not been given since 1921, when Massine had danced the Prince, while of those who had known the production in Fokine's day hardly anyone remained but Grigoriev, Tchernicheva, Kremnev and myself. We worked on the great ballet in Paris and tried to reconstruct it day by day. I felt

it was a bit hard, now that I was a principal dancer, still to have
to dance my old part as one of the twelve Princesses. Also, having
recently recovered from my operation, I felt it would be wise to
reserve my energy as much as possible for leading roles. I therefore asked Diaghilev during a rehearsal whether someone else
could not be a Princess in my place. I said I did not want to dance
in the *corps de ballet* any more. He was outwardly calm but in-
wardly furious. In front of everybody he told me I should consider it an honour to dance in his *corps de ballet*, which was only
good because principal dancers took their turn to dance in it.
He reminded me how Doubrovska danced with twenty-three
others in *Le Lac des cygnes*, and how Tchernicheva was one of the
Nurses in *Petroushka*. It was his right, he said, to decide which
ballets I should dance, not mine; and there was a clause in the
new contract I had signed the day before to that effect. I said
that if I had known this I should not have signed it, and that in
the next contract I would make a list of ballets I wished to
dance. He told me in that case we should part company for ever.
By this time tears were pouring down my cheeks. There were two
of us in the company whom Diaghilev could always make cry
whenever he wished, Nijinska and myself.

Golovine's old setting for *L'Oiseau de feu* had grown shabby,
and Diaghilev had commissioned a new one from Gontcharova.
The new design had its virtues, but I missed the magic of the old
scenery, which Diaghilev used to light so beautifully. The rostrum
had always been a problem in the old production: it was a very
high, steep wooden structure which had to be securely built up
and bolted before every performance, as every member of the
company came running down its steps in the course of the ballet.
It was expensive to transport and to renew, took a long time to
put up and take down, and often created complications on account of fire precautions. I have no doubt the stage staff were
delighted to see the end of this cumbersome piece of scenery,
but the beautiful groupings when the Princesses appeared in
turn on that high platform and ran down the steps with the moonlight on their hair, were never to be seen again. From 1926 onwards they continued to make some of the movements Fokine

had planned specially for the old production, but as Gontcharova gave them head-dresses and tucked up their hair, the back-bending and stroking movements became pointless. We now made our entrance through cut-outs in the forest set; and the big tree which used to shine with a magic light and from which the chief Princess used to shake down the golden apples, was now a flat with the fruit heaped at its foot.

So I was back in my old place as one of the Princesses, and although the production had changed I loved every minute of it. On the first night of the revival, *L'Oiseau de feu* was given as the middle ballet, following *Les Biches*. I noticed that there were several bouquets waiting for me; and one, especially beautiful, was an enormous mass of pure white flowers. On the envelope pinned to it was written 'After *L'Oiseau de feu*'. I told Grigoriev that I would not have this outstanding bouquet handed to me while I stood in a group of the *corps de ballet*, and that I should like it after *Les Biches*. He said 'It says on the envelope "After *The Firebird*"', and you'll get it then.' Our discipline was severe even in such matters as this. (I well remember the indignation of Nikitina during our very last season when Diaghilev refused to let her have an enormous stuffed dog handed to her on the stage.)

As we took our calls after *L'Oiseau de feu*, myself standing in the big semi-circle behind the principals, the enormous bouquet of white flowers was handed to me. I had a sensation of opera glasses being raised to every eye in the theatre, as the audience wondered what this girl in the background had done to be singled out with such flowers; and I longed for the curtain to stay down.

The card inside the envelope was inscribed with the words:

19

ILLNESS

Where the money went — A fatal walk — The dazzle of *La Chatte* — Abortive trip to Lourdes — Trying out treatments —Come-back at the Prince's — More Father-trouble — Collapse in Paris — Operations in Paris and Nice — An ordeal at Les Jasmins — Back to life and London — Two freak ballets and a masterpiece — Phantoms of the Opéra — Via Lourdes to Monte Carlo — The empty rehearsal room.

Before returning to Monte Carlo in 1928 we paid our first visits to Turin and Milan. In Turin, Massine rejoined us and arranged an attractive dance for Danilova, Lifar and himself in *Cimarosiana*. Spessivtseva also came back to us, and on the first night of *Le Lac des cygnes*, the orchestra, under Inghelbrecht, played so slowly that she and Lifar could barely get through their dance. Serge was used to Danilova and he was terrified of partnering anyone new (in the previous season at Monte Carlo he had almost dropped Doubrovska over the footlights), and his first appearance with Spessivtseva was altogether too much for him. I danced in the *pas de trois* with Petrova and Idzikovsky. Our début at La Scala, Milan, was not very well received.

Leon's gambling had become an obsession: I rarely saw him at home except when he came in to eat and sleep. If only he had been as reliable in his private life as he was in his professional life! He was loved and admired by the whole company. Watching the arrangement of a new ballet, he would take in automatically every step of every dance: he knew everybody's part in all the ballets and never had to be asked twice to show how something should be done or to teach a role. He was efficient in everything he undertook, did his own sewing and darning, and would trust no one to stitch elastic onto his tights or shoes.

The gambling ruined everything. Leon would ransack my cases for something of value to sell or pawn; I was in a continuous state of debt. As Natasha grew older her expenses increased; Father started more and more crack-brained schemes; Mother was desperately ill, and hardly a letter came from home without a demand for money. There was nobody in the company to whom I could confide my troubles, so I had to bear them alone.

One lovely evening about five o'clock, while Leon was playing poker in a café, I took a bus and went along the sea to Eze. When I got out of the bus the whole bay looked calm and still in the evening light. I climbed a grass slope, followed a winding path which petered out in some high stony ground and found myself in a ravine. I thought by then it was probably shorter to continue onto the upper road than to turn back. The higher I climbed, the steeper and stonier became the hillside: eventually I was obliged to walk sideways, taking all the strain on my left leg. It grew dark, but I kept on. At last I reached the top and lay down for a while on the ground to recover my strength. It was nearly nine o'clock when I found a café and asked for help. The proprietor stopped a bus full of tourists, and the driver squeezed me into the cab beside him and drove me back to Monte Carlo. Leon had not been home to dinner and never knew I had been out.

I felt uncomfortable in class the next day, and on the day after there was an awful wrenching in my left knee, and the ligament snapped. I kept on dancing for a while, but the pain was unbearable. One night, some days later, after hopping and jumping on my points as the Carnation Fairy in *Le Mariage d'Aurore*, I had to give up.

Villa Les Jasmins was further away from the Casino than the homes of any of the other dancers, so there was no question of my friends dropping in to visit me on their way to or from work. I was very lonely as I sat in my eyrie, nursing my leg. Had I but realised it at the time, I was suffering chiefly from an overdose of resentment against Leon, and if only I could have climbed out of the rut of self-pity I might have saved myself a lot of unnecessary suffering. As we so often do when in trouble, I turned more and more to God for help. I built myself a little altar, and placed on it some water I had obtained from the grotto at Lourdes. I made up my mind to go to Lourdes at the earliest opportunity: but for the time being I was on two sticks.

What I missed most, as I lay at the villa day after day on my own, was the music. Such silence after a life of sound can drive a dancer crazy. By the end of April a new ballet, *La Chatte*, was ready and I resolved to see the dress rehearsal. I hobbled down the long flights of steps on my sticks and a carriage took me to the Casino.

The most surprising element of *La Chatte* was its décor: we had had cubism, rayonnism, post-impressionism and surrealism, and the latest thing was constructivism. The two Russian brothers, Gabo and Pevsner, had built up and cut out structures and abstract objects from a new material, talc: rising against hangings of black American oil-cloth, these flashed, as they caught the light, their message of an amazing new plastic age to the incredulous and blinking public. Sauguet's score was gay and danceable, and Balanchine's choreography for Kochno's adaptation of the Aesop fable would have been delightful in any costumes, yet the shining transparent armour worn by the dancers gave it a heroic interplanetary quality, as if the little tragedy of the man who fell in love with a cat, saw her transformed into a woman, and died of a broken heart when she ran off with a mouse, was taking place in a society of god-like pioneers of a newly subjugated star. The form of these costumes was simple, and although Spessivtseva's talc *tutu* and Lifar's breastplate were sometimes distracting, there have been few ballets in which the beauty of young people's bodies in motion were shown to better effect.

Spessivtseva was the Cat at the first performance in Monte Carlo, but she hurt herself just before the season opened in Paris, and Nikitina learned and danced her role at a day's notice. *La Chatte* certainly became a ballet associated especially with Nikitina and Lifar. They were both so attractive, young, lithe and streamlined that they seemed as essential to Balanchine's beautiful work as Dolin had been to Nijinska's *Train Bleu*. The

Cat at one moment did *pirouettes* on her left point, supported by a finger held above her head, and as she spun round she sank in a deep *plié* to the ground, still remaining on the tip of her left toe. This has been done often since, but then it was new. Lifar's entrance, borne aloft by five men, like a warrior in a chariot, was unforgettable. The ballet ended with his being carried off dead, to Sauguet's funeral march.

Although the ligaments in my leg had healed, an arthritic condition had set in, and a disc had formed on the inside of my knee, so that I could not bend it at all. I began to wonder if it would ever be possible for me to dance again. When the ballet left for Barcelona I travelled across France to Lourdes.

It was hard to find a room in Lourdes, but at last I discovered some people who could take me in for two nights. Next morning at seven o'clock, I joined a long queue which was making for the establishment where one is submerged in water from the holy spring. Outside the grotto I knelt and prayed as the others did, and paid for candles to be lit. There was only room for a certain number of candles at the shrine, so many of these could never have been lit—and were probably sold again. I was the only one in the queue who was not wearing a cardboard label, and when, after hours of waiting, I arrived at the door, I was told that as I was not a member of any pilgrimage I could not go in. Later in the day I obtained the necessary ticket, but when I arrived once more at the shrine, there was a notice posted which said the waters were being replenished. I thought that my failure to gain admittance to the sanctuary at Lourdes was probably a punishment for going there under false pretences, as I was not a Roman Catholic.

I rejoined Leon and the company in Paris in the hopes of finding a more conventional cure for my knee. My first visit was to an eminent French surgeon, who said he could heal me. I sat in the chair while he burnt sixty-two *points de feu* on the inside of my knee with a live electric wire. He did not cure me and I suffered additional tortures for weeks from the burns. George Balanchine also had trouble with his knee, so we both went to a famous Russian surgeon, who recommended the removal of our cartilages. I refused this operation, and was later thankful I had, for after George lost his cartilage he was never able to dance or even kneel with ease, at least not during the existence of the Diaghilev Ballet.

While the company appeared again at the Sarah-Bernhardt Theatre, I was trying many different kinds of treatment. My left leg withered through lack of use, and my right leg grew over-developed. I used dozens of bottles of castor-oil in compresses on my knee, hoping to loosen the joints.

Then I was recommended to visit William Dempster, an English osteopath who treated athletes, and I went over to London to see him. He told me immediately that the seat of the trouble was in my hip and back, and he started to work my muscles with an electric treatment. My leg was so weak that the knee kept slipping out of joint, but Bill Dempster gradually got me dancing again. His bandages and adhesives were works of art. The Russian Ballet came to the Prince's Theatre, and by the end of July I was strong enough to dance Kikimora and my Carnation Fairy variation on the same evening. The man who had worked this miracle used to stand in the wings to manipulate my knee between ballets, and I shall always be grateful for all the work he put in on my wretched leg.

At this time there was no knowing what mischief Father would be up to next. He would borrow money from all kinds of people who then came to me for repayment. Sometimes he called at the stage door, demanding money. One of his projects was to give lessons in painting to children, promising their parents that if they passed certain examinations he would get them jobs in the Russian Ballet. When this fraud was exposed I suffered the unpleasant publicity. Finally, I took the terrible step of writing to tell Father that I disowned him.

The man who had paid an advance to take over the house at Hastings proved to be a crook. He walked out, leaving beds unmade and crockery unwashed and a number of creditors behind him. We had worry and expense over solicitors, and the contents of the house were all sold up. This was a great shock to Mother and brought on another heart attack. At the end of our season at the Prince's, I went down to the sale and spent fifteen pounds buying in a few of Mother's prized possessions. I paid twenty-five shillings for the crocodile my Uncle Tom had brought back from South Africa when I was a child. A woman friend in Hastings agreed to house these objects temporarily, but by the time Beatrice was able to go down and fetch them, this woman, too, had sold up everything and disappeared. I wonder where the crocodile is now—he was five or six feet long.

As my knee was still weak, it was decided that I should stay on in England for treatment while the company set off for a strenuous tour of Austria and Germany. After a cold, wet month with my family in a furnished house we had taken at Birchington in Kent, I settled down with some friends, Helen and Jim Ede, in their beautiful Georgian house in Elm Row, Hampstead.

For some reason Idzikovsky, too, had remained in London, and we used to practise together in a studio off Fitzroy Square. The only money I had was what Leon chose to send me. There was always the rent of the Monte Carlo flat to be found, and if Leon had been losing at poker we were in trouble.

As 1927 drew to a close my leg got better, but as the time approached when I was to rejoin the company in Paris, I began to feel unaccountable sensations of giddiness. The pavements I walked on felt as if they were made of some soft substance, which was disconcerting.

I joined Leon in Paris during the last week of 1927. Rehearsals were to begin on the following day, and he was to make an appointment for me with Diaghilev. We were staying, not for the first time, at an hotel in the Rue de Moscou, where we had a self-contained apartment across the courtyard at the back. Leon had hardly gone off to rehearsal the following morning when I was shocked by a sharp pain on my right side, and I began to be violently sick. The pain and sickness continued all day. A doctor who was called diagnosed appendicitis, but I told him I had lost my appendix eighteen months before. He gave me a drug and promised that I should be all right in the morning. This, however, was not the case. I urged Leon to telephone Diaghilev, for I knew the 'Old Man' would do something for me. Diaghilev sent me a Russian-Jewish surgeon of his acquaintance, who had a clinic at Neuilly, and who arrived to see me in his white overall, straight from performing an operation. He sent for an ambulance and, refusing to be carried down on the stretcher, I walked downstairs and got into it. As soon as I arrived at the clinic I was taken into the operating theatre. After giving me a lumbar puncture, the surgeon operated on my stomach, using only a local anaesthetic. My head and hair hung over the edge of the table and I complained that my hair was hurting before I passed out. Diaghilev came to visit me and was very distressed to find me too weak to talk. There was some doubt as to whether I should survive after a severe haemorrhage, and when the company went south Diaghilev telephoned several times from Lyon and Marseilles to enquire after me. I was cheered by his affectionate messages.

A time came when I could no longer bear the stifling atmosphere of the clinic, so when Camishov, the company's property man, who was in Paris to supervise moving scenery to Monte Carlo, came to see me I implored him to get me away at all costs. He had brought enough money to settle the bill, so I got out of bed, put on his overcoat over my dressing-gown, and went back to my hotel in a taxi.

Camishov engaged a Russian lady of good family to come twice a day to look after me. Another doctor found I had a streptococcal infection, for which he gave me regular injections. My hair fell out in great strands, and what remained had to be cut off. The proprietors of the hotel were good to me, sending up meals twice a day, but the bills mounted alarmingly. Friends came to visit me; Pablo and Olga Picasso brought their son Paolo, and Hilda Bewicke came with her daughter Leila, who was as clever as her mother and already spoke several languages.

Towards the end of February Leon suddenly turned up, having had a win at the Casino. He stayed twenty-four hours, paid part of the hotel bill and went off again, saying he had to catch the night train. I later heard that he had gone instead to a gambling club, lost everything he had, and left the following morning with nothing but his railway ticket.

I gradually grew stronger, but I still could not walk, so Olga

S   263

Picasso took me for drives in her car. Spring had come and when I saw the sunshine on the budding trees in the Bois de Boulogne, I thanked God to be still alive. I felt an urge to be back in my flat in Monte Carlo, so at last I packed and took a train at the Gare de Lyon.

It was wonderful to be home once more and to lie on the balcony in the sunshine, looking at the sea and mountains I loved. As soon as I could get about again I paid Diaghilev a visit at the Hôtel de Paris. Kochno was with him, and I was too overcome to say very much; but he kissed me and held me very tight against him as he said, 'It's good to see you here today, instead of on the hospital bed.' We had tea and he described the new ballet, *Apollon Musagète*, which was then in rehearsal. The 'Old Man' told me he had missed me and that he looked forward to my being well enough to dance again. I was so afraid of having an emotional breakdown in front of him, that I was quite glad when Leon came to take me away.

My friend Edith Gautier-Vignal was one of the kindest people I knew: she was one of three daughters of Alfred Schiff, the financier. Her sisters, Mrs Morley and the Baronne de Marwicz performed endless good deeds, and Edith herself was awarded a gold medal for her charitable work by the late Pope. (Their brother 'Stephen Hudson' was a writer, and translated the last volume of Proust into English, after the death of Charles Scott-Moncrieff.) Soon after the ballet left Monte Carlo for a tour of Belgium and Switzerland before their Paris season, my doctor, Mme Simon, decided that we should seek a second opinion on my condition, as I was making such slow progress; so I turned to Edith for help and advice. She took me to see Dr Pratt, a Paris surgeon who worked in Nice during the season. He told me that my various operations had left me in such a state that the only thing was to have everything removed. On the way back from seeing him we stopped at the Queen Victoria Hospital, which stood high above the coast road, and Edith persuaded the matron to take me in, which was difficult, as the place was run for English visitors and had practically closed down for the summer.

I was afraid that this major operation might not really be

necessary and that after it I should put on weight, but I resigned myself to taking the doctor's advice. When I came to afterwards, I could hear a voice moaning, 'Oh, my poor old leg!' At first I thought this was myself complaining about my injured knee, but I soon found I was sharing a room with a very old lady who had fractured her hip. My window opened onto a garden, and although I was in pain I suddenly felt at peace, knowing I was in good hands and in beautiful surroundings. I was looked after by two devoted nurses called Beecham and Sherriff. (Beecham has since died, but Sherriff and I still correspond.)

I was amused to hear that in Antwerp Leon had danced my part in *The Triumph of Neptune*, and had even worn my costume. In Brussels, where a big orchestra was available, Diaghilev revived *Le Sacre du printemps* with Bronia Nijinska in my role of the Chosen Virgin. I expect he thought I should never dance again and that it was wise to keep the ballet fresh in the memory of the company. Bronia, of course, had the strength and the understanding for this role, but her individual type of movement was so different from Massine's, that the dance she did was almost unrecognisable and had little in common with the rest of the ballet. With such complicated rhythms as Stravinsky's for *Le Sacre*, her gift for improvisation could not see her through, and apparently she finished her dance some time before the music. She only danced it once.

Three weeks after my operation I was taken home and carried up the steps by Edith's kind chauffeur. Thanks to Edith, I was beginning to mend at last, but she herself had gone away though not before making arrangements for the *concierge* to bring me two meals a day—and I was quite alone. When the rhythm of a woman's life is interrupted by an operation such as I had undergone, it tends to affect her in strange ways, and I had one more terror to face.

As the summer advanced the heat in my flat under the roof became more unbearable. The sea was like a vast, oily lake, with criss-cross streaks where the currents met. The air shimmered, and in the middle of the day there was nothing to hear but the chugging of a distant motor-boat. The nights were airless, with a big yellow moon and fireflies in the hillside streams. From my balcony, the drop into the tiny garden of the house below must have been nearly a hundred feet.

One morning as I lay on my bed with the window open onto the balcony, I was overpowered by an unfamiliar sensation. As strong as a great wave, the urge came over me to leave my bed and throw myself out into the void. I kept shutting my eyes, then cautiously opening them to see if the sensation had gone away, but it assailed me more strongly than ever. I was soaked with sweat as this battle between will and impulse raged inside me. Clutching the headboard of my bed, I screamed for help; and I seemed to suffer hours of torture before the *concierge* climbed the four flights of stairs and closed the window. I was held down by force until my doctor, Lillie Simon, arrived and gave me opium to put me to sleep. For days this temptation remained with me, so I slept on chairs in the dining-room, not daring to enter my bedroom or the drawing-room, which had balconies. When I grew calmer I opened the bedroom door a crack, and peeped in; but it took me a long time to rid myself of that dreadful sensation and to live peacefully in the room again.

One day Leon sent me the money for my fare; Lillie Simon put me on the train, and I was in Paris again. The proprietors of the Hôtel des Maréchaux in the Rue de Moscou were amazed to see me. It was a strange sensation to be picking up life once more, and I was afraid to let myself feel anything at all, for fear my new-found freedom would vanish. When the Paris season was over we crossed to London and I could hardly believe I was really seeing Natasha, Mother and Beatrice again.

Nikitina had made trouble between Diaghilev and Lord Rothermere, so backing had to be sought elsewhere for a second season at His Majesty's. It was now that Lady Juliet Duff, daughter of Diaghilev's first English friend, Lady Ripon, came to the rescue. By extracting the promise of small sums of money from a number of people, she got together the necessary amount. All this was repaid at the end of the successful season. Diaghilev not only had exceptional courage to rise above adversity, he also had very good friends.

At His Majesty's in the summer of 1928, I was able to see for the first time some of Diaghilev's recent ballets. *Le Pas d'acier*, dating from the previous year, was his only flirtation with Soviet Russia—at least since the red flag had been carried on in *L'Oiseau de feu* in 1917. The first scene in a railway station contained a regrettable episode in which fun was made of a starving aristocrat, but the second, which took place in a factory and which seemed to glorify the Communist ideal of labour, gave a chance to the designer Jakulov to indulge in a real orgy of 'constructivism'. One could not help being impressed by the closing moments when the whole décor came to life: wheels spun round, pistons thumped and the dancers wielded huge hammers in time to the noisiest music that even Prokofiev wrote.

Boris Kochno had devised the ballet *Ode* in collaboration with the painter Pavel Tchelitchev. This was an obscure but occasionally beautiful affair, the theme of which was nothing less than the marvels of nature and the insignificance of man in the universe. The dancers wound in and out, forming diagrams with white rope; there were transparencies and cinematic projections; and Lifar dressed as an eighteenth-century *abbé*, played with a gleaming globe in a shaft of iridescent light. This was the last ballet Massine arranged for Diaghilev, and a *pas de deux* called 'Adam and Eve' was outstanding. The man and woman performed slow, mysterious movements behind two gauze curtains hung from a pole held by themselves. At the end of the dance, which represented the birth of mankind, they appeared in the gap between the curtains, and in a series of tender gestures linked their fingers together to symbolise their sacred union.

If anything could have confirmed me in my resolution to dance again it was *Apollon Musagète*. This lovely work marked the return to classicism both of Stravinsky and Balanchine. In his score for string orchestra, Stravinsky aimed at reproducing in his own manner the serenity of Bach and Handel. Following his instructions to provide a series of traditional dances for Apollo and three Muses, ending in an apotheosis, Balanchine succeeded wonderfully in expressing the classical style of Petipa in his own terms and in those of the 1920's. Unwilling to let anything detract from the simplicity of this noble ballet, Diaghilev had gone to the 'Sunday painter', Bauchant for a charming but elementary set. Lifar looked splendid in his short, scarlet tunic, with a gold wig, belt and cross-garters; but I thought the women's white costumes, with their loose bodices and three-quarter length *tutus*—a cross between Greek draperies and the uniform of classical ballet—were unbecoming. Nothing, however, could spoil the perfection of the movements which Balanchine gave his dancers. Nikitina and Danilova alternated as the principal Muse; the others were Tchernicheva and Doubrovska. The final picture of Lifar walking up the slopes of Parnassus to the solemn, humming chords of Stravinsky's music, with the three Muses strung out behind him, their arms outstretched, and with the chariot drawn by four dark horses coming out of the blue sky on a puffy white cloud, was an awe-inspiring and memorable spectacle. There can be no doubt that some of the best ballets have been arranged for very few dancers. Watching *Apollon*, I was overwhelmed by the thought of what extremes of beauty can be presented on the stage.

That summer I did not go south but stayed with my family in England. My only excursion was a trip with Leon to Ostend, where he was disappointed to find only *boule* was played in the Casino. (In London he used to gamble at a Polish club in Camden Town.) In the autumn the Ballet set off on a Northern tour, visiting Liverpool, Manchester, Glasgow and Edinburgh; then crossed in December to Paris. Although I was still convalescent, I felt lost when I was away from the Russian Ballet, so I joined them to watch their performances at the Opéra.

The old theatre was full of memories for me: I thought of Leon's first kiss in the dark corridor, of the time Diaghilev put me in my place after the first night of *Le Astuzie Femminili*, and of the first time I had danced *Le Tricorne* in public and stood shaking my shoulders provocatively under Picasso's shawl in the middle of that great stage. Karsavina was back with the ballet as guest artist, and I somehow interpreted this as a good sign. I kept praying that I should be able to dance again—and dance just as well as before.

On the night when Karsavina was to appear with Leon and Lifar in *Petroushka*, Diaghilev, in the vain hope of shocking Nijinsky back to reality by showing him a familiar ballet on the stage, invited Romola to bring him to the theatre. I was watching in the wings when Diaghilev on the point of going through the pass door, stopped and said, 'Come with me'. Wondering if I had done anything wrong, I was led by him to the door of a box, where he said, 'Go in there and talk to Vaslav Fomitch.' A ballet had just begun, *Les Sylphides* I think, and as I entered the box Romola looked up in surprise. I asked Nijinsky if he remembered me, told him I had danced in his ballets, and had been with him in America, and that I was 'the English girl'. He looked at me intently, smiled and nodded his head. When I held out my hand he took it, but there was no grip or sensation of shaking hands. I did not stay long. When Diaghilev asked me later if Nijinsky had recognised me I could only say I did not know.

We saw in the New Year, 1929, with Russian Gypsy music in a restaurant near Montmartre. The company were to dance in Bordeaux and Pau before returning to Monte Carlo, and as I wanted to visit Lourdes again Diaghilev gave me leave to accompany them. This pilgrimage, however, was no more successful than my first, for when I got to the grotto the notice was up again saying that the waters needed replenishing.

Back at Monte Carlo, and rejoicing to see again the beloved Mediterranean, I looked round our flat at Les Jasmins and could hardly believe I had suffered so much there in the previous year. The year 1929 had brought me new hope and determination. On the very first morning, when Leon had gone off to work, I put on my tights and ballet shoes and stood looking in the mirror. I made a few arm movements, then did all the arm exercises, one after the other. I placed my feet in the first, second, third, fourth and fifth positions. Then I began to tremble, went hot and cold, and walked up and down in a panic. I had a bath, dressed and went down to the rehearsal room at the Casino. Meeting Grigoriev, I said to him, 'I'm going to start practising again. May I come and work here when the room is empty?' He looked at me as if I were mad, then answered after a pause,

'You can but try.' I thanked him and went to sit outside in the chilly sunshine.

Every morning I put on my practice clothes at home and exercised a little. When I tried rising on my half-points I could feel the pull on my stomach. It took some days before I could pluck up courage to bend forwards and backwards. I did this kneeling down. My confidence slowly returned.

One day at the end of January, when I knew nobody would be about, I went down to the rehearsal room. My heart beat like a drum as I entered the dressing-room which I knew so well and sat on one of the familiar chairs. I put my head on the table and wept. It needed a lot of courage to take my dancing kit out of the suitcase, but I managed to change and walked about in the dim light of the rehearsal room, staring at myself in the mirror. I did not look any different from a year ago, but I certainly felt it. I did some *pliés* at the *barre*, then became so nervous I had to walk about again. Suddenly overcome by depression, I changed and ran out into the open air. It was three days before I ventured near the *barre* again, but this time I was calmer and more assured. I did my exercises gently every day; and in two months I dared to join a class.

20

BEGINNING AND ENDING

Healing thoughts — Dancing for Diaghilev again — Dressed
by Chirico — *Le Fils prodigue* — Enthusiastic Berlin — *Le
Sacre* revived — Back to Covent Garden — Diaghilev's illness — The press meet Markevitch — 'LYDIA SOKO-
LOVA TRIUMPH' — Pat Dolin's party — Diaghilev bids
farewell — Holiday at Le Lavandou — The *Continental Daily
Mail*.

Once or twice a week I took the train along the coast from Monte
Carlo to Beaulieu, where Edith Gautier-Vignal had arranged for
me to have treatment at her villa from her Swedish masseuse. On
one of these journeys I found a copy of *The Christian Science
Sentinel* on the seat of the train, and began to read it with interest.
A week later I shared a carriage with a lady who was reading
a copy of this paper and I asked her if she had left another in the
train a week before. I told her, when she said she thought she
had, that I had taken it and read it, and I explained that I was in
need of a lot of help at that moment, and that I prayed continually
for the strength to begin dancing again. She said, 'Stop trying
to organise for yourself; relax your face; give up fighting and
leave everything to God. If you go about life with the knowledge
that love, which is God, is everywhere about you all the time,
then any unlovable thing like pain or fear will disappear.' Soon
after I had to get out at Beaulieu, and as I walked to the Villa
La Berlugane for my massage, I tried to puzzle out how to carry
out her advice.

At first I was afraid to give up the battle I had been fighting
for so long, but once I had the courage to let go just for a moment,

271

the sensation of well-being was glorious. Every day, when I started practising, I used to carry on a little light-hearted conversation with God. 'Here we are! On with the dance! You gave me talent and ability: now we'll put it into practice.' When I had done as much as I could I simply said, 'Thank You for helping me.' This is not as ridiculous as it sounds for, after all, all faiths can influence the body through the mind, and I have no doubt that it was by attaining a more favourable state of mind that I began to make such wonderful progress with my exercises. I gained in assurance daily and even managed to forget about my body, so that I sometimes amazed myself by jumping. This thrilled me as I had always been particularly proud of my elevation.

As the weeks went by I grew stronger and dared to hope that I might recover my position in the Russian Ballet. At the beginning of April I told Grigoriev that I should be grateful if he would let Diaghilev know I felt fit enough to appear again on the stage. To my overwhelming joy Diaghilev agreed to let me make a gradual return, dancing in only one ballet an evening. I was to be paid half-salary until I could be treated as a full-time member of the company. At the first rehearsal my legs shook like jellies.

It was sixteen years since I had first joined Diaghilev's company at Monte Carlo and I had five times been briefly separated from them: once by the outbreak of war, once through joining Massine, and three times by illness. Every time I returned to work in the extraordinary organisation which the 'Old Man's' will and genius had kept alive, I felt the joy of an employee who comes back to the firm where he knows he really belongs and where his worth is appreciated. In the Russian Ballet I not only had the satisfaction of doing a good job well—it was more than that: there was the privilege of working in a community devoted to the continual production of glorious works of art. To see masterpieces constantly created and to have a part in their creation was intoxicating; and I could imagine no other way of life for myself than that of dancing for Diaghilev.

My first role was to be the variation of the Carnation Fairy in *Le Mariage d'Aurore*. For this I only needed strong points and a firm spine; and in the *grand pas d'action*, luckily, Leon was to be my partner as before. So on April 8, 1929, I went to the theatre with my make-up case and all my accessories. Naturally I was not given back my nice corner dressing-room just off the stage: instead I had a little one downstairs next door to Leon's. I put my make-up out on the table ready for the evening and covered everything with a towel. When I came back later to prepare for the performance, I found the towel had been removed and my shoes and tights were laid out ready to put on. I could not understand this. Then my dear dresser who had done these things for me for thirteen years, since I was in the *corps de ballet*, came into the room. After embracing me she said, 'I've exchanged with Marie. She's gone upstairs, and I've arranged that whenever you are dancing I will dress you and help the girls down on this floor.'

When I was dressed and stood in the wings waiting to go on in the *Polonaise*, my friends wished me good luck and Leon kissed my hand. I took the plunge—and found the water wasn't cold after all. By the time we had reached the *Mazurka* at the end of the ballet, my self-confidence had completely returned. Countess Gautier-Vignal had brought Dr Pratt to see me dance, for they both took a personal pride in my recovery. This was an important evening for the two other English dancers besides myself, for Pat Dolin had returned to the Ballet and he danced for the first time *L'Oiseau bleu* with Alicia Markova. This was the beginning of a long and famous partnership.

The next role I tackled was my old one of the Odalisque in *Scheherazade*, which needed jumps and deep back bends, but I had no trouble at all; and by the end of the Monte Carlo season I was once more grovelling on the ground at Luba's feet pleading with her not to steal my lover. It was like old times.

Pat Dolin had the principal part in a new work called *Le Bal*, with music by Rieti and designs by Chirico. This was a *divertissement* for which Balanchine did some amusing choreography, and there were parts for most of us in it. I danced a gay *tarantella* with Lifar, but quite half the point of this dance was destroyed by the heavy costumes. Chirico's dresses were undoubtedly the most striking part of the ballet, being covered with architectural motifs and simulated parchment scrolls to give the impression of being made out of plaster or paper: but their weight and stiffness made them hard to dance in.

In his other new ballet, *Le Fils prodigue*, George Balanchine had to tackle for the first time a big, dramatic subject. In recent years the Russian Ballet had fought shy of the dramatic and passionate works for which they had originally been famous, and Balanchine's speciality was a kind of up-to-date classicism. Now he had to do something to match the grandeur of the parable and the force of Prokofiev's music. I thought the result was restrained and moving. Lifar was given the opportunity to let himself go in an emotional role, the like of which had not been seen in ballet since the days of Fokine. Yet, how differently Balanchine and Fokine set about things! It was interesting to consider the contrast between the orgy in *Scheherazade* with its sprawling girls and bounding Negroes, and the orgy in *Le Fils prodigue* with its weird atmosphere and acrobatic grouping. In the first ballet there were cushions, wine and fruit: in the second the only props were a hoop and a trestle table. Twenty years before, Diaghilev had astounded Paris with the colours of Bakst, which had seemed almost like a new vice: the décor of *Le Fils prodigue* was entrusted to the great modern religious painter, Georges Rouault.

Although Diaghilev was clearly losing interest in Lifar and no longer called for him at the end of rehearsals, he allowed him to work under our old friend Larionov on the choreography of a new version of *Renard*. Real acrobats were employed for this to echo the movements of the dancers in their own peculiar idiom. It was obviously meant to shock and did not belong to the Diaghilev Ballet. Lifar never showed any sign of minding the change in Diaghilev's attitude towards him. He always seemed to me to be without any depth of feeling.

We returned to the Sarah-Bernhardt Theatre in Paris, and I danced more of my old roles. When a dancer such as myself had been replaced in a role, and then came back to it, Diaghilev was always very fair: the original dancer and her successor would dance the part alternately. I still shared the Miller's Wife in *Le Tricorne* with Luba Tchernicheva, but it was announced that she was to retire at the end of the London season. We clubbed together and bought her an enormous topaz the colour of her eyes.

Diaghilev was evidently happy in his mind that I had made a complete recovery. Even so, it came as a shock when Grigoriev told me quite casually that *Le Sacre* was to be included in the programme for Berlin. Apart from Nijinska, who had danced my role once, nobody but myself had ever done the Chosen Virgin in Massine's ballet. I certainly had a sinking feeling, but not for the world would I have shown any surprise. I spent all the time I could going over the music and working up the dance again, step by step. My inside had healed, but I was unsure of my knee, and I had to be very careful not to give in to the temptation of fear. It seemed more than incredible that so few months after being a complete physical wreck, I should be going in again for this 'endurance test', surely the hardest dance that had ever been invented.

As I had not seen Natasha for six months, and she was now twelve years old, I decided to let her come with us to Germany. So during the Paris season my sister put her on the Channel steamer at Folkestone, which was not far from their new home at Birchington. She made her first sea trip alone, and told me afterwards that she had walked round and round the ship, hoping everybody would notice her hair, which for the first time was in a long plait looped up at the back of her head, with a large pink bow. I met her at Boulogne and took her back to the Hôtel des Maréchaux in Paris where we were staying. She was fitted up with new clothes at Le Printemps, and we soon made our journey to Berlin. I was glad I had brought her over, as she picked up some German—she was always quick to learn languages—and she was now old enough to appreciate the ballet. Natasha helped me to dress at every performance, and certainly felt she was one of the company.

The Stadtsoper, where we danced in Berlin was a huge auditorium, more like a concert hall than a theatre. This time the

Germans were mad about us: every performance was sold out and the critics were enthusiastic. One had the feeling that at last the Russian Ballet with its superb repertoire, which could be said to encompass the whole field of modern art, was honoured and made welcome everywhere, and Diaghilev's genius was acknowledged.

By the time the dreaded day arrived when we were to give *Le Sacre du printemps* there could be no doubt of our success in Berlin, which had proved a sticky town in the past. It had been a difficult day for me, trying not to be afraid, and during the awful period of suspense before my dance began I prayed that I should not fail Diaghilev, whose faith in me had been so great that he had risked putting on Stravinsky's masterpiece again. I had my reward when that huge audience stood up to shout and clap frenziedly at the end. The ovation was colossal and I had never known anything like it in my life before. Ansermet came round to congratulate me, and my dressing-room was full of enthusiastic friends. Natasha always remembered seeing *Le Sacre* in Berlin, and said afterwards that 'it was almost too much to bear'. Whatever Diaghilev thought during or after the performance I never knew, as he did not come round to see me and never mentioned it. I changed and went on in the next ballet as if nothing had happened.

In London we were back at Covent Garden for the first time in years. Although this was delightful and although our season was exceptionally brilliant, with Dolin back to dance in *Le Bal*, Spessivtseva in *Le Lac des cygnes* and Karsavina in *Petroushka*, and although the faithful London public seemed to love us more than ever, we could not help recognising the fact that Diaghilev was ill. He looked grey, with deep black shadows under his eyes, he walked painfully leaning on his stick, and he very seldom came to the theatre. Even so, when he dined with Florrie Grenfell he was gay and drank champagne, which was bad for him as he was diabetic. When she remonstrated he said, 'Do not be disturbed, *ma fidèle*. I will take saccharine with my coffee.' He always called Florrie '*Ma fidèle*'; and Juliet Duff he called '*Chère chérie*'.

But Diaghilev was not too ill to have a new enthusiasm in his life. He was enraptured with the personality and talent of a young Russian composer, Igor Markevitch, who was only sixteen. This boy was to play his first piano concerto in the interval between two ballets at Covent Garden, and on the day before, Diaghilev held a rehearsal and a reception for the press, to which we were invited. We all assembled in the bar and the principal female dancers were asked to act as hostesses. Diaghilev took me aside and said, 'I am going to have some of the important press men brought to you. I want you to tell them what a brilliant composer Markevitch is.' Opening my eyes very wide, I protested that I knew nothing about him. Diaghilev said, 'You are English and you can talk to them. You will know what to say.' When the time came I told them that though they would, of course, form their own opinions, I felt sure they would agree with Diaghilev about Markevitch's brilliance. I think, however, that few of them did.

I had not seen Father since the season at the Prince's Theatre two years before. Now, once again, he began to haunt me, waiting at the stage door or sending up desperate messages. One day a friend told me that he had heard a man telling a group of people outside the theatre he was my father; they had laughed at him. My conflicting feelings—pity, fear and shame—made it hard for me to get through that performance. There was nothing to be done: I had written to Father that he must fend for himself, and I resolved to be firm, as much for the sake of the Diaghilev Ballet as for my own. This menace, which amounted to blackmail, continued for a long time: but I am happy to say that Father's last years were spent in a home for old people, where I secretly contributed to his upkeep, and where, removed from temptations, he painted his watercolours and was loved and respected by all who came in contact with him.

The bookings at Covent Garden were so good that the management put in extra seats: even so we were sold out well in advance. The last time I had danced *Le Sacre* in London was on the small stage of the Prince's Theatre, with two grand pianos visibly protruding from the wings. It was therefore a joy to have the

scope of a big stage at the Royal Opera House. The excitement of
the audience before the ballet began could be felt on the stage.
Unlike the Berliners, people in London knew me as a dancer
and were aware that I had recovered from a serious illness, so
they had a sense of anticipation of seeing me again, as well as of
hearing Stravinsky's score. It was a tremendous night for me.
Friends who came to see me told me that crowds of people who
could not get tickets were walking up and down outside the
theatre. It is impossible to describe the gratitude one feels for
an audience which pours out as much affection and appreciation
as the public did that night after *Le Sacre*. Beecham and Sherriff,
the two nurses who had looked after me in the Victoria Hospital
at Nice, were now in London. They asked me for tickets, but
there were none to be had, so I seated them on two stools in the
wings. They could hardly believe their eyes when they saw what
I had to do in *Le Sacre*.

The critic of the *Morning Post* wrote: 'Mlle Lydia Sokolova
quite carried away the audience with her spirited grotesqueries'
—which was an odd way of alluding to Massine's choreography.
Under a headline 'Lydia Sokolova Triumph—Famous dancer's
ovation at Covent Garden', the music critic of the *Daily Express*
recorded that: 'Mlle Lydia Sokolova, capturing the mood of
primitive ecstasy with all her former genius, received an ovation
quite as tremendous as that accorded, two months ago, to Mlle
Rosa Ponselle, the singer. People nearly fell out of their seats
and boxes to cheer her back after her long and arduous illness.'
The writer of 'Talk of the Day' in the *Evening News* wrote: 'The
dancing of Sokolova was utterly enchanting. I liked the comment
of my companion . . . when she stood forlorn in the middle of
the stage he whispered to me, "She's like Lillian Gish." He meant
it for high praise.'

Pat Dolin gave a party towards the end of the season at his
studio at Glebe Place in Chelsea. We all tried very hard to be gay
and unconcerned, but there was a sense of strain as it was known
that Diaghilev, who had been away from the theatre for several
days, would be present. There was a hush as he appeared standing
in the doorway. His face was ashen, the flesh was loose round his

cheeks, his eyes were sunken and his grey hair showed through the dye. He sat down on a chair near the door and folded his hands on the top of his cane, just as I remembered him doing when I went for my audition at Covent Garden sixteen years before. He looked as if he were suffering and spoke very little. I began to edge towards him through the crowd, and I think he saw what I was doing, for he looked up and gave me a genuine smile. I would have given anything to have sat quietly on the floor beside him for a few minutes.

After our last performance at Covent Garden Diaghilev came on the stage to speak to us, looking rather stronger and more cheerful. He told us how pleased he was the season had been such a success, and thanked us for all our hard work. Then he explained what we should be doing the following year, and said how satisfied he was to have a series of engagements booked far ahead. It really seemed that the Diaghilev Ballet was due for a period of prosperity. Nevertheless, there was a wistful air of sadness about the 'Old Man' when he said good-bye to the company, shaking each dancer by the hand. To some he would say a few words, in the manner of royalty; and as I stepped forward to take his hand he said to me, 'Rest well'. I replied, 'Thank you, Sergei Pavlovitch. You too.' As he left the stage he turned and gently waved his hand.

Diaghilev went off to Paris, Munich and Salzburg with Markevitch. We were to dance one week in Vichy before our holiday.

Leon and I were spending the first part of our holiday in the south of France at a little place on a sandy bay called Le Lavandou. The hotel was right on the beach. Leon's great hobby had always been fishing, and now even I learned to catch little fish on hooks fixed to a line, held over the side of a boat.

Every day I would walk along the beach to a kiosk in the village street to buy the *Continental Daily Mail*. I used to read this to Leon in Russian just as I had read him many books in this way.

One very hot morning I left Leon lying flat on his back, roasting in the sun, and went as usual for my newspaper. Unlike English papers which are folded double, newspapers in France are folded in four, then again across the middle. As I took the

paper from the rack, I saw the words 'DEATH OF' standing out
in heavy black type. With a sudden sense of foreboding, I cried
out 'Oh, no! Oh, no!'

Even before I turned the paper over I knew what was printed
there. When I got back to Leon all I could say was, 'Leon, Diaghilev!' I handed him the paper. Reading the first lines he said,
'Yesterday morning in Venice.' As the awful truth sank into my
consciousness, my knees gave way and I lay on the sand, burying
my face in my hands. When I looked up at last Leon had gone.
Then I saw him in the distance walking along the edge of the
sea, kicking the water with his foot.

INDEX

Addison, Errol, 191
Aga Khan, the, 64
Aïda, 19
Alfonso XIII, King, 76, 82, 84, 85, 105, 125, 175
Anello, shoemaker, 199
Ansermet, Ernest, 68, 75, 162, 163
Antonova, Elena, 83, 84, 86, 149, 155
Apollon Musagète, 264, 267, 268
Après-midi d'un faune, L', 30, 38–41, 213
Astafieva, Seraphine, 36, 212
Astolfi, Zelita, 122
Astruc, Gabriel, 44
Astuzie Femminili, Le, 149, 152, 153, 169, 214, 268
Atwell, Winifred, 8
Auric, Georges, 218, 235
Aurora's Wedding. See *Mariage d'Aurore, Le*

Bakst, Leon, 7, 28, 30, 36, 41, 52, 53, 56, 68, 81, 86, 98, 129, 139, 186, 188–91, 274
Bal, Le, 273, 274, 276
Balakirev, Mily, 140
Balanchine, George (George Balanchivadze), 225, 229, 230, 239, 248, 252–4, 259–61, 267, 268, 273, 274
Balanchivadze, George. See Balanchine, George
Baldina, 28
Balla, 101
Barabau, 239, 240
Barrocchi, Randolfo, 86, 139
Baton, René, 48

Bauchant, André, 268
Bax, Arnold (later Sir Arnold), 140
Beatrice (the author's half-sister). See Gaulton, Beatrice
Beaumont, Comte Etienne de, 229, 248
Beaumont, Cyril, 130, 183
Beecham, Nurse, 265, 278
Beecham, Sir Joseph, 45, 64
Beecham, Sir Thomas, 45
Belle au bois dormant, La. See *Sleeping Princess, The*
Benois, Alexandre, 7, 30, 61, 68, 185, 186
Berners, Lord, 140, 250, 252
Bewicke, Hilda, 78, 156, 159, 178, 192, 202, 263
Biches, Les, 209, 214–17, 223, 226, 229, 237, 238, 250, 254, 256
Birley, Oswald (later Sir Oswald), 157
Bolm, Adolf, 34, 59, 60, 74, 75
Boot, Hilda (Butsova), 8
Boris Godounov, 7, 44–6, 63
Bourman, Anatole, 138
Boutique fantasque, La, 112, 134, 137–139, 143, 148, 169, 177, 186, 226, 249
Bowen, Vera (Mrs Harold Bowen), 199
Braque, Georges, 218
Brianza, Carlotta, 189, 190
Bromova, Anna (Annie Broomhead), 15, 31
Broomhead, Annie (Bromova), 15, 31
Browne, Winifrede, 8
Busby, Mr, 3, 4
Butsova, Hilda (Hilda Boot), 8

Camishov, 143, 174, 263
Campbell, Herbert, 45
Carnaval, 55, 59, 66, 68, 71, 93, 97, 119, 120, 130, 148, 169
Caruso, Enrico, 19
Casse-Noisette, 186
Cecchetti, Enrico, 31, 33, 39, 46, 47, 48, 55, 70, 86, 99, 138, 189, 190, 209, 229, 232, 238
Cecchetti, Giuseppina, 31, 86, 99, 100, 138
Chabrier, Emmanuel, 214
Chaliapin, Fyodor, 44–6, 63, 64, 211
Chamié, Tatiana, 240
Chanel, Gabrielle, 145, 167, 201, 222
Chant du rossignol, Le, 146–8, 229, 233
Chaplin, Charlie, 93, 103
Charlotte of Monaco, Princess, 202, 205, 206, 219
Chatte, La, 259, 260
Children's Tales. See Contes russes
Chirico, Giorgio di, 273
Chout, 176, 179, 180, 183, 204
Chu Chin Chow, 185
Churchill, Randolph, 249
Cimarosa, Domenico, 149, 152
Cimarosiana, 214, 226, 237, 257
Clark, Vera. See Savina
Cléopâtre, 35, 67, 74, 75, 77, 92, 108, 129, 130, 172, 226
Cloustine, Ivan, 27
Cochran, Charles B. (later Sir Charles), 175, 183, 200, 242
Cocteau, Jean, 37, 97, 102–4, 221
Colombe, La, 214
Contes russes (Children's Tales), 101, 131, 169
Coppélia, 17, 20
Coq d'or, 62, 63, 144, 204
Courtauld, Mrs Samuel, 249
Courtenay, Sheila, 15
Crocker, Mr, 127
Cuadro flamenco, 179–81, 183

Dalbaicin, Maria, 143, 176, 181, 192, 236
Dalcroze, Jacques, 42
Danilova, Alexandra (Shura), 74, 225, 228, 231, 238, 248, 249, 254, 257, 268
Daphnis et Chloë, 53, 54, 213, 214, 226
Debussy, Claude, 39, 41, 97
Delaunay, Robert, 129
Dempster, William, 261
Derain, André, 139, 186, 248
Devillier, Catherine, 143, 175, 236
Diaghilev, Sergei Pavlovitch, first mentioned 7; first appearance 31. From then on, *passim*.
Dieu bleu, Le, 36, 37, 87, 97.
Dolin, Anton (Patrick Kay, also called Patrikeeff), 187, 212, 213, 218, 220–2, 224, 228–30, 232, 233, 236, 238, 259, 273, 276, 278
Dolly Sisters, 178
Dormer, Daisy, 67
Doubrovska, Felia, 192, 231, 233, 248, 249, 255, 257, 268
Dove, Alfred, 127
Drobetsky, 86, 87
Duff, Lady Juliet, 266, 276
Dukelsky, Vladimir, 230
Duncan, Isadora, 51
Dying Swan, The, 10

Ede, Mr and Mrs James, 262
Edward VII, King, 8
Efimov, Nicholas, 225
Egorova, Lubov, 194
Ernst, Max, 245, 248
Estampielo, 181
Evina, Wanda, 86, 102, 138, 229

Fâcheux, Les, 214, 218
Faithful, Doris, 15, 18, 19, 31, 34
Falla, Manuel de, 141, 142
Fauré, Gabriel, 82
Fedorova, Sophie, 130

Felix (Felix Fernandez), 113–16, 122, 134–7, 175, 176, 221
Femmes de bonne humeur, Les, 98–102, 130, 140, 143, 226
Fernandez, Felix. See Felix
Fête de Versailles, La, 206, 207
Fils Prodigue, Le, 274
Finch, Flora, 93
Firebird, The. See Oiseau de feu, L'
Fireworks (Stravinsky's Opus 1), 101
Fokina, Vera, 52, 57
Fokine, Mikhail, 7, 28, 30, 38, 51–64, 68, 88, 143, 148, 185, 213, 226, 231, 232, 244, 254, 255, 274
Frohman, Margarita, 87

Gabo, Naum, 259
Gabrielita, La, 181
Galitzine, Princess, 169, 170
Gaudin, 34
Gaulton, Beatrice (the author's half-sister), 2, 4, 5, 6, 12, 22, 78, 126, 157, 197, 210, 211, 220, 227, 262, 266, 275
Gautier-Vignal, Comtesse, 178, 264, 265, 271, 273
Gavrilov, Alexander, 69, 112, 119, 120, 138
Geltzer, Katerina, 14, 16, 18
Giselle, 17, 194
Gish, Lillian, 278
Glinka, Mikhail, 140
Golovine, Alexander, 255
Gontcharova, Natalie, 62, 68, 70, 82, 203, 204, 255, 256
Gounod, Charles, 214
Grenfell, Florence (Lady St Just), 157, 184, 225, 239, 244, 276
Grigoriev, Serge, 31, 33, 34, 39, 43, 45, 48, 67, 73, 84, 86, 89, 95, 102, 105–8, 110, 116, 117, 119–21, 125, 137–40, 146–8, 159, 170, 171, 172, 177, 185, 199, 201, 213, 217, 228, 229, 243, 244, 251, 254, 256, 269, 270, 272, 275

Gris, Juan, 213, 214
Grock, 128
Guinsbourg, G., 214
Gunzburg, Baron, 48, 49

Hamnett, Nina, 235
House Party, The. See Biches, Les
Hoyer brothers, 202

Idzikovsky, Stanislas, 65, 66, 69, 84, 85, 86, 99, 132, 138, 143, 146, 153, 191, 229, 232, 236, 248, 249, 253, 257, 262
Inghelbrecht, D. E., 257
Ivan the Terrible, 63

Jack-in-the-Box, 248
Jakulov, 267
James, Blanche, 15
Jasvinska, Mme, 110
Jeux, 38, 41, 42
Jones, Robert Edmund, 89
June (Lady Inverclyde), 200

Kahn, Otto, 68, 77, 79, 80, 88, 90
Karsavina, Tamara, 7, 36, 37, 39, 41, 52–56, 59, 63, 64, 135–7, 143, 146–8, 151, 153, 169, 175, 177, 244, 245, 249, 268, 269, 276
Kay, Patrick (Patrikeeff, later Anton Dolin). See Dolin, Anton
Kchessinskaya, Matilda, 233
Kellerman, Annette, 66
Keynes, John Maynard (later Lord Keynes), 239
Khovanschchina, 44
Kikimora, 132
Kirby, Mr, 253
Knight, Laura (later Dame Laura), 46

Kochno, Boris, 103, 150, 151, 174, 175, 201, 202, 218, 223, 224, 230, 252, 259, 264, 267
Kokhlova, Olga (later Mme Picasso), 33, 83, 84, 86, 130, 223, 263, 264
Koribut-Kobutovitch, Pavel, 202
Kosloff, Alexis, 28, 29, 30
Kosloff, Theodore, 27–31
Kostetzky, Stanislas, 138
Kostrovsky, 91, 92, 106
Kremnev, Natalia (Natasha, the author's daughter), 109, 110, 111–119, 123, 124, 126, 127, 132, 154, 157, 196, 197, 210–12, 220, 227, 258, 266, 275, 276
Kremnev, Nicolas, 57, 58, 60, 64, 65–71, 77–9, 86, 87, 89–91, 94, 96, 97, 100, 102, 105, 107–9, 114–16, 119, 120, 123, 124, 131, 132, 138, 139, 143, 145, 149, 150, 154, 155, 157, 161, 168–70, 173, 174, 178, 192, 238, 254
Kuznetzova, Maria, 60, 61
Kynaston, Virginia, 8

Lac des cygnes, Le, 186, 214, 218, 229, 255, 257, 276
Lambert, Constant, 243–5
Lapitsky, 202
Larionov, Michel, 62, 68, 70, 71, 82, 83, 131, 174, 179, 180, 204, 274
Laurencin, Marie, 215, 216
Laurier, Jay, 200
Laye, Evelyn, 200
Legat, Nicolas, 57, 238, 239, 247
Légende de Joseph, La, 60, 61, 140, 144
Lenglen, Suzanne, 221
Leno, Dan, 45
Leno, Dan, Jr., 8
Lifar, Serge, 202, 224, 225, 230, 232, 233, 234–8, 240, 244, 245, 249, 252, 254, 257, 259, 260, 267–9, 273, 274
Littler, Mrs Emile (Cora Poole-Goffin), 8
Liturgie, 69

Lopokova, Lydia (Lady Keynes), 14, 17, 73, 74, 84, 85, 86, 99, 104, 132, 137–40, 143, 183, 192, 194, 195, 198, 199, 239, 249
Louis II, Prince of Monaco, 201, 202

Maikerska, 53, 54
Mariage d'Aurore, Le, 201, 207, 209, 229, 258, 272
Markevitch, Igor, 277, 279
Markova, Alicia (Alicia Marks), 225, 227, 228, 233, 273
Marks, Alicia. See Markova, Alicia
Marks, Mrs, 227
Marra, Eleanora (Mme Massine), 242
Martel, El, 181
Marwicz, Baronne de, 264
Mary, Queen, 239
Massine, Leonide, 56, 57, 60, 61, 67–77, 82–4, 86, 97–100, 104, 106, 107, 112–14, 116, 129, 130–2, 134, 135, 137–43, 146–50, 152, 153, 154, 159–71, 172–6, 179, 181–3, 185, 198, 199, 203, 221, 225, 226, 229–35, 239, 242, 248, 254, 257, 265, 267, 272, 275, 278.
Matelots, Les, 233–5, 237
Mateo, el sin pies, 181, 183
Matisse, Henri, 146
Mavra, 201
Meniñas, Las, 82–4
Michael, Grand Duke, 233
Midas, 59, 60
Mikolaichik, Nicolas, 192
Milhaud, Darius, 222
Minareta, La, 181
Miro, Joan, 245, 248
Mitchell, Michael, 13, 21, 23, 199
Montague, Ethel, 15
Montéclair, Michel, 214
Monteux, Pierre, 48, 89
Mordkin, Mikhail, 10, 11, 13, 14, 23, 66
Moreno, El, 181
Morley, Mrs, 225, 264

Morosoff, 11, 17
Moussorgsky, Modeste, 45, 218
Munnings, Sir Alfred, P.R.A. (the author's kinsman), 2
Munnings, Emma (the author's mother), 1–12, 126, 142, 143, 157, 196, 197, 227, 258, 261, 262, 266
Munnings, Frederick (the author's father), 2–12, 22, 126, 157, 196, 227, 249, 258, 261, 277
Munnings, Henrietta (the author's paternal grandmother), 3
Munnings, Jack (uncle of the author), 3
Munnings, John (the author's paternal grandfather), 2
Munnings, Tom (uncle of the author), 2, 262
Mutter, Patricia, 8

Narcisse, 55, 78, 79, 105, 108, 160, 163, 169, 214, 226
'Natasha', the author's daughter. (Natalia Kremnev, now Mrs Edward Sumner), 109, 110, 111–19, 123, 124, 126, 127, 132, 154–7, 196, 197, 210, 212, 220, 227, 258, 266, 275, 276
Nelidova, 36
Nemtchinova, Lida, 69
Nemtchinova, Vera, 69, 74, 140, 151, 177, 191, 215, 216, 229, 234, 242, 243, 244, 250
Niccolini (shoemaker), 25
Nijinska, Bronislava (Bronia), 68, 78, 79, 188, 192, 201–3, 212–18, 221, 223–5, 226, 229, 231, 232, 255, 259, 265, 275
Nijinsky, Mme (Romola) (Romola de Pulszka), 46, 48–50, 77, 80, 89–93, 106, 110, 269
Nijinsky, Vaslav, 7, 30, 31, 36–50, 51, 71, 76–80, 86–93, 105–7, 110, 159, 161, 162, 170, 202, 203, 226, 244, 269

Nikitina, Alice, 228–31, 238, 256, 259, 260, 268
Noces, Les, 203–6, 249
Nouvel, Walter, 174, 197, 202
Novak, Sigismund, 83, 86
Nuit sur le Mont Chauve, La, 218, 219

Ode, 267
Oiseau bleu, L', 273
Oiseau de feu, L', 30, 35, 42, 97, 102, 129, 183, 254–6, 267

Papillons, Les, 59, 169
Parade, 102–4
Pas d'acier, Le, 267
Pastorale, La, 248
Patrikeeff (Patrick Kay, later Anton Dolin). See Dolin, Anton
Pavillon, d'Armide, Le, 55, 57, 201
Pavlova, Anna, 7, 8, 10, 11, 13, 23–8, 30, 50, 77, 193, 226, 245
Pergolesi, Giambattista, 150
Petipa, Marius, 51, 186, 187, 188, 195, 201, 267
Petroushka, 30, 35, 42, 60, 78, 97, 129, 134, 140, 164, 169, 178, 226, 255, 269, 276
Petrova, Vera, 250, 257
Pevsner, 259
Pflanz, Fanny, 87
Phi-Phi, 200
Pianovsky, 25
Picasso, Pablo, 7, 42, 102, 103, 130, 141, 142, 150, 151, 174, 179, 180, 181, 220, 223, 263, 268
Piltz, Maria, 34, 36, 43
Polignac, Prince Pierre de (later Prince Pierre of Monaco), 202, 205, 206
Polignac, Princesse Edmond de, 202
Polunin, Elizabeth, 70
Polunin, Vladimir, 70
Ponselle, Rosa, 278

Poole-Goffin, Cora (Mrs Emile Littler), 8
Porter, Mr and Mrs Cole, 237
Poulenc, Francis, 215
Pratt, Dr, 264, 265, 273
Prince Igor, 30, 35, 63, 64, 157, 169, 223, 231, 232
Prokofiev, Serge, 174, 180, 267, 274
Pruna, Pedro, 234
Pulcinella, 149–53, 164, 169, 177, 180, 181, 226
Pulszka, Romola de (Mme Nijinsky), 46, 48–50, 77, 80, 89–93, 106, 110, 269

Rabinoff, Max, 13, 20, 21
Rainier, Prince (of Monaco), 219
Rambert, Marie, 34, 39, 40, 42, 47, 48, 49
Ravel, Maurice, 53, 97, 140
Redhead, Rita, 245
Renard, 201, 202, 274
Respighi, Ottorino, 112
Revalles, Flora, 75
Ricketts, Charles, 130
Rieti, Vittorio, 273
Rimsky-Korsakov, Nikolai, 28, 52, 57, 62, 70
Ripon, Marchioness of, 64, 266
Robertson, Rae, 160
Rodin, Auguste, 46
Romanoff, Boris, 61
Roméo et Juliette, 243–5, 248, 249
Rosen, Mr, 66
Rossignol, Le, 61, 146
Rossini, Gioachimo, 112, 134
Roszovska, Zoia, 134, 173, 178, 220
Rothermere, Viscount, 243–50, 254, 266
Rouault, Georges, 274
Rubia de Herez, La, 181
Russian Wedding, 17

Sacre du printemps, Le, 38, 42–5, 159–168, 181–3, 187, 226, 235, 265, 275–8

St Just, Lady. See Grenfell, Florence
Satie, Erik, 102–4, 140, 248
Sauguet, Henri, 259, 260
Savina, Vera (Vera Clark, later Mme Massine), 131, 138, 153, 159–61, 163, 167, 168, 170, 171, 172, 173, 198, 211, 220, 225, 229
Scarlatti, Domenico, 98, 130
Scheherazade, 28–31, 35, 52, 55–7, 93, 119, 120, 130, 140, 178, 273, 274
Schmoltz, Helena, 11, 17, 20
Schollar, Ludmilla, 41, 191, 228
Sedova, 14, 16, 20
Sergeev, Nicolas, 186–8
Sert, Jose-Maria, 60, 82, 83, 152, 153
Sert, Misia (born Misia Godebska, married (i) Natanson, (ii) Edwards, (iii) Sert), 60, 83, 163, 167
Sevillano, El, 181
Strabelska, Gala, 69
Shabelska, Maria, 69, 86, 104, 131
Sheraiev, 27
Sherriff, Nurse, 265, 278
Sickert, Mrs Walter, 183
Sierra, Martinez, 141
Simon, Mme, 264, 266
Sitwell, Osbert (later Sir Osbert Sitwell), 131
Sitwell, Sacheverell, 250, 252
Slavinsky, Thaddeus, 116, 151, 174, 176, 177, 179, 180, 198, 199, 201, 234, 243, 244
Sleeping Princess, The, 185–95, 201, 212, 218, 223
Snowmaiden, The (Snegoroutchka), 70
Soleil de nuit, 70–2, 74, 204
Soumarokova, Luba, 69, 192
Soumarokova, Nura, 69
Spectre de la rose, Le, 30, 45, 52, 53, 92, 93, 97, 108
Spessivtseva, Olga (Spessiva), 87, 191, 193, 194, 257, 259, 276
Statkevitch, 247
Steinberg, 59

Stoll, Sir Oswald, 28, 123, 127, 195, 223, 238

Strauss, Richard, 60, 88, 89, 97

Stravinsky, Igor, 7, 30, 38, 42, 45, 52, 61, 68, 101, 146, 149, 150, 160, 162, 164, 165, 167, 168, 174, 175, 182, 185, 186, 188, 201–3, 265, 267, 268, 276, 278

Such, Henry (the author's maternal grandfather), 1, 12, 22

Such, Mrs (the author's maternal grandmother), 1, 12

Sudeikina, Vera, 190

Svetlov, Nicolai, 71

Swan Lake. See *Lac des cygnes, Le*

Sylphides, Les, 30, 35, 36, 55, 93, 97, 100, 119, 128, 133, 140, 160, 169, 172, 220, 231, 269

Tarasoff, 30, 31, 33

Tariat, 83

Tchaikovsky, Piotr, 185, 188, 192, 195

Tchelitchev, Pavel, 267

Tcherkas, Constantin, 177, 238

Tchernicheva, Lubov, 34, 36, 56, 57, 67, 69, 75, 84, 86, 99, 120, 129, 132, 138, 139, 143, 151, 177, 191, 192, 216, 217, 219, 231, 236, 247, 249, 254, 255, 268, 273, 275

Tentations de la bergère, Les, 214, 217

Tetrazzini, Luisa, 19

Thamar, 35, 55, 81

Till Eulenspiegel, 88–91, 179

Tommasini, Vincenzo, 98

Train bleu, Le, 221, 222, 224, 226, 238, 259

Trefilova, Vera, 193, 194, 218, 249

Tricorne, Le, 134–7, 141–3, 148, 169, 175, 176, 178, 220, 221, 226, 236, 268, 275

Trini, 200

Triumph of Neptune, The, 250–4, 265

Troubridge, (Una) Lady, 46

Unger, Serge, 202

Utrillo, Maurice, 239

Vadimova, Dora, 235

Valois, Ninette de, 209, 210, 212, 213

Vassili (Vassili Zuykov, Diaghilev's servant), 76, 117, 140, 171

Vaudoyer, Jean-Louis, 97

Versailles, La Fête de, 206, 207

Victoria-Eugenia, Queen ('Queen Ena'), 82, 84, 85

Vladimirov, Pierre, 64, 191, 193, 232, 233

Volinine, Alexander, 20

Wilson, President, 78

Wilzak, Anatole, 228

Woizikovska, Mme (Leon Woizikovsky's mother), 209–12, 220

Wollheim, Eric, 123, 127, 199

Wood, Christopher, 243

Woizikovsky, Leon, 57, 83, 84, 85, 86, 99, 116, 132, 134, 137, 138, 142, 143, 148–50, 152, 153, 154, 155, 157, 158, 161, 166, 167, 171, 172–8, 183, 184, 186, 192, 197–201, 207, 208, 209–12, 217, 220–5, 227, 228, 232, 234, 236–41, 249, 257, 258, 260, 262–6, 268, 269, 273, 279, 280

You'd be Surprised, 198

Yousoupoff, Prince, 169

Zalmani, Rita, 15, 66

Zambelli, Carlotta, 14, 16, 18

Zéphire et Flore, 230, 231, 233, 235, 236, 238

Zuykov, Vassili, 76, 117, 140, 171

Zverev, Nicolas, 30, 31, 91, 92, 93, 104, 106, 242, 243